PROGRESS IN PHILOSOPHY

THE REVEREND CHARLES A. HART, PH.D.

PROGRESS IN PHILOSOPHY

PHILOSOPHICAL STUDIES
IN HONOR OF
REV. DOCTOR CHARLES A. HART

Editorial Board

HONORARY CHAIRMAN

HIS EMINENCE, FRANCIS CARDINAL SPELLMAN, D.D.

EDITOR

JAMES A. McWILLIAMS, S.J.

ASSOCIATE EDITORS

JAMES D. COLLINS GERALD B. PHELAN
LEO A. FOLEY, S.M. VINCENT E. SMITH

THE BRUCE PUBLISHING COMPANY
MILWAUKEE

NIHIL OBSTAT:

JOHN A. SCHULIEN, S.T.D.
Censor librorum

IMPRIMATUR:

✠ ALBERT G. MEYER,
Archiepiscopus Milwauchiensis

August 11, 1955

CONTENTS

Part One PROLEGOMENA

Part Two METAPHYSICA

Part Three NATURALIA

v

73989

Part Four ETHICA

Part One   PROLEGOMENA

FATHER HART

BY JAMES D. COLLINS

The present collection of philosophical essays is intended by his associates and friends as a testimonial to Reverend Doctor Charles Aloysius Hart. The volume is being published with the support of the American Catholic Philosophical Association, for which Father Hart has just rounded out twenty-five years of faithful service as secretary. The essays are composed as independent contributions to philosophy on the part of a representative group of American Scholastic thinkers. They provide a cross section of the speculative interests and scholarship of contemporary Scholasticism in America.

Father Hart was born in Ottawa, Illinois, on September 6, 1893, the son of John J. Hart also of Ottawa, Illinois, and Mary Etta Donovan Hart, who was born near Galesville, Illinois. He attended the public grade and high schools of Ottawa, Illinois, after which he taught in public schools in Serena, Illinois, and at Sheridan, Illinois, in which latter town he was principal of the grade and junior high school. His college work was done at St. Viator College, Bourbonnais, Illinois, from which he received the bachelor's and master's degrees. He studied for the priesthood at St. Paul Seminary and was ordained a priest by the Most Reverend Edmund M. Dunn at Peoria, Illinois, on September 20, 1919. He was then sent to the Catholic University of America for theological and philosophical studies, obtaining S.T.B. and J.C.B. degrees in 1920 and the doctorate in philosophy in 1930. Father Hart has been associated with this institution throughout his teaching career.

3

In 1921, he received an appointment as instructor in philosophy at the Catholic University of America. He advanced steadily through the academic ranks of instructor, assistant professor, associate professor, and full professor in the School of Philosophy. In addition to his main work at the School of Philosophy, Father Hart has also taught at the Catholic Sisters College and has been professor of philosophy at the College of Notre Dame of Maryland in Baltimore since 1932. As public recognition for his services to Catholic education, his alma mater, St. Viator College, awarded him the honorary degree of Doctor of Laws in 1936.

Among the more than 5000 undergraduate and graduate students whom he has taught during his thirty-four years, Father Hart's teaching has been influential in arousing interest in the basic philosophical issues. His own example of devotion to metaphysics has kindled a similar enthusiasm in the minds of a generation of his students. His cycle of graduate courses on problems in metaphysics has served to introduce his numerous students to the main sources of the Greek and medieval traditions in first philosophy. Father Hart's lifelong interest in the theater and other arts has found educational expression in a valuable course on the relation between beauty, art, and the artist from the philosophical viewpoint. An article in the *Journal of Aesthetics and Art Criticism* (1941), entitled "Aesthetic Theory of St. Thomas Aquinas," presents some of his views in the field of Thomistic aesthetics. He hopes shortly to organize his lectures in this field in a volume for publication. Perhaps the major fruit of this educational effort is the series of over thirty doctoral dissertations, all in the field of metaphysics, written under his direction. The majority of these have been published by the Catholic University of America Press. In addition, he has directed nearly one hundred master's dissertations on more particular metaphysical problems. Both doctoral and master's dissertations have made a systematic investigation of the Aristotelian and Thomistic teachings on the nature and unity of metaphysics and its proper object, the transcendental perfections, the categories and causes of being, the problem of individuation, and Thomistic aesthetics, as well as on God, the supreme Being and Culmination of metaphysical reflection. It is typical of Father Hart's broad interest, however, that he has also encouraged and directed doctoral and master's studies in the metaphysical doctrines of Duns Scotus and other medieval thinkers in the non-Thomistic tradition. Another group of dissertations reflects his concern for establishing some intelligent and critical contact between the wealth of medieval doctrines and the systems of Whitehead, Santayana, Dewey, Croce, and other contemporary philosophers.

Father Hart has also found time to interest himself in the general activities of the student body at the university, acting for a number of years as faculty adviser for freshmen students. During this time, he secured the establishment of the Catholic University of America chapter of Phi Eta Sigma, national freshmen academic honor society, for which he continues to be the faculty adviser. He also aided a university social group in securing its establishment as Omega chapter of Phi Kappa, a national Catholic social fraternity, of which he has been adviser for the past thirty years. Father Hart is a member of the Committee on Student Activities of the college of the university and also a member of the Committee on Philosophy in the college curriculum.

Father Hart has always shown a central interest in the development of the American Catholic Philosophical Association (of which he is a charter member), assisting the late Doctors James H. Ryan and Edward A. Pace of the Catholic University faculty in the organization meeting at the university in January of 1926. At the sixth annual meeting, held at Loyola University in Chicago in December, 1930, he was elected secretary-treasurer, a post previously held by Doctors James H. Ryan and Fulton J. Sheen. He has served continuously since that date as secretary, guiding the destinies of the Association during the past quarter of a century. He was also treasurer until 1943, when this office was given separate status. During his term of office he has also been instrumental in the organization of regional conferences of the Association in various parts of the country, for the greater participation of the membership in the work of the Association by more frequent meetings at the local level. Throughout the years, successive officers and committee members have benefited greatly from Father Hart's experience and devoted energy. Among his pioneer efforts was the regular use of radio and, more recently, television to publicize the annual meetings. It is due in no small part to his foresight that the Association and its publications are operating on a sound financial basis. One of Father Hart's chief tasks has been the editing of the annual *Proceedings of the Association.* He has also edited the *Studies* of the Association and served for an appointed period of years on the editorial board of *The New Scholasticism.* Since 1949, he has conducted the column, entitled "From the Secretary's Desk," in *The New Scholasticism,* as an organ for establishing more effective communication among the members of the Association.

Father Hart's published doctoral dissertation was *The Thomistic Concept of Mental Faculty* (1930). He edited a volume of essays, sponsored by the Association in honor of Monsignor Edward A. Pace (vice-rector of Catholic University of America and first president of the Association) on his seventieth birthday, entitled *Aspects of the New Scholastic Philosophy* (1932). As his own contribution to this volume, Father Hart made a survey of the progress of Scholasticism in America since 1879: "Neo-Scholasticism in American Catholic Culture." A good portion of his other writings has appeared as papers in the *Proceedings of the American Catholic Philosophical Association.* In addition to round-table discussions and radio addresses, he has written the following papers: "America's Response to the Encyclical 'Aeterni Patris'" (1929); "Religion in the Philosophy of Society" (1933); "The Church and the State" (1939); "The Metaphysical Foundations of the Natural Law" (1950). The common thesis running through these studies is that the Christian philosopher has the obligation and right to contribute something valuable to civil society in our time. His function is to supply a rational explanation that is adequate both to the facts of human nature and to the requirements of right order and social peace. Recently, Father Hart has contributed a series of articles to *The New Scholasticism* to suggest the revolutionary character of Thomistic metaphysics in its more recent appraisal: "The

Metaphysics of Man's Nature and Peace" (1947); "Twenty-Five Years of Thomism" (1951); "Participation and the Thomistic Five Ways" (1952). The 1951 article sums up the development of American Scholasticism during the period of Father Hart's own intimate contact with most of the leaders of the field. For the *Catholic University of America Bulletin* he has contributed a number of articles on philosophical subjects, including more recent articles on the subjects: "An American Center of Neo-Scholastic Philosophy" (1942); "The Significance of Thomism for Our Times" (1947); "Reason and the Great Revelation" (1950). To a symposium on *Integration of the Curriculum of Catholic Colleges and Universities* under the editorship of Dr. Roy Deferrari, he contributed an article on "Logic in the Integration of the Curriculum of Catholic Colleges and Universities." He has also published articles and reviews in *The Catholic Educational Review, The Ecclesiastical Review, The Thomist,* and other journals.

Amid all his activities, Father Hart has always remained first and foremost a priest of God. In addition to a number of sermons preached over the national radio networks for the National Broadcasting Company's "Catholic Hour" and the Columbia Broadcasting System's "Church of the Air," his priestly work has extended to the parks and public auditoriums of Washington. In 1932 he organized the Washington Catholic Evidence Guild, with which he has remained as director. After the manner of the London Catholic Evidence Guild organized by Frank and Maisie Ward Sheed, the Washington Guild conducts outdoor religious forums on Catholic doctrine in several of the parks and other public places of the city on Sunday afternoons and evenings. The Guild's members are composed primarily of lay men and women, who attend regular weekly training classes in Catholic theology and its popular presentation, conducted by Father Hart. He has also acted as chaplain of the Washington Council, Knights of Columbus, and assisted the Council in its Columbus University teaching program, with classes in philosophy.

Father Hart has been active as a Catholic representative in the speaking programs of the National Conference of

Christians and Jews. During World War II, he served as the Catholic speaker in many trios of priests, ministers, and rabbis in the extensive religious programs in behalf of good will and understanding among the various religious faiths, and for the more active participation of enlisted men and officers in the religious services of the various establishments. Father Hart also gave the National Conference's annual lecture on "Religion in American Life" in 1940, at the University of Miami in Florida.

In line with his work in this area, he was selected to write the chapter on Roman Catholicism in the symposium, *Religion in the Twentieth Century,* edited by Vergilius Ferm (1948). In a relatively brief compass, this article gives considerable information on the Church in its foundation, organization, history, and relevance for the modern world. Within the Catholic community, Father Hart has steadily maintained the position that the present-day relevance of Catholicism depends in large degree upon the intellectual competence and integrity of our metaphysical analysis of human nature, in its individual and social aspects, in relation to God. This conviction has provided a steady beacon for all his own work in philosophy.

In a characteristic way, the following text sums up Father Hart's viewpoint as a teacher of philosophy in a Catholic university.

As a priest and teacher, I do not believe that, strictly speaking, there can be a "philosophy of life" for a Christian college or university student. Man can live fully only by the whole truth of the mysteries of Christianity, whose influence alone can save him from destroying himself. But a real theology of life cannot ordinarily be achieved except through the medium of a sound philosophy. Not only does ultimate philosophy provide a rational foundation for theology proper, but it also equips the student for such inquiry into the meaning of the mysteries of the Trinity and the Incarnation as is open to the human intellect. I have tried to give increasing emphasis on this proper and necessary relation between ultimate philosophy and theology throughout the thirty-four years of my university teaching, stressing the proper autonomy of philosophy as worthy of independent study for itself, but also urging the obligation of the Christian philosopher to look beyond his own field to divine revelation for the fuller understanding of a true way of life. It has always seemed to me that this aspect of philosophy is not sufficiently stressed in our Catholic colleges and universities. We often fail to convey the full meaning of what is properly called a "Christian philosophy," in our effort to appear before the nonreligious public as offering a system of ultimate reasoning which has had no relation of any kind with a theology proper. This misrepresents our deepest tradition. There can be proper autonomy in each of these two fields of wisdom which does not require us to sell our birthright for a mess of pottage. If it is said that Christian theology can be presented entirely without relation to metaphysics, then the exponents of such a view will nevertheless admit that philosophy is at least the ordinary door by which the trained mind may enter into the domain of the supernatural truths, inasmuch as revelation is made primarily in terms of the very existence of God, man, and man's relation with his Creator.

St. Louis University
St. Louis, Mo.

THE MEETING OF THE WAYS

BY JAMES A. MC WILLIAMS, S.J.

In its more than a quarter century of existence, the American Catholic Philosophical Association has done much intensive work. Formal studies on a high level have been presented at the conventions, in the Association's journal, and in other publications sponsored by the Executive Council. It has been our hope that as we have profited by encounters with non-Scholastic philosophies, we in turn may have a beneficial impact on philosophical thinking outside Scholastic areas. There has been, in fact, a general veering toward the same objectives we have been pursuing. It would be invidious, certainly, for one side to take the credit for all this. Hence it seems more proper to note some points of accord between ourselves and others, and at the same time to signalize certain hazards that endanger that accord and imperil the whole philosophical enterprise.

Philosophy as such is not a "faith once delivered to the saints," and containing all the truths which man is privileged to know from that source; it is instead a human enterprise endeavoring to discover the basic principles of all reality as far as the best efforts of human reason by itself can succeed in doing so. Consequently, philosophy is not a thing peculiar to any particular church or nation; it is open to the whole human race or to any of the race who have the interest and the competence to enter into it. In that spirit everything that follows herein will be set forth.

To indicate the immediate antecedents of the recent turn in philosophical thinking, let us put it this way: previous phi-

11

losophers were more concerned about ideas than about things. Philosophy was preoccupied with what the mind was doing when thinking, rather than what the thinking was about. Scientists, it is true, tried to forget the mind and concentrate on the objective world, in particular the subatomic world, but that world, under the manipulation of mathematics, by which alone it could be reached, became so mysterious that many speculative scientists were drawn back into the mind-complex, becoming concerned with ideas or symbols instead of things. It is from this recurrent "egocentric predicament" that contemporary philosophers are endeavoring to extricate both themselves and the scientists.

To succeed in this, the first impasse to escape from is the idealist contention that ideas are things, and indeed the only things that can ever be known. The Idealists have their own trouble with this, because their various ideas do not agree with one another. That raises the harrying question: Can irreducible known fact be incompatible with irreducible known fact? Many philosophers are refusing to succumb to such despair. They are saying that there must be other things besides ideas, things where there are no contradictions. Moreover, to maintain his position the Idealist must show not only that there are no other things, but that it is inconceivable that there could be other things. Yet, when he denies other things he must have some conception of what he is denying.

The only way out is to accept the fact that we have no immediate and direct awareness of ideas but only of things. To illustrate this point, let us enlarge the term "idea" to include sense image (without insisting for the moment on the distinction between the two) and introduce as a witness Professor Emeritus W. H. Sheldon. He is speaking of eyesight, "which," he says, "typically involves in the sensing beholder no noticeable subjective change, *nothing but the object seen.*"[1] In this primitive experience there is simply a burgeoning of *things.* What, if anything, goes on in the beholder is not seen nor in any way experienced. Later on we do reason that something must have happened within the beholder, and if you

---

[1] *God and Polarity* (New Haven, Conn.: Yale University Press, 1954), p. 479. Italics added.

wish to give the name "idea" to whatever happened there, then you are saying that idea is something you must reason to; not a matter of direct awareness but a conclusion therefrom. With that distinction we can say that what we directly experience are things, and by inference we can know many other things which we do not directly experience; such as the processes that go on in the dark recesses of the optic thalamus and which enable us to see, yes, but to see *other* things.

The next impasse from which to escape is the fact that the image can be recalled in the absence of the object which originated it. But here we need only note that the image in its inception is identical with some aspect or form of an actually existing thing. The "when" and "where" of the object are not constituents of the thing or of its form. All sensations are, as a matter of fact, later than the phenomena they record; often so late that the place and condition of the object have changed, as with the rocket plane we hear or the stars we see. Putting aside, then, the time and place of the originating cause (which are things to be reasoned to), we need only maintain that the form which the image has is the form of something other than the process that brought it about. The process is a *quo*, a "by which," not a *quod*, not the thing known. As in the clear light of day the light itself is not seen but only the bodies therein, so knowledge is visible reality in the daylight of awareness.

Somewhat in this fashion philosophers are currently endeavoring to free themselves from the trammels of "ideation" and get at their proper task of piecing together the elements of reality. A well-known example of this is the group of essays under the title, *Return to Reason*[2] And there are many other instances of the same trend. On the Scholastic side surely the intense concentration on "being" is a striving to get away from mere "ideas" and back to reality. Some may even feel that the Schoolmen are overdoing it by urging Aristotle's description of knowing as the *mind becoming the object*.[3] That might seem very like the contention of the American New

[2] *Return to Reason* (Chicago: Regnery, 1953).
[3] *De Anima*, III, ch. 2, 425^b–26; ch. 4, 430^a–4 ff.

Realists that the awareness is "out there," in the external object. As Francis H. Parker says, these "Pan-Objectivists" resorted to the "flinging of Hume's impressions and ideas outward into the 'objective' world."[4] Yet Parker himself endorses Aristotle's dictum that "the soul is in a sense all reality." All this surely gives priority to objective reality. But the difference is this. When Aristotle says a subject "becomes" something else, he means it acquires a form it did not have before. And since all reality is the object of intelligence, the soul, to the degree it knows all reality, has become all reality. However, the object has the form first, and the mind acquires it. The Pan-Objectivists held that the *object* acquires the form; and so the object "becomes" the mind, and we are back in idealism.[5]

A valid realism must therefore maintain that the existent is prior to knowledge of it. And whatever efficient causes may be involved in producing an image, the image is *form*, not producing agent or process. Form, to be explicit, is any distinctive quality or "kind," so that if a thing is like or unlike another it is so by its form.[6] Contrary to Kant, the mind does not posit the forms, but instead lets the existing world in. While remaining entitatively distinct, the mind takes on the forms of that world without assimilating the matter, so that the image and the object are formally identical. And since things are knowable by their forms, the forms existing in awareness are the knowledge of existing things.

Admittedly we have been ignoring some problems of sense perception, such as the "elliptical" penny (when viewed at an angle) and the oar "broken" at the surface of the water. These questions greatly perplexed the Neo-Realists because seemingly they forgot that the senses make no judgment, and in any case considerable sense experience (called *experimentum*

---

[4] *Return to Reason*, p. 161.

[5] These and other Neo-Realist attempts at realism the writer has discussed in "British Neo-Realists," *The New Scholasticism*, III, 3, July, 1929, and "Realism in Science," *Modern Schoolman*, XVII, 2, January, 1939.

[6] Cf. St. Thomas: "Quum diversarum rerum sit distinctio ratione propriarum formarum, necesse est ut quod alicui secundum propriam formam simile fuerit, alteri dissimile inveniatur." *C. G.*, I, 54, n. 2.

by the ancients) is required before any significant idea can be formed or judgment elicited. On the purely sense level, realism has no meaning. Nor are genuine Realists primarily concerned with the noetic process itself. They are seeking the nature of the existential world. Too often, though, they are frustrated by surreptitiously introducing as prime data what are conclusions derived from such data. When, for instance, I see or hear things, I readily conclude that there must be some operation within me that caused the things to be seen or heard, and I am tricked into saying that all I experienced was a modification of myself; whereas I actually experienced something *else*. This error leads to the hopeless attempt at comparing my subjective states with the objective world. In this I am defeated at the start, because to make a comparison on that basis I must ideate them both; the result being that I could do no more than compare idea with idea, never with the existing world. But this impasse is due to mistaking for a prime datum what is in fact a conclusion therefrom.

It is admittedly difficult to uncover the simon-pure prime data of awareness, buried as they are under the conclusions and associations of adult life. The association may sometimes be disrupted. Thus a patient recovering from a total anesthetic will hear coughing without knowing that it is he himself who is coughing. Still his past experience supervenes to classify the sound as a cough. Genetic psychology, it is true, seeks to explore the earliest infant experiences, the very first awakenings of awareness. But here again adult experience presents as propositional knowledge what could hardly be reported except by exclamations and, if possible, pointings. Nevertheless, many a philosopher, anxious to find *being* in every awareness, has wondered how it could possibly be found in the most primitive.

By reducing awareness to its very minimum, we must at least say that in every sense experience, whether infant or adult, things simply spring up out of nothingness, they begin to be: a sounding thing, then another; a savory thing, then another; an odorous, and so on. Each is in contrast to the others, and in contrast to its own previous nonbeing. And into nonbeing they (so far as sense is concerned) subside again. However, the things just enumerated have no spatial spread, no distinction of place; they are "immaterial" qualities with no intimation of an extended world. But with visual experience there occur astonishingly new things, colors spread out. With touch, these extended things have a feel; and a three-way expanse, giving play to motion. Not simply qualities now, but extended colors and feels: bodies, outside of and distant from one another; things "out there" and distinct from the body I discover to be my own.

Hence, in the very origin of experience, sense data occur as distinct beings. Intellectual knowledge of being literally starts with sense. Not after it. The attempt to sever *any* human knowledge from the deliverance of sense is futile. Knowledge, however come by, is an awareness of existing things, not of thingless "ideas." Furthermore, apart from any "out there," the experience of the continuous change of qualities, as well as the *return* of past experiences, contain an awareness of an enduring subject, supplying the basis for the distinction of perceiver and perceived, entitatively distinct, even if not spatially so.

While we may assume that realistic philosophers will proceed *pari passu* thus far, there is danger of mere verbal agreement in subsequent steps. Instances of this are the meanings attached to "substance," "possibles," and "being." As to the first, let us concede at once that the senses themselves never make any distinction between substance and accident. To intelligence alone is it evident that some things are resident in another as their immediate subject — which indeed may again be resident in another, but there must ultimately be some subject not resident in another, and that is substance. However, some accidents, the specific properties, cling to the substance as long as the species endures. But it is a mistake to include these inseparable accidents under the term "substance," leaving only the contingent to be called "accidents." Scholastics have endeavored to avoid this error by reserving the term *essence* (in the strict sense) to designate substance. Certainly no finite substance can exist without accidents but that does not make them identical. On the other hand a substance together with all its accidents, both proper and contingent, is a single existing being. As the accidents vary, so does the one existence vary; but not the essence. And here we glimpse the beginning (though not the end) of the famous distinction between essence and existence in one finite being.

Although "essence" in a broad sense means anything intelligible, we must be careful not to jump to the conclusion that essences are simply nonexistent objects of thought, or the pure possibles. That unfortunately is what Sheldon does when he says, "The two poles are the existence and the essence or *possibility*."[7] There are no *existing* pure possibles, but there *are* existing essences. As to possibles, the only existent is their foundation, from which the mind selects the elements which it puts together in a nonexistent combination. The possible as such is not actual; it is not even a potency, active or passive. As Aquinas warns us, "A thing is denominated 'absolutely possible,' not because of a potency at all but because of the compatibility of terms that are not repugnant to one another."[8] Only existing things have potencies. So, before equating essence with possibility, we should remember that pure possibles are such only because and only so long as they are being thought of. (Also it is well to observe that by "possible" St. Thomas *usually* means an existing thing, any existing thing with a passive potency to be changed, as a body, or the "possible" intellect.) About the "absolutely possible" it can be said that the constituent "terms" get both their character and their compatibility from the essence of God, as their ultimate foundation.

Empirical psychology has so engrossed the attention of the epistemologist and even the metaphysician that it has too often distracted them from their own proper quests of establishing the conditions of certainty and of investigating reality in its entirety. Nor has psychology itself been immune from subversion by physics and biology. All this is an emphasis on the efficient causes of knowledge and is misleading, because knowledge, however it may be produced, is not a case of efficient but of formal cause. Nevertheless there is one point we

---

[7] *Op. cit.*, p. 688. Italics added.
[8] *S. T.*, I, 46, 1, ad 1.

must note here. Only an existing thing can act as an efficient cause. Hence, regardless of the means by which it does so, only an existing thing can cause a knowledge of itself. And any discipline that professes to be seeking knowledge must admit the absolute priority of existing being and not allow the "thinker" to usurp that priority. Kantian rationalism pretended that the mind could efficiently fashion its own world; reasoning was what the mind did to the object. Bluntly put, it is the other way around: reasoning is what the objective existing world does to the mind.

Farther back in history Descartes did not indeed rate knowledge as an efficient cause, but by his insistence on his own "clear and distinct idea," he shifted the basis of his philosophy from the object to the subject. For surely the objective existing thing itself cannot be anything but what it is, excluding any confusion with what it is not. If there is any confusion or fogginess, that must come from the subject. But since Descartes is often accused of getting modern philosophy off on the wrong foot, we would do well to remember that he lived at a time when subjectivists and objectivists, particularly in religion, were engaged in a real world war. Yet both sides conceded that in the moral order the sincere personal conviction of the individual is a valid norm for the moral rightness of his own conduct. To extend that rule, however, as many more than Descartes were doing, to mean that the sincerity of any conviction warrants its objective verity, is philosophy's suicide. Conviction does not determine the objective fact. The contrary must be the case if philosophy is to live.

It is important here to note that even in moral matters where the judgment of the individual conscience is the un-impeachable guide, objectivity must remain supreme; because, for the conscience to be genuine, the individual must make every reasonable endeavor to square his judgment with the existing objective situation. If he does not do that, his "conscience" is unworthy of the name, and any error he makes is inexcusable. Realism views every individual human nature as having, like any other nature, a definite character with definite tendencies and needs ingrained in it, so that these remain there as long as the nature remains. Any misuse, therefore, of that nature, whether well intentioned or not, must inevitably have bad results on the perpetrators themselves and on the race. Likewise, any treatment in harmony with that nature will have beneficial effects. Philosophical errors in regions seemingly remote from human happiness work their way at last into human conduct and by prompting mistaken moral judgments become a detriment to human well-being. False philosophies equally with false consciences are, willy-nilly, a menace to the dignity and happiness of man.

That there has been a veering toward this objectivism by non-Scholastic writers is evident from the current professional literature.[9] On the other hand, the Existentialists, even in moral matters which they claim as their forte, and despite their name, cannot, as a school, be classed as Realists. In their revolt from the Idealists (as Hegel) who reveled in detached essences evolving by dialectic necessity, the Existentialists started from the presupposition that no ideas or essences are ever realized in human beings; that there are no such things as essences existing there and never will be. Consequently, for them essences are sheer nothingness, and to entertain any idea that could be called an "essence," is to plunge into the chasm which they dread and from which they are ever struggling to escape. Hence they cannot tolerate the thought of the human being having a specific nature or "essence," with an innate natural law. Still, if they were to grant man a rational nature (they need not call it an essence), then, but only then, would they be right in maintaining that the individual builds up his own moral personality. The good act must be in conformity with some nature; if there is no enduring nature, there is no building.

The human will, of which the Existentialists make so much because it is not fixed or predetermined, is an appetite. Man has an option about how to gratify this appetite, and so he is not predetermined. However fixed a nature may be, it can still be conceived as free, so that the existing individuals are not necessitated in all their actions. And if "essence" is said

---

9 Random examples are: Foster, *Masters of Political Thought,* Vol. I; Ebenstein, *Man and the State;* Veach, *Intentional Logic.*

to limit act, that only refers to the obvious fact that any substance cannot give or take more than it is capable of.[10] Minerals can act on one another but they cannot learn or acquire habits, vegetal organisms have irritability but no sensation, brute animals have sensation but no intellection. Yet within the range of its potentialities, every essence is capable of innumerable actions and changes. As for man, the potential *objects* of his intelligence are limitless, nevertheless subjectively he is limited (in his corporeal life) to acquiring knowledge through his senses. Likewise his will is limited to the options offered by that knowledge. All this should be obvious to anyone. But the important point is that the will's options are for weal or woe accordingly as it chooses or refuses the goods that are in accord with the *de facto* rational nature of man. In that way the will freely improves or damages the moral and even, by its insidious influence, the intellectual character of the individual.

In the existing world each thing has its individual form. It is by their distinguishing forms that existing things are revealed in awareness. Intelligence can indeed range them in classes and can discern in them many connections, implications, and bases for inference to other things not directly given. But if the cognoscitive powers are so dominated by the actual existents, error would seem to be impossible. Yet error is a fact admitted by all. What is the answer?

By default of other explanations the search for an answer leads to the orectic tendencies, the appetites, of the knowing subject. Even on the irrational level an analogous thing happens. The trout strikes at the artificial fly, the greyhound courses the synthetic hare, migrating birds in a storm seek fatal refuge by dashing into a beacon light. Orectic tendencies overreach the cognoscitive data. In a similar manner man's eagerness for a certain conclusion often prompts a judgment without sufficient evidence. It is not a case of the intellect's being forced to judge without *any* evidence (that would be impossible) but of its being induced to accept a thing under some partial aspect as the only distinctive form of the existent

---

[10] Cf. St. Thomas, *Compendium Theologiae*, I, c. 18.

being. Thus, because man is biological, to judge that he is only that is to ignore a great part of the evidence. Likewise, if, with the Existentialists, I am avid to vindicate the individual as the only really existent object of knowledge (and this is commendable), I may refuse to consider the formal character that is equally as real and evident as the individual peculiarities, and which is seen repeated in other individuals. In all this the will cannot be exculpated from the charge of an initial refusal. All other propensities respond positively and find gratification in so doing. Only the will's response, because it is free, can be a simple negative; the will can enjoy declining. But after it has induced a first misstep in judgment or attention, others follow logically, leaving the fallacious impression that this consistency insures consistency with fact.

Whether the will or the intellect be at fault, must philosophers forever oscillate between individual and universal? between nominalism and conceptualism? Must we accept one of these hard alternatives to the exclusion of the other? It is from that predicament that realism is trying to free itself. When we say that all our knowledge begins with sensation, we do not mean that sensation is first had, then put aside before intellection begins. For the human being the primitive elements of intellection (or of metaphysics, if you like) are, as we have said, born simultaneously with every sensation. The sensible is also intelligible; in every sensation the existent is contrasted with nonexistence, and one existent with all others. Being is the first object of intelligence, and we have it here. Only when that is attained can abstraction begin. Abstraction is an operation of the intellect but it does not take something away from sense data and carry it off to some separate realm totally immune from sense. Abstraction takes place *within* the very things of direct sense awareness. Our own experience tells us that we keep in attentive awareness the individual differences of two or more things equally, at the very time and in the very act of recognizing a common trait. Besides, if that were not the case, we would never know where our abstractions came from nor know to what to apply them in predication. Hence the individual and universal are not inimical and mutually exclusive; they exist together.

It is clear, then, that the common trait is just as existent as the individual peculiarities. The crux comes, though, when we discover that *after* we have perceived the common trait we can separate it in thought from particular individuals and, disregarding its origin, consider it apart from them all, and even endow it with a new set of peculiarities which no existing individual has ever had. In this way the science-fiction writers picture rational animals on other planets who differ widely from earthmen except in the common trait of rational nature. In the same way we can fashion many possibles to which we ascribe no existence whatever. We can even refine our universals to a stage at which they could not exist at all, as a mathematical line or plane, and other *entia rationis*. Yet all these achievements have their foundation in sense experience, and it is a matter of conscious awareness that particular phantasms hover about even these concepts (perhaps by operation of the "cogitative sense") to keep us reminded, as it were, of their existential origin.

But even this is not the full account. Besides sense data and concepts, there is the most important knowledge of all, judgmental knowledge. Thus when an existing being is *increasing* continuously, the very analysis of the being compels the judgment that there is a continuing subject, and that there is some other existing being which is causing the change. To cite St. Thomas on this question would be superfluous, but there is one insight of his that should be signalized. It is that the very nature of continuous change requires it to be in the *existing* order. "Being moved is not said of non-existing things. . . . We do say that non-existents are conceivable or imaginable or even desirable, but not that they are being moved. Being moved implies an actual existent."[11] Here then is judgmental knowledge that there is a subject and a cause actually existing. This knowledge cannot be neutral to actual existence as imaginations and concepts can be. And by a similar necessary inference we come to a judgmental knowledge of existing spiritual beings.

Images and concepts, although they formally contain the

---

[11] *In IX Meta.*, L. 3, nn. 1805–1806 (Marietti).

factual existents that have been experienced, are not the most important part of knowledge. We must note that even contingent existents have consequent necessities that force intelligence to the knowledge of other existent things that are implicit in the immediate data. That most important knowledge is called judgmental, and it always attains to existing things. And to such alone. If that statement seems excessive, then, putting aside all scruples about the extent of its impact, we should consider that, since concepts are formally the essences of things, there is nothing left for the judgment but to attest the extramental existence. Images, it is true, arise from existing objects but they can be refined to such elements as do not or cannot exist in just that way; still these elements do exist in some complex. Judgment attests the whole complex that is required to assert: There *is* (or was) something that actually has this characteristic. Negative judgments, on the other hand, simply mean that the intelligence finds no existent that is, or ever was, such a subject of such a predicate. Hence to ignore the existential import of judgment is to yield to the illusion that knowledge can be divorced from the existing world.

In résumé, then, realism requires (*a*) that prior to the fact of knowing, the faculty is ontologically distinct from the object to be known; (*b*) that the object actuates the faculty, never the reverse; (*c*) that the actuating effected by the faculty's reaction is simply awareness; (*d*) that the actuating effected by the object is the image or concept produced in the faculty; (*e*) that the consequent judgments attest extramental existence. The first four requirements are generally accepted by Realists, but they are futile without the last. By the last, too, we learn that both object and faculty are efficient causes but the ontological object is the *only formal cause* of the awareness that we call knowledge. Formally, the *actus* of the faculty is identical with some *actus* of the objectively existing thing. There is therefore no mystery about the maxim: "*Sensibile in actu est sensus in actu, et intelligibile in actu est intellectus in actu.*"[12] The actuating done by the object as sen-

---

[12] St. Thomas, *S. T.*, I, 14, 2, (c).

sible is the actuation of the sense, and the actuating done by the object as intelligible is the actuation of the intellect — whether the actuation be concept or judgment.

In contemporary philosophical literature the emphasis on *being* is indeed an insistence on the primacy of the existent object. But many readers are baffled by the constant repetition of the word. To them, the term "being" is so vague that, instead of explaining anything, it is more like a series of dull blows on the head. "Being?" Why, everything is that. Whether permanent or changing, absolute or relative, everything merits the term. And what is so common to all must be so vague and meager in content, so near to nothingness that we can scarcely form any notion of it. This difficulty of course comes from attempting the impossible task of forming a universal concept of existence, as something totally detached from all existents. We then fancy that by adding something that is *not* existence we get the different classes of beings. But that would be to add nothing. Hence, unlike a universal, existence cannot be set off in an exclusive category by itself; it pervades all the categories. Philosophers should be humble enough to accept a fact that they cannot categorize; and frank enough to admit that there is a judgmental knowledge that goes beyond the conceptual.

As all subjects of judgment are ultimately existent things, so all genuine predicates ascribe to them a greater or lesser existence according to the concepts formed from the sense data. But once the conceptual barriers are dissolved, "existence" stands ready to be applied to the totality of any subject which the judgmental act may discover in illimitable reality, and thus the endless wealth and variety of existing things flood the intellect without let or hindrance. In the expanding horizon of this knowledge, worlds mount above worlds. From the intricate structure of the atom to the man who contemplates it, from the flora that carpets the earth to the seemingly lifeless island universes of outer space, from the instinctive fauna to the subsistent spiritual substances — all are burgeonings of the richness of existence. In this growing abundance of things the mind's hunger also grows; by their vanishing, its quest is only heightened for the inexhaustible source from which these contingent particulars are but derivatives. And the ascent from lesser to greater, from good to better, is a direction set by the very existents themselves.

But abundance is not all. Still more are we inspired by the existential compatibility that excludes contradictions and impels the mind to form compatible judgments and inescapable conclusions. Axiomatic truths, nay, logical necessity itself is imbedded in existential reality. And although the will, prior to its choice, has an option as to what things it may make exist, once a thing does exist, that fact can never be undone, so that in the most contingent and transient existents necessity is revealed, and their very differing from one another remains a fact immutable. These necessities reigning throughout the mutable world are ingredients of every awareness. Underived from anything in that world, unalloyed by time, they tower above individual things, and above all the speculations I may rear thereon, objectively guiding the mind to existence's ever increasing unfolding.

By reason of the necessary priority of existence over knowledge, my thoughts are subsequent and adventitious to existent reality; reality must ever be there awaiting my loftiest explorations. Hence judgment, refusing to halt at the abstractions achieved within the manifold of experience, cannot rest until it attaches itself to some extramental, unabstracted existent. Be it knowledge of cause, of substance or accident, of matter or spirit, the judgmental operation, grounding itself in the sense data and the conceived essences thereof, reaches out to existing things not *prima facie* present in immediate awareness but which it is forced by these very data themselves to affirm. Confronted thus with boundless existence beyond ourselves, existence as the exclusive source of the very possibles themselves, we are both awed and heartened by the looming up of a supremely subsistent eternal Fact that is the foundation of all knowledge and consistency.

St. Louis University
St. Louis, Mo.

Part Two   METAPHYSICA

On the Notion of Subsistence*
Further Elucidations (1954)

BY JACQUES MARITAIN

The first draft of the "Note on the Notion of Subsistence" contained in Annex IV of *Les Degrés du Savoir* appears in all previous editions. It has been reprinted in the present edition since it represents a certain typical approach to the problem which has seemed true to us now for a long time, and also because it has furnished one of the themes discussed in the recent controversies on the problem. At present, however, we consider that it requires revision, not in its fundamental insights, but in regard to certain corollaries against which the criticisms addressed by Father H. Diepen seem to be justified.[1]

Father Diepen, moreover, is quite correct in suspecting[2] that the philosophical considerations in question have been inspired by reflection on the theology of the Incarnation, especially by reflection on the thesis of the Thomistic school which

---

* The following article was prepared for the new English translation of M. Maritain's *Les Degrés du Savoir* (Charles Scribner's Sons, New York). In response to the editors' request, M. Maritain was pleased to allow it to appear also in this volume as a tribute to Doctor Hart.

[1] Father H. Diepen, O.S.B., "La Critique du Baslisme selon saint Thomas d'Aquin," *Revue Thomiste,* 1950, I, and 1950, II. Particularly does the author seem right in noting (p. 115), against what we wrote in the first draft, that the act of existing "is of itself perfectly adapted and accommodated to the essence which is its formal principle; so perfectly that it can be joined to no other essence in the actuation of the latter." Whence it follows that it ought to be considered "an impossibility for one essence to be joined to another essence in a common actuation, hence in an act of existing in so far as it is the actuation of the essence" (cf. also *ibid.,* p. 304).

[2] *Ibid.,* p. 117.

affirms that just as there is but one subsistence, that of the Verbum, in Christ, so also there is but one existence, the uncreated existence of the Verbum, in virtue of which exists also the human nature assumed by Him. Father Diepen attacks this thesis of "the ecstasy of existence" (according to which the human nature of Christ, deprived of its own existence is enraptured so to speak in the eternal *esse* which holds it outside nothingness).[3] He maintains that the human and created nature has been actuated in Christ by a human and created existence, and asserts that on this point Cajetan and all the great Thomists of the school have forced the thought of their master. After carefully weighing them, it now seems to me that Father Diepen's arguments can hardly be refuted. But when the same author, in explaining how there is nevertheless only one personal *esse* in Christ, as St. Thomas formally teaches, endeavors to show that the created existence of the human nature concurs with the uncreated existence of the Verbum in that personal *esse*,[4] then the least we can say is that it remains very obscure as far as we are concerned.

Not being a theologian by profession, it is no business of ours to take sides in this debate and to choose between the Thomism of Father Diepen and the Thomism of Cajetan, John of St. Thomas, Gonet, Billuart, and Garrigou-Lagrange. If, moreover, we have recourse to the texts of the Angelic Doctor himself, we are not freed, at least at first sight, from the difficulty. For we find on the one hand that he teaches:

> Sic igitur cum humana natura conjungatur Filio Dei hypostatice vel personaliter, et non accidentaliter: consequens est quod secundum naturam humanam non adveniat ei novum esse personale, sed solum *nova habitudo esse personalis praeexistentis* ad naturam humanam, ut scilicet persona illa jam dicatur subsistere non solum secundum divinam naturam, sed etiam secundum humanam [*S. T.*, III, 17, 2].

and again:

---

[3] This thesis is defended in particular by Father R. Garrigou-Lagrange, *De Christo Salvatore* (Turin, 1946), p. 314 ff. Father Diepen's criticism of it is presented in the *Revue Thomiste*, 1950, II.

[4] *Revue Thomiste*, 1950, II, pp. 521–524.

Illud esse aeternum, Filii Dei, quod est divina natura, *fit esse hominis,* in quantum humana natura assumitur a Filio Dei in unitatem personae [*ibid.,* ad 2].

But on the other hand he declares in an opusculum of which the authenticity is today recognized,[5] and which antedates the Third Part of the *Summa Theologiae* by a few years:

> Sicut Christus est unum simpliciter propter unitatem suppositi, et duo secundum quid propter duas naturas: ita habet unum esse simpliciter propter unum esse aeternum aeterni suppositi. *Est autem aliud esse hujus suppositi,* non in quantum est aeternum: sed *in quantum est temporaliter homo factum.* Quod esse, etsi non est accidentale, quia homo non praedicatur accidentaliter de Filio Dei, ut supra habitum est, *non tamen est esse principale sui suppositi, sed secundarium.* Si autem in Christo essent duo supposita, tunc utrumque suppositum haberet proprium esse sibi principale, et sic in Christo essent simpliciter duo esse [*De Unione Verbi Incarnati,* a. 4].

In any case, simply as a philosopher, we may learn a lesson from the mishap to which theology exposed us in the first version of our discussion of the notion of subsistence. Henceforth, while we shall always recognize the fact that it is the theology of the Hypostatic Union which has led philosophy to become aware of the problems concerning the person and subsistence, we will abstain from linking our philosophical reflections on subsistence to a particular theological theory, especially to one subject to controversy and which may eventually be discredited, and force ourselves to proceed on a basis and within a frame of reference that is purely philosophical.

The following three are the fundamental considerations on which, in our opinion, we must rely:

In the first place, it is things, subjects, *existents* that we experience. From these existents our intelligence disengages by abstraction *essences* — "suchnesses" or intelligible "struc-

---

[5] If previously we did not take into account the *De Unione Verbi Incarnati,* it was because relying on Cajetan we doubted its authenticity. But contemporary criticism following Father Pelster now maintains that authenticity to be definitely established. Hence, even if the text of Article 4 is the only one of its kind in the work of St. Thomas, it is proper nevertheless to emphasize with Father Diepen (*art. cit.,* pp. 296–297) the incontestable importance of such an ἅπαξ.

tures." These are the object of its first operation (simple apprehension) and of eidetic vision. Though these essences are found in a state of universality in our mind, where they are known as such, they exist really in things — in a state of singularity, as individual natures. To deny or to put in doubt this extramental reality of (individuated) essences would be to put in doubt the noetic value of the human intelligence.[6] But for a sufficiently attentive analysis, what is the absolutely precise and "pure" data of the intelligence as far as essences are concerned? Because they are derived from existents by the operation of the intelligence, they do not give the existents themselves as these are present to us, but quite precisely something immanent in the existents and which determines the existents to be what they are. The intelligence seizes them and gives them to us as *that by which* the things, subjects, or existents are such or such. Hence in its very notion, essence is a principle *quo*.

In the second place, essence is potency in relation to existence, to the act of existing, which is act and perfection *par excellence*. Essence is form or act in a certain order (the order of specification), but potency or capacity in another (the order of exercise) or in relation to *esse*. Between essence and existence there is a relation analogous to that which we observe between the intelligence and the act of intellection, the will and the act of volition.

> "Esse rei consequitur principia essentialia rei sicut operatio virtutem."[7] "Sicut enim potentia se habet ad operationem ut ad suum actum, ita se habet essentia ad esse."[8] "Sicut autem ipsum esse est actualitas quaedam essentiae, ita operari est actualitas operativae potentiae. Secundum enim hoc utrumque eorum est in actu: essentia quidem secundum esse, potentia vero secundum operari."[9]

In the third place, there is an intuition of existence, which is the first act of any authentic metaphysics, and in virtue of which, within the very analogy to which we have just referred

---

6 Cf. our *Introduction Générale à la Philosophie*, pp. 141–155.

7 *In II Sent.*, dist. 15, q. 3, a. 1, ad 5.

8 *Ibid.*, q. 79, a. 1.

9 *De spiritualibus creaturis*, a. 11.

between the *esse* in relation to essence and the act of intellection or of volition in relation to the intellect or the will, the *esse,* is perceived quite precisely — even as in their own order intellection and volition — as an *exercised act,*[10] exercised by the thing or the existent subject, or as an activity in which the existent itself is engaged, an energy that it exerts. Existence is therefore not only received, as if by *esse* essences were pinned outside nothingness like a picture hung on a wall. Existence is not only received, it is also *exercised.* And this distinction between existence as received and existence as exercised is central for the philosophical theory of subsistence. It was not made explicit in the first draft of this "Note," which was thus open to the criticisms of Father Diepen. Truly — one can rightly maintain — since it is the potency to *esse,* essence as such suffices by that very fact to limit, appropriate, or circumscribe to itself the existence that it *receives* (in order to bring the subject to existence). But to *exercise* existence something besides the bare essence is necessary, namely the supposit or person. *Actiones sunt suppositorum,* actions are proper to supposits, and especially and above all the act of exercising existence. In other words, to exercise existence the essence must be completed by subsistence and thus become a supposit.

By way of parenthesis we might note that a consideration of the *esse* proper to operations, and more generally to accidents, brings remarkable confirmation to the necessity of distinguishing between existence as received and existence as exercised. In effect the nature is the radical principle *quo,* powers or faculties the proximate principle *quo* of operations. It is the supposit (*quod*) which produces or accomplishes them. What does this mean if not that the supposit *exercises* the diverse accidental *esse* which are proper to its diverse operations — as well as the diverse accidental *esse* proper to its powers or faculties. But neither the faculties nor the operations *exercise* the (accidental) existence proper to them.[11]

---

[10] Cf. H. Diepen, *art. cit.,* p. 303.

[11] When the faculties pass into act, they exercise (in a secondary fashion and as instruments of the supposit) their operations and the accidental *esse* proper to the latter. But precisely as powers or faculties they do not exercise their own accidental *esse,* which is exercised only by the supposit from which they emanate (and which uses them as instruments only when they pass into act).

They are activated by it, they *receive* it in the substance in which they inhere and "to which" they belong, they do not *exercise* it. It is the supposit that exercises existence — its own substantial *esse* and the accidental *esse* of its operations. And so we have here a similar situation in that the *esse* which is *received* by the accidents is not *exercised* by them, but is *exercised* by the supposit.

In regard to the substantial *esse,* it is *received* by the nature and (by means of the nature) by the supposit. It is *exercised* by the supposit.

It was no mistake to insist on the most important significance of the difference of order between essence and existence and of the "transcendence," so to speak, of existence in relation to essence. But what inference should be drawn from that? Since existence by its very notion demands, as we have just seen, that it be not only received but exercised, and since this exigency, pertaining as it does to the existential order, places us outside and beyond the order of essence, it must be said that (substantial) essence or nature can *receive* existence only by *exercising* it, which it cannot do as long as it remains in its own essential order. In other words, it can receive existence only on condition of being drawn at the same time from the state of simple essence and placed in an *existential state* which makes of it a *quod* capable of exercising existence. This *state* which completes, or rather surcompletes the essence — not at all in the line of essence itself, but in relation to a completely other order, the existential order — and permits the essence (henceforth supposit) to *exercise* existence is precisely subsistence.

Nor was it a mistake to affirm that if existence is received

Nor do the *operations* exercise their own accidental *esse*. The latter, like themselves, is exercised by the supposit (principally) and by the faculties (instrumentally).

In short it is only when an accident (such as an active power or a *habitus* . . .) is actually used by the supposit to produce an operation that it exercises — secondarily and instrumentally — an accidental *esse* (that of the operation). In all other cases it is the supposit alone which exercises the *esse* of the accidents, which is received but not exercised by them. In this we have one of the characteristic signs of the fact that there is only analogy between substantial *esse* and accidental *esse*. Any other conception of accident makes it an additional little substance.

by the essence as act by potency, it is by (the existence) *itself holding* (not certainly by efficient causality, but by formal or intrinsically activating causality) the essence outside the realm of simple possibility,[12] since the *esse* is not received by the essence as in a pre-existing subject which would thus already be in existential act. The essence which receives existence holds from it, in what concerns the existential order, absolutely all its actuality, in short is nothing without it. But what must be inferred from that? Exactly the same as in the preceding observation. Since existence is by its very notion an exercised act, the essence can be so held outside the realm of simple possibility only on condition of being at the same time carried by subsistence to the state of subject or supposit capable of *exercising* existence.

And so the proper effect of subsistence is not, as we thought at the time of the first drafting of this "Note," to confer on the individuated essence or individual nature an additional incommunicability (this time in relation to existence) or to make it limit, appropriate, or circumscribe to itself the existence it receives, and hence prevent its communicating in existence with another essence or receiving existence conjointly with another essence; it is simply to place it in a state of *exercising existence*, with the incommunicability proper to the individual nature. The individual nature does not receive a new incommunicability from the fact of subsistence. Facing existence as a subject or supposit capable of exercising existence, it is enabled to transfer into the existential order, to exercise in existence itself the incommunicability which characterizes it in the order of essence and as an individual nature distinct from any other. This is not a new kind of incommunicability, but the promotion onto a new plane of the incommunicability which defines singularity. Subsistence renders the essence (become supposit) capable of existing *per se*

---

[12] On this point, as with regard to the "transcendence" of existing, we are happy to be in agreement with Rev. Father M. Corvez, O.P. ("Existence and Essence," *Revue Thomiste*, 1951, II). And with him we hold that "we may believe that the fear . . . that in writing *holds, sustains the essence*" we have "unconsciously envisaged efficient causality, is without foundation." (*Ibid.*, p. 324, note 1.)

separatim,[13] because it renders an individual nature (become supposit) capable of exercising existence.

It appears, then, that subsistence constitutes a new metaphysical dimension, a positive actuation or perfection, but under the title of a *state* (according as a "state" is distinguished from a "nature") or of a terminative mode. Thus do we understand, with however certain important modifications, the position of Cajetan.[14] Let us say that the *state* in question is a state of *active exercise,* which by that very fact makes the essence pass beyond the order of essentiality (terminates it in the sense) and introduces it into the existential order — a state by reason of which the essence so completed faces existence not in order to receive it only but to exercise it, and constitute henceforth a center of existential and operative activity, a subject or supposit which exercises at once the substantial *esse* proper to it and the diverse accidental *esse* proper to the operation which it produces by its powers or faculties.

And when the subject or supposit is a person, subsistence, from the fact that the nature which it "terminates" or "sur-completes" is an intellectual nature — whether a pure spirit, or a spirit animating a body (in which case the body subsists by the subsistence of the spirit) — brings with it a positive perfection of a higher order. Let us say it is then a state of active *and autonomous* exercise, proper to a whole which envelops itself (in this sense that the totality is in each of its

---

13 Cf. *S. T.,* III, q. 2, a. 2, ad 3.

14 Some precisions may be useful here. If for us subsistence terminates nature, it is not, as we for a long time believed, following Cajetan, as a *terminus purus.* With Father Diepen we think that this substantial *mode* or *state* is a positive reality or a positive perfection added to the nature (but not in the line or order of nature), and that between subsistence and essence there is a real distinction (cf. Diepen, *art. cit., Revue Thomiste,* 1950, I, pp. 104–105, 110–111). But for us this positive reality is defined by the notion of *state of exercise* rather than by state of independence or of possession of self, by the self (which belongs to person, not to supposit in general); and it does not result from the nature without any causality being required for it (as Father Diepen grants following Cajetan, *ibid.,* pp. 108 and 110); it is an actuation received by the nature under the efficient causality of the First Cause, at the very instant that the latter makes the nature exist — an actuation which belongs to the existential order and does not confer any specification, but which, like existence itself, approximates *formal causality* without being a form properly so called (see number 3, below).

parts), therefore interior to itself, and possessing itself. Such a whole, possessing itself, makes its *own* in an eminent sense, or reduplicatively, the existence and the operations that it exercises. They are not only *of it*, but *for it*, for it as being integral parts of the possession of the self by the self-characteristic of the person. All the features we have just indicated belong to the ontological order. They refer to the ontological depths of subjectivity. Precisely here lies the ontological basis of the properties of the person in the moral order, of the mastery that it has over its acts by free choice, of its aspiration to liberty of autonomy, of the rights it possesses — these latter in reference to goods which are *due* to it as pertaining to what we have elsewhere[15] referred to as the sphere of its possession of itself by itself and of its mastery of itself, or its autodetermination.

From all this it is clear that the conception we are here proposing, and the very distinction between existence as received and existence as exercised, is understandable only in the light of the axiom *causae ad invicem sunt causae.*

From the side of formal causality, it is by reason of the existence *received* by the essence — or because the essence is actuated by *esse* — that the supposit exists.

And from the side of dispositive causality (material causality), it is on condition that subsistence carries the essence beyond its own order and constitutes it a supposit capable of *exercising* existence, that the essence receives *esse* and is actuated by it.

In other words it is by being received by the essence that existence is exercised by the supposit, and it is by being exercised by the supposit that existence is received by the essence. Subsistence plays (but in an absolutely different order) a role *analogous* to an "ultimate disposition," or is, so to speak, a kind of ultimate disposition for the exercise of *esse*. This involution of causes is at the core of the problem.

Finally we have pointed out that St. Thomas establishes a relation of analogy between the couple essence and *esse* and the couple active potency and operation,[16] and we have stated

---

[15] Cf. *Neuf leçons sur les concepts premiers de la philosophie morale,* p. 165.
[16] See footnote 9.

that it is the supposit or person that *exercises* existence (its own substantial *esse*) and *exercises* its operations, as well as the accidental *esse* proper to them.[17] We shall now note the difference between these two kinds of exercise. The supposit has an efficient power over its operations. These latter emanate from it and are produced by it by means of its active potencies or faculties — though, when it is a question of the perfectly immanent operations of intellection and volition, such operations, in as much as they are of themselves not predicamental "actions" but "qualities" and kinds of superexistence, are more properly exercised and lived than produced.

But with regard to existence the supposit obviously enjoys no efficient power. Its *esse* is neither produced by it nor does it emanate from it. If it can be said that the supposit actively exercises existence, it is in the more profound sense — and this is the privilege, and the mystery, of the act of existing — that for *esse,* to actuate the supposit is (in virtue of the divine action compenetrating it) to be the fundamental and absolutely first activity of the supposit in its substantial intimacy and depths — activity eminently *its own* when the supposit is a person — by which it is other than nothing.

The views put forward in the preceding pages constitute an emended version of our position concerning subsistence, this time elaborated from a purely philosophical perspective without depending on any particular theological thesis. Nothing now prevents our crossing for a moment the threshold of a domain not our own and returning, by way of a brief intrusion into the theological controversy mentioned at the beginning, to the texts of St. Thomas which we have cited, so as to test in their context the validity of the philosophical notions we have just used. Perhaps it will devolve that if we use instrumentally the notions in question, these texts admit an interpretation bordering on that of Father Diepen, but nevertheless different, and which mediates in a certain way the positions of the eminent Benedictine theologian and those of the great Dominican Commentators.

Our remarks are situated in the context of the articles of

---

[17] See footnote 10.

Father Diepen already cited. And it is in the form of questions subject to the judgment of theologians that we submit them. We would like to know whether, in order to have the best chance of understanding the thought of St. Thomas, it might be best to express it in the following fashion.

1. Just as there is in Christ only one single *subsistence,* so also there is only one single *personal existence* (*esse personale* is St. Thomas' expression; that is to say, the *esse* in virtue of which the supposit as such or the person as such exists). And this unique personal existence is the divine existence, as the great Commentators maintain.[18]

2. There is however in Christ, as he says in the *De Unione Verbi Incarnati,* and as Father Diepen maintains, a created *esse,* by which the human nature is actuated, as it demands to be insofar as it is potency in regard to the act of existing.

3. But this *esse* is only *received* by the human nature, it is not exercised by it (since in no case is it the nature, but the supposit, which exercises existence). Nothing human exer-

---

[18] This thesis, in our opinion, manifestly derives from the article of the *Tertia Pars* from which we quoted a few lines at the beginning and which we quote more fully here:

"Illud esse quod pertinet ad ipsam hypostasim, vel personam secundum se, impossibile est in una hypostasi vel persona multiplicari; quia impossibile est quod unius rei non sit unum esse . . . Si contingeret quod post constitutionem personae Socratis advenirent Socrati manus, vel pedes, vel oculi, sicut accidit in caeco nato, *ex his non accresceret Socrati aliud esse,* sed solum relatio quaedam ad hujusmodi; quia scilicet diceretur esse non solum secundum ea quae prius habebat, sed etiam secundum ea quae sibi postmodum advenerunt. Sic igitur cum humana natura conjungatur Filio Dei hypostatice vel personaliter, ut supra dictum est, et non accidentaliter; consequens est quod *secundum humanam naturam non adveniat ei novum esse personale,* sed solum nova habitudo *esse personalis praeexistentis* ad naturam humanam, ut scilicet persona illa jam dicatur subsistere non solum secundum divinam naturam, sed etiam secundum humanam" (*S. T.,* III, q. 17, a. 2).

"*Illud esse aeternum* Filii Dei, quod est natura divina, *fit esse hominis,* inquantum natura humana assumitur a Filio Dei in unitatem personae" (*ibid.,* ad 2).

Cf. *ibid.,* q. 19, a. 1, ad 4: "Esse pertinet ad ipsam constitutionem personae; et sic quantum ad hoc se habet in ratione termini; et ideo unitas personae requirit *unitatem ipsius esse* completi et personalis." And *Compendium theologiae,* c. 212: "Si esse accipiatur secundum quod *unum esse unius suppositi,* videtur dicendum quod in Christo *sit* tantum unum esse." And it is clear that for St. Thomas this *unum esse* is the pre-existing existence of the Word, the eternal and uncreated existence.

cises this human *esse*. It is exercised (secondarily) by the pre-existing divine Person, without entering for all that in any way into the constitution of the *esse personale* of Christ.

4. If in effect the created and human *esse* of the human nature is exercised by the person of Christ, it is in a way similar to that by which are exercised the multiple *esse* of the operations that this Person produces by the instrumentality of the human nature, without this created *esse* received by the human nature contributing anything to the *esse* in virtue of which, absolutely speaking, the Person of Christ exists, and which is eternal.

5. Thus the created and human *esse* does not at all concur in the constitution of the *esse personale* of Christ. And yet, being the substantial *esse* of a nature in which the Incarnate Word subsists, and being exercised by the Person of Christ, it is sovereignly *possessed* by that Person, it is sovereignly *His;* and that is why St. Thomas can call it *esse secundarium sui suppositi*.[19] It is a substantial *esse* which belongs to the divine Person, which is *His*, but which does not enter into the constitution of the *esse personale* of this Person, or of the *esse* in virtue of which it exists as person, and which is the un-created existence. We can say that by this existence of the human nature, which it exercises and possesses, which is its own, the divine Supposit exists humanly. But from this existence of the human nature it receives absolutely nothing in order to exist purely and simply, or to exist as supposit, to *exist personally*.[20] In other words, the created existence of the human nature is integrated or "attracted," just as that nature itself, to the *ens personale*, to the subsistent whole (the accidents themselves and their accidental *esse* most certainly are!);[21] but it cannot be integrated into the *esse personale* of Christ, concur in the constitution of the existence — eternal

---

[19] *De Unione Verbi Incarnati*, a. 4 (quoted at the beginning).

[20] Cf. *S. T.*, III, q. 3, a. 1, ad 3: "Non enim ex natura humana habet Filius Dei quod sit simpliciter, cum fuerit ab aeterno; sed solum quod sit homo." *Summa contra Gent.*, IV, c. 49, ad 4: "Verbum Dei per solam naturam divinam *simpliciter esse habet*, non autem per humanam naturam; sed per eam habet quod sit hoc, scilicet, quod sit homo."

[21] Cf. *Compendium theologiae*, cap. 211: "*Accidens trahitur* ad personalitatem subjecti."

and uncreated — in virtue of which the subsistent whole exists *both as supposit and as person.*

6. Although it be a substantial and not an accidental *esse,* the created and human *esse* of Christ would thus not compromise the unity of Christ as subject *(aliquid)* and as person *(aliquis),* nor the unity of the *esse personale* any more than do the multiple *esse* of the accidents, powers, and operations which emanate from the human nature. On the other hand, if the humanity were joined to the Son of God *accidentaliter* — and if in saying "this man" I designated a human subject accidentally united to the divine Word — the temporal and created *esse* proper to the human nature would obviously constitute another *esse personale* than the divine *esse personale.* But it is *hypostatice* or *personaliter* that the humanity is joined to the Son of God; so that in saying "this man" it is the uncreated Person the divine Word Itself that I designate.[22] Hence what occurs is only a new relation *(nova habitudo)*— to the human nature — of the pre-existing *esse personale:* it becomes the *esse personale* of "this man," that is to say, of the divine Supposit which subsists henceforth *according to this human nature also,* and no longer only according to the divine nature;[23] and the temporal and created *esse* proper to the human nature, while being a substantial *esse* sovereignly *possessed* by the divine supposit, remains outside the *esse personale* by which the latter exists — eternally — as supposit.

7. In this way it becomes quite clear, we believe, in what very precise sense St. Thomas teaches in the *De Unione Verbi Incarnati* that the temporal and created *esse* of Christ is not in the same relation as the *esse divinum* with the eternal supposit,[24] and that it is *secundarium.*[25] It is, if I may say so, a simple temporal and created echo — in the human substance

---

[22] Cf. *Sum. contra Gent.,* IV, c. 49, ad 10: "Ipsum Verbum supponitur cum dicitur *hic homo.*" And *S. T.,* III, q. 16, a. 9: "Oportet quod in hoc quod dicitur: *iste Homo,* demonstrato Christo, designetur suppositum aeternum."

[23] Cf. *S. T.,* III, q. 17, a. 2, corp., and ad 2 (quoted above).

[24] "Esse humanae naturae non est esse divinae. Nec tamen simpliciter dicendum est quod Christus est duo secundum esse: *quia non ex aequo respicit utrumque esse suppositum aeternum"* (*De Unione Verbi Incarnati,* a. 4, ad 1).

[25] *Ibid.,* a. 4, corp.

of Christ — of His uncreated personal existence. It is received by a human nature without human subsistence, it is exercised by an uncreated supposit which pre-exists it and for whose existing as supposit, or personally (for its existing *simpliciter*), it in no way contributes.

And it is also clear that these positions of the *De Unione Verbi Incarnati* in no way contradict the doctrine which, we believe, springs obviously from the *Summa Theologiae,* and according to which the unique *esse personale* of Christ is the eternal *esse* of God.[26]

---

[26] As for the very notion of subsistence, which we have tried to clarify above (cf. note 13), we see, if we pass from the philosophical plane to that of theology, that St. Thomas, in his doctrine on the Hypostatic Union, teaches that the human nature of Christ has no subsistence of its own. This created subsistence is replaced by the uncreated subsistence of the Word. Does St. Thomas' teaching on this point indicate that the uncreated subsistence acts as subsistence for the human nature by divinely conferring on it the completion which created subsistence, of which this nature is deprived, would confer on it? Or does it indicate that the uncreated subsistence *renders useless* the human nature's being perfected or completed by such a completion? For our part we believe that it is the second interpretation that is better founded. In other words, a human nature, on which this mode or state in which subsistence consists is not at all conferred, is assumed, possessed, and used by the eternally subsisting Person of the Word.

It seems to us that in this way a more satisfactory account is given of the fact that the divine subsistence "terminates" the human and created nature of Christ without entering into composition with it and plays an informing role in regard to it. It terminates it in the sense that this human nature cannot exist without a subsistence which assumes it and possesses it, but this subsistence which assumes it and possesses it and in virtue of which a pre-existing Whole makes it a part of itself, does not perfect it itself and render it itself subsistent; it dispenses it from subsisting, or from being itself achieved and completed by that mode or state in which subsistence consists. Thus, on the one hand, the humanity, become nature and part of the divine supposit and principle *quo* of the life and operations accomplished through it, becomes for the eternal *esse* of that supposit the term of a new relation, in as much as it is with the eternal *esse* (*esse personae*) that *iste homo,* this man, this divine subject which has humanity, exists. On the other hand, the human nature of Christ receives a human and created existence (*esse naturae*) without itself being rendered capable (by subsistence, and as a supposit) of exercising this existence, because it is the eternally pre-existing supposit which, making use of it as a principle *quo* of activity, itself exercises the human and created act of existing proper to the human nature, as it exercises also the human operations accomplished by means of the latter, and the accidental *esse* which are proper to them.

A final remark can be made on the subject of the Thomist theory of subsistence or of supposit. It is the supposit that *lives* and *acts,* but it lives and acts only *by* the nature. Hence it follows that in Christ the Person, who is divine, lives and acts at once in two totally distinct orders: on the one hand in virtue of the divine nature with which it is identical, on the other hand in virtue of the human nature which it has assumed.

If we meditate on what St. Thomas has written on this subject,[27] we are led, we believe, to the following positions. The Incarnate Word lives and acts according as He is God, or in virtue of the divine nature, within the uncreated Trinity. He lives and acts according as He is man, or by His human nature, among us on earth. In His terrestrial life He has lived and acted in all things by His human nature and its operations — acting also to be sure by His divine nature but insofar precisely as it used, as instrument, the human nature and human operations (*super hominem operabatur ea quae sunt hominis,* as Pseudo-Dionysius said).[28] It is by His humanity, or always humanly, always by the exercise of His human operations — moved by the divinity more perfectly than any purely human man could be — that the Son of God has accomplished everything He did here below, has spoken, acted, suffered, accomplished His divine mission.

Hence it follows that besides the uncreated divine *science* that He possessed as God He had a human manner of knowing in His terrestrial life.[29] And according as He was man, that which pertained to His state as *comprehensor* was reserved, so to say, for heaven by reason of the exigencies of His state

---

[27] See especially *S. T.,* III, q. 19, a. 1.

[28] Quoted by St. Thomas, *ibid.,* III, q. 19, a. 1, ad 1. In the *ad* 2, St. Thomas explains that "operatio quae est humanae naturae in Christo, inquantum est instrumentum Divinitatis, non est alia ab operatione divinitatis; non enim est alia salvatio qua salvat humanitas Christi et divinitas ejus." Cf. q. 43, a. 2.

[29] Cf. *ibid.,* III, q. 9, a. 1: "Christus cognovit omnia per scientiam divinam operatione increata, quae est ipsa Dei essentia: Dei enim intelligere est sua substantia, ut probat Philosophus. Unde hic actus non potuit esse animae humanae Christi, cum sit alterius naturae. *Si igitur non fuisset in anima Christi aliqua alia scientia praeter divinam, nihil cognovisset:* et ita fuisset frustra assumpta; cum omnis res sit propter suam operationem" (*ibid.,* ad. 1). Cf. also ad 3.

as *viator*. Even the share of His human soul in the divine life — the beatific vision which it enjoyed here below — remained a paradise above, sealed off from its faculties. The vision, says St. Thomas, did not reverberate from the superior part of the soul in the inferior part, nor from the soul into the body: *"Dum Christus erat viator, non fiebat redundantia gloriae a superiori parte in inferiorem, nec ab anima in corpus."*[30] For indeed the beatific vision, being of itself strictly ineffable, shone on the highest part of the soul without being expressed in any concept or communicable idea.

We ask ourselves, or rather we ask theologians, if the conclusion to be drawn from this is not that the supreme evidence that Christ, in His human soul, had of His own divinity by the beatific vision not passed into the experience of Himself proper to the *homo viator* in the form only of an absolute certitude or knowledge which was surconscious or superconscious (I mean retained at the supreme spiritual point of consciousness), and neither signifiable in concepts nor communicable? And that, in His human soul, it was by His infused and prophetic knowledge employed as an instrument by His own divine nature and His own divine science that He knew with *communicable and reflexively conscious knowledge* that He was the Incarnate Word? May not the same things also be said of the knowledge He possessed of His redemptive mission?

It seems to us that these considerations, whether they simply express, or extend by inference the positions of St. Thomas, remain quite close to the Gospel text, and assist us in understanding, for example, how the Son of God was pleased to call Himself the Son of Man, and that He did everything in obedience to the Father, and that He could say the Father was greater than He, and on the cross could quote the psalmic plaint[31] of being abandoned by God. It also seems to us that these considerations show how the Thomistic principles throw light more profoundly than do the hypothesis correctly criticized by Father Diepen,[32] on the problems that

---

[30] *Ibid.*, III, q. 46, a. 8; cf. q. 14, a. 1, ad 2, and q. 15, a. 5, ad 3.

[31] Ps. 21.

[32] Cf. H. Diepen, O.S.B., "La Psychologie humaine du Christ selon Saint Thomas d'Aquin," *Revue Thomiste*, 1950, III.

contemporary minds, having a particularly lively sense of the Saviour's humanity, have raised concerning the human psychology and psychological consciousness of Christ.

Princeton University
Princeton, N. J.

Metaphysics and Unity

BY ELIZABETH G. SALMON

I

We probably cannot count the times we have thought of the formula: *ens et verum convertuntur*. But less often have we reflected on the strange developments that can take place when we have substituted our understanding or rather our limited expression of the truth of being for being.

Many historical examples can show us the results of this tendency, but perhaps if one is followed through to a concrete conclusion, it would make clear what such a stand entails with respect to the basic conception of metaphysics. For it seems that the difficult problem of plurality of metaphysics goes back to this seeming harmless equation of truth, according to a certain mode, with being.

Now Descartes has difficulty in understanding certain points regarding God's knowledge and action as found in the works of certain scholastics, perhaps in St. Thomas himself. In an attempt to understand his difficulties, it appears that they arise from his starting point.

He starts with a position with respect to the notion of being different from that of St. Thomas. Having doubted the existent which for St. Thomas is first the sensible, material thing, he replaces it by knowledge of clear and distinct ideas. In his view, what we can be sure about is what we are immediately aware of, and what is distinctly known. The "clear" is the immediately given and the distinct is what is definitely itself and not anything else. Alone intelligible notions intuitively grasped, simple natures or essences, such as the essence of a triangle or ultimately the essence of extension, is what is clear and distinct and is what one must begin with in the study of creatures and God.

Thus if clear and distinct ideas are basic and are substituted for being, you have clear and distinct essences, intelligibles, in place of an existent which, though it is known as given, is not fully expressed by our conception of it. As being given and being more than any one conception, it can remain the source of further understandings. In other words, the actuality of its existence is not equated with any one of our understandings of it. So the mystery of being always remains for us, but yet remains as given and as also needing an explanation. Thus to explain the "to be" of a thing, it does not suffice to explain that there is a cause of its mode or essence or its intelligibility as far as we can seize it, but we must also explain that it exists as a being among beings. One must explain not only that this mode is a mode of being but for any beings "to be," to be actual, the only answer is a cause of existence which is Itself Act, Existence Itself. To posit such a Cause still does not mean that one grasps the full intelligibility of being, but one can see that it is true that being Existence Itself, it is fully intelligible to Itself, the Divine Mind, and other beings through the being of God as the Source and Creator of them. A being for us remains in itself what it is with its actualities, potentialities, its dynamic mode of existence which cannot be possessed in one clear conception or idea.

Also, as N. K. Smith well points out, depending on how one conceives being one explains choice.[1] A particular being, as an existent, can to the Thomist offer different aspects to desire. As a particular mode of being it has a particular degree of perfection, but as a being in the realm of being it also presents itself merely as a mode within the vague totality of being, and it is only the totality that can be necessitating for the will.

On the other hand, if being is equated with the clear and distinct idea, with the intelligible essence, the will could only

---

[1] N. K. Smith, *New Studies in the Philosophy of Descartes*, pp. 148–169.

acquiesce in what is clear and distinctly presented, for its very distinctness eliminates any other aspect or alternative. So liberty in Descartes is seen as the spontaneous assent to exclusive, distinct, circumscribed-intelligible contents. The clearer its intelligibility the more spontaneous would be our assent.[2]

Now if one conceives being in terms of clear and distinct ideas, and this liberty is also conceived in these terms; and if God and His ways are interpreted in these terms, one creates strange problems.

If clear and distinct ideas are beings or are equated with them, there is an intelligible world of the true — the eternal truths. These eternal truths are seen of themselves to be what they are, and also being what they are they are the good.

This notion of eternal truth is very intriguing.[3] Eternal truths for Descartes are simple natures or essences that are in themselves distinctly intelligible. And are they not eternal for are not simple natures always these intelligibles? For how can this intelligible such as a triangle or extension be at any time not the intelligibility of a triangle or extension? If these truths are these truths, they have been and will always be such truths.

But then the problem is: can one say such truths are not created by God? Descartes sees that if one makes them eternal, or necessarily to be what they are, are they not then posed with a certain priority before God to be what He must create? But if one says that then these clear and distinct essences or ideas, eternal truths which as being just such truths are limited and finite, are yet prior to God, God would have to assent to them and choose them if He wills to create

---

[2] Descartes, *Oeuvres de,* ed. by Adam and Tannery (1897–1910), *Meditationes IV,* t. 9, p. 47.

[3] Descartes, *op. cit.* A Mersenne, 15 avril 1630, t. I, p. 145, l. 5–16. Cf *Gilson, Commentaire sur le Discours de la Methode,* p. 335 (p. 35, l. 5, n. 3), also p. 372 (p. 41, l. 12). Here M. Gilson gives the references to the chief texts of Descartes concerning eternal truths as given in the Adam and Tannery edition of his works: a Mersenne, 15 avril 1630, t. I, p. 145, l. 5–16; to the same, 6 mai 1630, t. I, p. 149, l. 21 — p. 150, l. 27 — p. 151, l. 1 — p. 153, l. 3; to the same, 27 mai 1638, t. II, p. 138, l. 1–15; A Mesland, 2 mai 1644, t. IV, p. 118, l. 6 — p. 119, l. 14; VIae Resp., t. VII, p. 431, l. 26 — p. 433, l. 10 — p. 435, l. 22 — p. 436, l. 25.

a world. However Descartes admits that as limited these eternal truths are creatures, and he also wishes to maintain creation *ex nihilo*. So God must create the eternal truths as well as existents. So if in the very way being is explained, one comes to the point in which one must say that God can from the point of view of intellect only behold the true, the only alternative is, if creation is to be maintained, that these truths must depend not on His intellect but solely on His will. Descartes insists that the intellect and will are one in God, but the emphasis is put on the will. The eternal truths or essences are such because God has willed them to be such. Our minds grasp them to be necessarily what they are since God has willed them to be such as they are.

From this it would follow that God can evidently, if He so wills, create the contradictory. God could make the contradictory of $2 + 2 = 4$ or the essence of a triangle. The only other alternative seems to be that these truths are not creatures.

The problem, it seems, is so acute because being has been identified with intelligible contents as such contents have been conceived by our minds.

Would not the acuteness of the dilemma vanish once one considered, for example, material being in its material mode of existence? As such it is not difficult to see material being as changeable, mutable, and not eternal. It could always not be. But the changeable, temporal, ordered, and relational world since it is existing can give rise to a science of mathematical order and relation which as a certain intelligibility of that order, or as a science of it, is unchangeably such an intelligibility of that order. On the supposition that the mode of being, the material quantitative, is, there can be an understanding of it in our minds such that $2 + 2 = 4$ or that the angles of a triangle are in a certain manner related to its sides. This science as a science is unchangeable on the supposition of the creation of the material world and a human intellect to formulate it. For mathematics as such is after all a human science. God, in order to understand material order and relation, does not need to formulate it according to the science of mathematics.

But one can push it further and say, even if the material

existent world is the foundation of this intelligibility is not this intelligibility as in the material existent, eternal? — For being in its turn is founded in God and particular being is created by Him. Thus is not God still faced with eternal truths and must not one say that if He wills He could make to be the contradictory of mathematical and moral truths?

Yes, God is the Source of being and its truth. But it is far different to see God as being, to see Him, He who is, and to see that He cannot contradict Himself, than to see Him as limited by truths conceived according to our mode of conceiving them. In the first point of view, God could not make to be what could not be a mode of being, but He need not make the kinds or modes of being He has made. If He creates, which He need not do, He must make, or rather what He makes to be, must be a mode of being and as a being one mode is not an absolute contradiction of another mode of being. They are both beings and the only contradiction to being is nonbeing, which would be a negation of God Himself. Therefore, though the mode of being that is, depends on God's will in creation, it also depends on His knowledge, that is His knowledge of being which is Himself and in the light of that wisdom He wills these modes to be. But having created this being, He cannot will this being not to be what it is.

However, if one sees creation concerning not modes of being, or existents, but concerning eternal truths, one is posing the problem on a different plane. One, in this point of view, is considering the nature or some intelligible aspect of a mode of being and then is placing such concepts or ideas in the mind of God. One then juxtaposes the contradictory of that nature or that intelligible as another possible being. Actually such a juxtaposition of "being" is really a juxtaposition of two ideas or intelligible aspects of the same being — one contradictory of the other. It is as if one were posing the problem in this fashion: This sort of being exists. I have a certain understanding or science of it. Could then some understanding or concept of the science which is the exact opposite or contradictory be, while the being of which it is the science, still exists? This absolute contradictory can only be posed with respect to our intelligible expression of the nature of a thing.

From this point of view, one can with full assurance say that a nature of an existent thing intelligible in this fashion cannot be and be intelligible in an absolutely contradictory fashion. Moreover, God could not make this contradictory to be, once having created the nature of the being of which our concept or idea is an intelligible expression. But He need not have created the mode of being from which we have drawn our intelligible conception.

The difference here is that in one case one is talking of a contradiction of a nature that is created and explicitly expressed in a positive, distinct, intelligible fashion; in the other case one is talking not of the contradictory of a nature of a being, but of an entirely other mode of being. The notion of being as analogical does not exclude the notion of another being as a contradictory; but a univocal expression of a nature excludes its contradictory.

The penalty for Descartes in substituting clear and distinct ideas for the mystery of the existent and for the vague though real understanding of being was to establish the possibility of the unintelligibility of things, because their essences, as solely dependent on God's will, could not be used to reach anything of His wisdom. The intelligibility of one's ideas was such because He so willed them. God's intellect then becomes unfathomable and perhaps arbitrary and the clear and distinct ideas really unintelligible.

Now if the metaphysician avoids the clear and distinct ideas of Descartes and their identification with being and all its consequences, yet he very often does not avoid the attraction of his *Cogito*. Yet these two notions are closely connected in Descartes, and will, I think, ever be closely connected. Many a metaphysician who would reject the "clear and distinct" idea as being would yet stress being in terms of the I, conscious, living, knowing as giving a privileged and primary meaning to being as existent. But this tends in a subtle fashion to bring us back to understanding existence not as it is, but after the manner we conceive it in our mind.

Metaphysicians that stress this "I" as existent see clearly that metaphysics to be a science of the real must be of the existent real. It seems most evident that even in doubting or knowing, one cannot but know that one exists. Thus, it seems, in the Ego one has a living, conscious experience of existence, and in our conscious life one has an experience of the unity of an existing being.

This point of view is attractive and seems secure, especially when one considers the sensible world in its flux, its lack of definiteness, concreteness and individuality, and also in its possibility of being a source of illusion in knowledge. There is none of this indefiniteness or uncertainty in the "I knowing that I know." But what is overlooked is that I know myself *in* knowing, and knowing is knowing reality. And reality is not intelligible ideas in mind, but it is first given to me in the sensible existent world. Thus that this world is, and is with a certain nature, is the latticework through which and in which we know we are. And it is in reflecting on how we know sensible material unity that we get an appreciation of the unity of the one understanding it. It is true that the "I" has a certain experience of its own existence and an experience of its own activity, but it has not directly an experience of the act by which it is a spirit, and not directly of the unity of its activity except through the existence, nature, and unity of the thing understood. One does not, except partially in the sensible order, experience the existence of the world, but one, in knowing at all, understands that this world is and is something. And it is in understanding reality, sensible reality or being, that one experiences understanding as being; but one does not directly, fully, or clearly experience the being of understanding. Thus for us to say "I am" is already to have said the world is. It is that actuality that raises the experience of any other actuality. Moreover, if we try to render intelligible the actuality of the "I" independently of the actual world, we must do so in terms of ideas. "To be" will then be seen as the "to be" of ideas.

II

Once the metaphysician sees that his object is being and not idea or eternal truths, he will also become aware that he cannot speak of a system or a plurality of metaphysical systems, one contradicting the other. This will become clearer if we stress with St. Thomas that knowledge is a grasping of being, and fundamentally, of existing being, not an intuition of an idea. Basically being is the existent, and for us it is first the existent in all its sensible, material, living, sensitive, intelligible conditions; in all its richness, its limitations, its relatedness, and its independence, with all its actuality manifesting itself in all the ways in which it exists. It is almost a truism then to say that no one experience, no one concept or notion about being is going to express it fully. Mind nibbles upon it. It is given; we are fully aware it is there, and the life of knowledge is to render it intelligible according to the manner of our rational soul. We must respeak its reality in a spiritual expression which terminates for us in concepts and then in judgments, then in the conclusions of reasoning with understanding growing through our reflection on our understandings. But we must not permit concepts and judgments to lose their role of means by which we are expressing this reality, this totality, this unit complexity which is the existent. Otherwise we no longer consider, as we have seen, being itself. If we concentrate on the concepts or judgments themselves, they become beings in their own right and are works or fabrications of mind whose purpose is to enable us to grasp some aspect of reality. Considering them as such works and reflecting upon them, we can simplify them and through the making of other concepts, reduce their complexity. Thus we can delimit, construct, and fabricate what to us will become clear and distinct notions; then their definitions with this rigid clearness are unchangeable and immutable. With certain relations that we likewise define in the light of these notions, we can form first principles and can make deductions with consistency and so form a system. But the basic notion of metaphysics — being — is not like such constructed notions. The notion of being must never lose its touch with that total reality which is known to us through sense experience, concepts, and judgments. And it is reality in all its richness, together with what it implies, which is given through this notion, being. This reality is so given that we see that no expression totally expresses it, but it is this reality that we know we mean when we say we are thinking or writing about being.

Thus the notion of being as a primary notion in metaphysics is not seen as a logical notion, a genus, nor as a mathematical clear and distinct idea — these notions are notions tailored by our minds for our purposes — but it is a notion that bespeaks reality. Yet to know reality is not to live immersed in its temporal changing diversity, as perhaps a worm is immersed in the dust or earth surrounding it. No! It is to be part of reality, to exist in this world that exists, but also to be aware of it, to seize it, to seize it in understanding. In that moment there is a vision of unity. As I have said elsewhere, "to know what it is 'to be' is to have a notion that grasps a certain understanding of all that is; it thus gives a unified understanding which is an understanding also of a certain unity in being, but yet it is an understanding that must bespeak the diversity of what it is, and so possesses the very minimum of unity. We express this by saying this notion is analogical."[4]

Thomistic metaphysics in seeing being so understood as its primary notion, sees also what it means by its primary notion of unity. This notion as notion is analogical because it expresses existents, existing in diverse ways and so expresses a universe of existents with intimations of all that is or is able to be. For the Thomist, I think, analogy in its truly irreducible character refers only to being as existentially understood and not to natures or formal perfections as such. It is not expressive of a similarity of participation of two formal notions in a third; nor is it expressive of an over-all intelligibility that varies as it refers to one polarity or another. In that latter sense you have a point of view that as a point of view is unitary and univocal, and only as embodied in the polarities is diverse, or it reduces itself to a purely relational notion. Moreover, as a point of view or as tied to the polarities, it is only partial and so always leaves the possibility of referring to some other formal aspect of this thing, or just some particular concept of it, or some other relational reference. While analogy in St. Thomas gets its specifically irreducible character from the fact that it is always referring to the totality which exists as itself, and as a distinct being, and yet can

---

[4] *The Good in an Existential Metaphysics* (Milwaukee: Marquette University Press, 1951), p. 5.

express everything, as all are distinct existences. Thus the basic unity of being expressed through the analogical notion is not a point of view but the totality of the existent as existent, and all beings as existents. This notion of being does not permit of any other point of view that is not already implicitly in it — just as reality does not permit of reality outside it. So to unify everything under the notion of being is not to squeeze everything into one point of view, or into one concept or clear idea — but it is through intellectual notions to express all the richness and complexity of what reality really is. "Being" so understood can be considered as a notion that does not explicitly differentiate the modes of perfection, but neither does it eliminate them. It primarily expresses that "to be" being, something must be. This is far from a logical notion or algebraic sign or clear and distinct idea. Nor is it possible to speak of it as a notion in one-to-one correspondence with reality. It is not even a correspondence — if intellectual understanding can be called a correspondence — of an apprehension to a formal aspect. It is a recognition of what is and is according to its mode — and for us as we first meet being, it is, as it is, and as it is related.

Analogy as it may be extended to notions other than being and its transcendentals, remains truly analogical only as it refers to the mode of existence. For example, as intellect in man is to his mode of existence, so intellect in the angel is to his mode of existence. The perfection of intellect apart from reference to existence is not a strictly analogical notion, but rather one expressing a similar perfection varying in degrees, but basically such degrees express a univocal similarity. This follows unless the meaning is switched to refer to the mode of existence of spirit.

As has been noted, if the notion of being expresses the very reality of what it is "to be," it follows that the total expression is an endless task. Yet in another sense, our knowledge can never get to any beyond of being because there is no real outside of reality. But as we can never grasp the full meaning of being, our first notion in metaphysics is both an end and a beginning.

Without going through the full understanding of all the

transcendental notions, one can also see that in the under-standing of being there is implicit not only the notion of unity, but also of truth and goodness. Each of these views in a sense is as immediate as the understanding of being, as Maritain says: it suddenly arises from an angle of vision. In other words, we are forced to have many notions to express what we call being or reality. Each vaguely, totally expresses it; yet each explicitly expresses more without revealing the depth of the mystery. But as each makes explicit another aspect, it also implicitly expresses the other aspects.

What then is the basic reason for many transcendental no-tions? Not a radical, ultimate plurality of being within itself but a distinction in being of essence and existence which though not separable so as to form two beings and thus the possibility of two definitions as absolutely excluding each other, yet as giving rise to judgments that one is not reducible to the other, though each speaks of the other. To put this in another way: we seize things as kinds but also all as existent kinds. We seize them as actually existing but in terms of the manner of existence yet the manner does not fully explain the actuality because if it did it would exclude the actuality of any other manner or mode of being. Thus the mystery of act or existence in which all share presents us with a mystery of unity which forces us to seek its source, which we reason must be, but whose perfect being still is shrouded in mystery.

Moreover, we are forced to analogical notions because we are created beings knowing this duality of created being as well as the plurality of beings and their relations. We are beings in the conditions in which we are: existing as oneself, not another; and above all existing as in the relation of know-ing and loving the complexity of other things wherein we seize the intelligibility of being, its truth, its perfection, and tend to its lovableness and its restful completeness. Besides, it is in that knowing and loving that we can glimpse that the reality and unity of being as we know it is a developing finalized act that comes to its full act and unity only through its actuality in spirit knowing it and loving it as the reality it really is, and so returning it in the finality of a spiritual being to its Source and End.

That vision of unity exceeds, of course, the mystery of an individual; it is the tremendous unity of all being and no mind can fully encompass it, and none more than St. Thomas recognized that. Yet also it can be said that any mind with philosophical power grasps something of that vision of being. St. Augustine, for example, whose mind was of no ordinary power, spoke deeply of some transcendental aspects of being. He stressed unity; he certainly saw all things as true and in that aspect he stressed not only the intelligible image but something of the necessity of being to be what it is. St. Thomas was clearly educated by that metaphysical insight and vision — as well as we might say by the metaphysical insight of Avicenna who in a certain fashion stressed existence. But an important point St. Thomas stressed was that the transcendental aspect of being was rooted in existence and so there was an irreversible order to the transcendentals. For him being primarily means "to be" — then "to be" something — "to be" itself, and "to be" not other — "to be" true — and "to be" good. For him existence is fundamental, and he makes that angle explicit while other philosophers make other transcendental notions such as truth the primary notion, and never make existence explicit. Yet any transcendental notion, though explicitly it may express one aspect of being, yet implicitly it expresses all the others. But, of course, unless the root of the transcendental aspects is made explicit and a decision is made as regards their order, there is a certain metaphysical dimension lacking. However, while some transcendental aspect is stressed, one metaphysics is not simply contradictory or in absolute error with respect to another, for one transcendental aspect does not absolutely exclude the other. This sort of contradiction can happen only on the plane of purely formal perfections, or as we have shown, if one implicitly speaks of the truth of things in terms of clear and distinct ideas.

However, one transcendental notion as explicit is not the identically same notion as the other, nor is the understanding it connotes absolutely independent of the order in which it is understood, for order here is not extrinsic but is also of being and of intrinsic intelligibilities so ordered. Yet the dimension in intelligibility given each transcendental through the understanding of order is not such as to totally vitiate the understanding of each transcendental taken separately.

So it seems that no philosophy that grasps some transcendental vision of being poses for us a radical problem of plurality. This is posed in insoluble terms only when one sees "philosophies" each as an organized body of notions understood as one radically distinct system entirely distinct from a second radically distinct system of notions. Then one position is as a clear idea juxtaposed to the other and they cannot be seen to meet in being. Any true metaphysics is a negation of system in that sense. But metaphysics also has the problem of making explicit not just one but the various transcendental aspects of being, and in making them all explicit, it also makes explicit their order. For us, especially since Descartes but not necessarily for St. Augustine or St. Bonaventure, it is clear that we must make a decision as to the root of the transcendental character and so of transcendental notions.

But what I wish to stress is that if one has some metaphysical understanding of being and seizes one transcendental aspect, by that one seizes, in a sense, the others; and if in this seizing one makes one aspect explicit, the view cannot be regarded as one possible theoretical interpretation of "metaphysical facts," allowing for another utterly distinct possible interpretation. As long as some transcendental vision is involved, one can proceed and one does not utterly exclude other angles of vision. Thus, in a way, there may be alternative treatments that yet do not exclude one another. Each is not another possible theoretical explanation, but rather each is a necessary aspect of being which together with the others vaguely expresses the unity of reality. The plurality of transcendental notions arises from the complexity of reality and though there are in reason many notions one notion does not explicitly exclude the other. That is the peculiarity of a transcendental "notion."

Thus the whole of metaphysics can be gone through in the light of any one of these transcendental notions, but, as has been said, these are not alternative systems of explanation, each is fundamentally being, reality as understood, but our discursive thought must ask whether or not it has made explicit the root source of the transcendental notions and what all the notions are, and whether or not it has made manifest an order and made it explicit. In other words, we must see clearly that our metaphysical understanding is a resaying according to our minds of the complexity of reality. This reality has a certain unity which is the very root of why we try to understand it and, correlatively if we do understand it, we understand it is in some sense one. Metaphysics of its very nature expresses unity. St. Thomas has not made explicitly intelligible the whole complexity of reality; neither has he elaborated all that can be elaborated in metaphysics. What he has made explicit is that the root of the transcendental notions is existence and in so doing he has made in broad outline explicit their order. From this insight it is evident that if we take being as it exists formulated in knowledge, we are going to lose the mysterious unity of the existent that allows for an endless deepening of metaphysical insights. In place of this mystery given to mind but not fully fathomed we shall have a plurality of understandings, one excluding the other as contradictory.

Fordham University
New York, N. Y.

WHAT IS REALLY REAL?

BY W. NORRIS CLARKE, S.J.

What is now widely known as the existential interpretation of Thomistic metaphysics has definitely come of age.[1] (By existential I mean that interpretation which sees in the act of existence the source of all perfection and intelligibility, hence the center of gravity of St. Thomas' whole philosophy.) The professional literature on both sides of the water gives increasing evidence that Thomists in many different quarters are engaged in a systematic and highly fruitful program of rethinking the whole of Thomistic philosophy in the light of this great central insight.[2] As speculation and text work proceed hand in hand, each illuminating the other, it is becoming more and more evident that this perspective is by no means some short-lived fad borrowed from the contemporary Existentialist movements and superimposed extrinsically on St. Thomas' own thought, but rather that it is that one luminous center which Bergson speaks of as the key to every great

---

[1] The aim of this essay is not to validate this interpretation but to explore some of its implications. For the explanation and defense of the whole approach, the reader is referred to the many well-known writings on the subject, such as Gilson, *Being and Some Philosophers* (2 ed., Toronto, 1952); Maritain, *Preface to Metaphysics* (New York, 1939), and *Existence and the Existent* (New York, 1948); J. de Finance, S.J., *Etre et agir* (Paris, 1945); the entire volume of the *Proceedings of the American Catholic Philosophical Association,* 1946, devoted to the subject, etc.

[2] Two fine examples from our own side of the water are the recent articles of Joseph Owens, C.SS.R., "A Note on the Approach to Thomistic Metaphysics," *The New Scholasticism,* XXVIII (1954), 454–476; and George P. Klubertanz, S.J., "Being and God According to Contemporary Scholastics," *Modern Schoolman,* XXII (1954), 1–17.

philosophy, in the light of which alone the total body of St. Thomas' texts takes on full intelligibility and coherence.

As this process of systematic rethinking advances, however, it is inevitable that one should not only uncover new insights into the strength and unity of the system but also that one should run up against certain doctrines or modes of expression long imbedded in the school tradition which seem somehow out of harmony with this primal intuition. When this occurs, intellectual integrity and true loyalty to tradition demand that the apparently unassimilable items be critically reexamined and either be proved capable of organic integration in some modified form or be resolutely amputated for the good of the whole organism. Such is the task now being carried out step by step by progressive-minded Thomists on many different sides. The operation is admittedly a delicate one. But the responsibility for it must be met by each new generation of Thomists if they wish the original lifeblood to continue coursing vigorously through the veins of the tradition as it grows through the ages.

It is the purpose of this essay to present for discussion and further exploration one such instance of a point of doctrine long current in the Thomistic school tradition but which seems to us — and to an increasing number of others — to have its roots in quite a different metaphysical tradition and to be seriously out of harmony with the basic premises of a metaphysics centered on existence. We refer to the traditional practice among Thomistic metaphysicians (traditional, that is, for the past three or four centuries) of describing the content of "real being," the object of metaphysics, as "that which is or can be," thereby including within its extension two classes of beings, actual and possible. Both of the latter are thus presumed to verify the note of real in some proper and intrinsic way and hence to stand opposed to the so-called "beings-of-reason" (*entia rationis*), which all Scholastic philosophers admit do not fall under the proper object of metaphysics. Inseparably linked with this inclusion of the possibles within the order of real being is the analysis of being taken as a noun (the object of metaphysics) as signifying essence with some relation to existence but prescinding from the actual exercise of this existence. The point at issue is therefore whether or not it is legitimate to characterize "real being," the object of metaphysics, as a noun signifying essence prescinding from the actual exercise of existence and thus including in a proper and intrinsic sense the possibles; and if not, what is the proper way to describe their ontological status and relate them to the object of metaphysics.

It may seem to some that after the writings of Gilson and other leading exponents of existential Thomism the question should be considered as already settled. Such is by no means the case. We have been told that Professor Gilson himself has complained that many Thomists read and admire his writings, but that not nearly so many have the courage to follow out consistently in their own teaching the message he has been trying to convey. And outside of the work of Gilson and a few others,[3] this particular consequence of existential Thomism does not yet seem to have received any widespread explicit attention, let alone acceptance by the broad central stream of teachers. The fact is that a large majority of contemporary Thomists, including many who are quite sympathetic in general to the existential perspective, still adhere quite solidly to the traditional analysis of real being as including possible being and therefore as signifying primarily essence prescinding from the exercise of existence.[4] Many of the latter make it

---

[3] Some of those who have explicitly committed themselves to the essentials of the position we are holding are, aside from Gilson himself (*op. cit.*, Chaps. V–VI): F. Van Steenberghen, *Ontology* (New York, 1952); G. Klubertanz, S.J., *Introduction to the Philosophy of Being* (New York, 1955) pp. 24, 188; J. Isaac, O.P., veteran metaphysics reviewer in the *Bulletin thomiste*, VIII (1952), 490, 550–551; I. Bonnetti, C.P.S., "Il valore dell'esistenza nella metafisica di S. Tommaso," *Divus Thomas* (Piacenza), LIV (1951), 359–371; H. Grenier, in the fourth edition only of his *Cursus Philosophiae*, II (Quebec, 1952), who from his first to his fourth edition has undergone a remarkable evolution from a strict traditional position almost all the way to our own; also the doctoral dissertation of Norbert Huetter, S.J., *The Eidetic Existentialism of St. Thomas* (Fordham University, 1952), devoted entirely to the place of the possibles in an existential Thomism; and D. J. B. Hawkins, *Being and Becoming*, p. 33 ff., 105 ff.

[4] Thus the very recent and excellent Thomistic text by H. Gardeil, O.P., *Initiation à la philosophie de S. Thomas d'Aquin*, IV: Métaphysique (Paris, 1952), defends it most explicitly. And even Prof. Maritain, ardent pioneer and champion of existential Thomism, in his otherwise vigorously existential

quite clear, too, that they hold to this position not merely out of love for tradition but because they fear that any impugning of the reality of the possibles will weaken or destroy their absolute objective validity and thereby undermine certain all-important and universally accepted truths of the *philosophia perennis*.

Such an attitude deserves the sincerest respect. Those who hold it have every right to be assured that if they change over to a new mode of expression, no important or necessary truth of Christian philosophy will be jeopardized. It is to this group of thinkers in particular that the present essay is directed, in the hope that it may place the issue squarely before them and lead them to a serious and sympathetic consideration of what we believe to be the truth of the matter, namely: (1) that the so-called traditional analysis of real being is not the original tradition of St. Thomas himself or of his two greatest commentators; (2) that a clear-cut existentialist interpretation of being as the object of metaphysics not only will bring a more satisfactory unity and consistency to their whole metaphysics but will leave intact the genuine objectivity of the possibles and explain even better how they come under the scope of the science. The ramifications of this whole question, however, especially as regards the nature of the possibles, are so vast that within the brief limits allowed us we must be pardoned for being able to do little more than sketch the main outlines of both the problems and our suggested solutions.

First, let us look at some typical examples of the traditional modern Thomistic analysis of the meaning of "real being" as the object of metaphysics. The first is taken from the representative and deservedly praised textbook of general metaphysics currently used at the Gregorian University in Rome, one of the most influential centers in the world for the training of future seminary professors:

> Therefore being taken as a participle signifies "that which actually is or exists," whereas being taken as a noun signifies "that to which existence is suitable or due, that whose act is existence,"

Preface to Metaphysics, pp. 21–22, seems to have felt compelled to adhere at least partially to the current tradition.

whether it actually exists or not. . . . Being taken as a noun, which is the object of metaphysics, has a wider extension than being taken as a participle, since it embraces not only existing beings but merely possible beings. For it is evident that not everything which can be *de facto* is. In addition to actual beings there are objectively given (*dantur*) possible beings, and the description of being as a noun applies to both.[5]

An even clearer statement of the same position can be found in the first edition of another text perhaps even more widely known on this continent, representing the Laval John of St. Thomas tradition:

> Wherefore being taken concretely, as the participle of the verb "to be," is used in two ways:
> 1) as a *participle* or formally, including to be or to exist as actually exercised, i.e. the very exercise of the act signified by the verb, just as *currens*, as a participle, means one who is actually running;
> 2) as a *noun* or materially, designating the essence or subject which is ordered to actual existence, but prescinding from whether or not it actually possesses this existence. Hence being as a noun signifies being *in actu signato*, i.e. as designated or denominated from the act of existence, although it neither affirms nor denies the exercise of this act.
> In one word, being as a participle is that which actually is; being as a noun is that which is or can be. The object of metaphysics is being as a noun, and can thus be described: that to which existence (*esse*) is suitable or belongs (*competit*) in any way whatsoever.[6]

If one turns now to the classic texts reflecting the more strictly Dominican stream of the tradition, such as Gredt, Maquart, etc., the analysis begins on a much more existential basis, drawn directly from the texts of St. Thomas himself. But the final result is about the same. Thus Gredt quickly passes from St. Thomas' "that which is" to "that which is or

---

[5] P. Dezza, S.J., *Metaphysica Generalis* (Rome, 1945), pp. 24–25; same doctrine in 3 ed., 1952.

[6] H. Grenier, *Cursus Philosophiae,* II: Metaphysica (Quebec, 1937), p. 7. This popular work has been translated into both French and English. In his third edition, however (cf. n. 3 above), he has completely abandoned the distinction of being into noun and participle, though he still retains the object of metaphysics as "that which is or can be." In his fourth edition he has dropped the "can be" entirely, though elsewhere he still classifies the possibles among "real being" as opposed to beings-of-reason.

can be," in order to include the possibles.[7] Maquart's exposition exhibits an amazing semantic *tour de force*. He begins with an excellent existential analysis closely following the texts of St. Thomas, in which he insists that being as the object of metaphysics means "that which actually is," explicitly including existence as exercised rather than prescinding from it as others have said. Then he suddenly pulls back into the tradition at the last moment with the astonishing statement that the actual existence he is talking about means also possible existence, so that a being means "a thing possessing existence, either actual or possible, or, that which exists or can exist."[8]

What is to be said of this now solidly entrenched distinction between being as a noun and as a participle and of the interpretation of the respective contents of each? When one reads the neat, clear expositions of the doctrine in modern Thomistic textbooks, one gets the impression that here is a point so obvious and universally accepted that it commands assent without further discussion or examination. Yet if one undertakes only a little probing into the latent suppositions behind it as well as into the history of its evolution in the Thomistic school after St. Thomas, one is struck with consternation at the mare's-nest of ambiguities, confusions, oversimplifications, and dubious underlying principles which have marked its career from the beginning. There is space here to single out only a few.

In the first place, one gets the impression from these expositions that the Latin participle allows of only one noun use and another participial, presumably nonsubstantival use. This is not the case. The Latin present participle allows of three uses, one participial and two substantival. In ordinary grammatical parlance the participial use is strictly adjectival, requiring always the presence of some substantive which it modifies. Since the participle understood in this way could not stand by itself as the subject of a sentence, it obviously

---

[7] J. Gredt, O.S.B., *Elementa Philosophiae Aristotelico-Thomisticae* (ed. 7a; Freiburg, 1937), II, 4–6.

[8] F. Maquart, *Elementa Philosophiae* (Paris, 1937), III, Pars II, 13–17.

could not apply to being as the object of metaphysics and hence can be eliminated at once as irrelevant.

There remain two noun uses. According to the first it signifies the subject of an action understood as actually exercising this action. Thus: *Studens non debet simul audire musicam* ("Someone studying should not simultaneously listen to music"). In the second it signifies the same subject as one whose characteristic or proper activity is the action expressed by the participle but prescinding from whether or not he is at present actually carrying on this activity or state. Thus: *Studens debet satis dormire* ("A student should get sufficient sleep").

Now it is extremely difficult to determine from the studied ambiguity of the Latin textbooks (they seem to avoid carefully such full sentence examples as the above) just how they understand the participial use of being, whether as a pure adjectival or as one of the two substantival meanings. This, of course, is favored by the ambiguity of the Latin, devoid of any definite or indefinite article, which would usually settle the question. It is impossible to maintain the same ambiguity in English. Hence Thomists writing in English are forced to commit themselves, and almost universally interpret participial as synonymous with adjectival. But then they blandly ignore all but the second or nonexistential noun use, which without further ado they identify with being as the object of metaphysics. It is my strong impression, however, to judge from their examples and explanations, that most of the Latin writers understand what they call the participial use as really one of the two noun uses, capable of standing alone as the subject of a sentence. If this is so, they ought to say so clearly and remove the unnecessary ambiguity that has so long enveloped this distinction and that causes such dangerous confusion when one attempts to transpose their thought into the modern languages. It would be far clearer, too, to adhere to ordinary grammatical terminology and reserve the term "participial" for its proper adjectival use instead of using it to describe what is really just as much a substantival meaning as what they technically call the noun use.

Once the ambiguity of terminology is cleared up, the truly

metaphysical problem remains: Which of the two theoretically possible noun uses of being is the one most appropriate to express being as the object of metaphysics, i.e., real being? The analogy commonly drawn with examples like studying, running, etc., to legitimate the noun use of a participle as signifying a subject in terms of its characteristic activity but prescinding from the actual exercise of this activity, is misleading and deceptive. It is clear enough that when the participles in question express some kind of accidental activity or state of a subject, without which the subject can still continue to exist, then the above-mentioned noun use finds a legitimate application. Thus a student or runner can still continue to exist as a real subject even when not studying or running. But the situation changes radically when it is a question of an absolutely ultimate and transcendent predicate such as being. Here we are in the presence of a participle which expresses an activity or state so absolutely primary and fundamental to its subject that it constitutes the very subject itself as real subject, so that without it there simply would not be any subject at all outside the mind to talk about. Does not the peculiar intelligible content of such a participle render impossible a nonexistential noun use of itself which pretends to speak of a subject as though it were somehow still real or present, while amputating intellectually the very act which renders the subject intrinsically real or present at all in any proper sense?

The above criticism is not implying that the same term, "being," cannot be used to refer both to possible essence and to actually existing essence. Since it is our absolutely ultimate category and the formal object of our intellect, every intelligible object of discourse must be understood in some way in terms of being. Thus even "beings-of-reason," though no one claims they can be called real beings, must still be called "beings," but always with the qualification "of reason," i.e., those contents of thought whose only being is a mental existence produced by the mind itself and remaining therein, that which the mind treats *as though* they were beings within its own mental universe. But we are implying that the term "being" as applied to actual and possible being is used in two radically and intrinsically different senses which, though related by dependence and analogy of extrinsic attribution, cannot be reduced to any one single meaning applicable to all by proper and intrinsic analogy.

The serious danger in attempting to include both actual and possible being under the single, apparently more ultimate category of real being is that it almost inevitably misleads one into believing, and at the very start of metaphysics, that there is some common element intrinsic to both of these orders which constitutes them to be real precisely as real, that is, a kind of ultimate constitutive note of reality as such. The trouble is that the only element common to both is intelligible essence precisely and exclusively as intelligible, since a possible essence has no more in it than that. Hence the inevitable inference that the ultimate note which properly constitutes reality as such is the intelligibility of essence. Thus at the very first step in metaphysics the act of existence is implied to be some kind of extrinsic, though substantial element added on to the real as such already constituted by intelligible essence.[9] Does not this eviscerate from the beginning the fundamental metaphysical insight of St. Thomas, which sees in the act of existence "that which is most intimate in every being," the innermost root and core of all perfection, all forms, and the source of all intelligibility?[10]

Nor does it remove the difficulty to say that what is com-

---

[9] Cf. the indictment of the early great Thomistic commentators for their tendencies along this line in expounding the real distinction of essence and existence, by I. Bonnetti, "Il valore dell'esistenza nella metafisica di S. Tommaso," *Divus Thomas* (P.), LIV (1951), 359–371.

[10] "Esse autem est illud quod est magis intimum cuilibet, et quod profundius omnibus inest: cum sit formale respectu omnium quae in re sunt . . . " (I, q. 8, a. 1; ed. Leonina); "Omnis enim nobilitas cuiuscumque rei est sibi secundum esse" (C. G., I, 28; ed. Leonina); "Unde patet quod hoc quod dico esse est actualitas omnium actuum, et propter hoc est perfectio omnium perfectionum" (*De Pot.*, q. 7, a. 2, ad 9m; ed. Spiazzi, *Quaestiones Disputatae,* Marietti, 1949); "Omne ens inquantum est ens est actu" (I, q. 5, a. 3); "Impossibile est quod sit aliquod ens quod non habeat esse . . . " (*De Ver.,* q. 21, a. 2); "Unumquodque, quantum habet de esse, tantum habet de cognoscibilitate" (C. G., I, 71); "Unumquodque cognoscibile est secundum quod est actu et non secundum quod est in potentia, ut dicitur in IX *Met.* Sic enim aliquid est ens et verum, quod sub cognitione cadit, prout actu est" (I, q. 87, a. 1).

mon to both orders is not essence alone but essence as ordered to existence.[11] For in the possible essence this ordering is still only a purely rational relation, the essence as related by *thought* to its possible existence as *thought,* whereas in the actual being the relation is a real one between real essence and real existence. There still remains the unbridgeable gap between real and nonreal relations, and we are still left with the minimum note of intelligibility as the ultimate constitutive note of reality as such. Such a position, it is true, is quite compatible with the notion of real being as the object of metaphysics which is adopted by Scotus and still more clearly by Suarez.[12] This is entirely consistent with their whole metaphysical outlook and the subsequent elaboration of their systems. We have no quarrel with them at all in this paper, though we do not believe theirs is an adequate, or at least the best way of constructing a metaphysics of the real as real. But we do feel that the same position is dangerously misleading and inconsistent within the perspective of the existence-centered metaphysics which is now so widely accepted by Thomists as the peculiar original achievement of their master.

A glance at St. Thomas' own habitual way of analyzing the notion of being will bring out the contrast more clearly. It has been asserted that the distinction between being taken as a noun and as a participle does not appear in St. Thomas.[13] Ordinarily, it is true, he ignores it entirely, perhaps because he considered the meaning he was following sufficiently clear from his analysis of the content of being — as indeed it is. But there is one text in which he commits himself clearly on the subject. Apropos of the question whether it is possible to speak of the three divine Persons as "three things or three beings," he takes the occasion to analyze the difference not

---

[11] The traditional doctrine in the Thomistic school has always insisted, against Scotus and Suarez, that the notion of being signifies essence, not as prescinding entirely from *esse,* but always with some relation or ordination toward existence, as in the case of the possibles. Cf. the masterly exposition of André Marc, S.J., "L'idée de l'être chez s. Thomas et dans la scolastique postérieure," *Archives de philosophie,* X (1933), cahier I.

[12] Cf. Marc, *op. cit.*

[13] Maquart, *Elem. Phil.,* III, Pars II, 14–15: "Distinctionem inter ens ut participium et ens ut nomen, non adhibuit S. Thomas."

only between thing and being (*res et ens*) but also between being as a participle and as a substantive. As regards thing and being, there are two elements, he says, to be considered in a thing, its quiddity and its act of existence. *Res* or thing, since it derives from "to think" (*reor*), signifies the intelligible quiddity as such whether it is existing inside the mind or outside in nature. *Ens* or being, since it derives from "to be" (*esse*), signifies the thing according to its actual existence. Since *res* here clearly means a genuine quiddity or essence, hence a true possible, not a being of reason, could there be a clearer indication of the strictly existential meaning of being in contrast to thing? Next, as regards the noun and participle use of the term "being," whose meaning he has already defined, he identifies the participial sense explicitly with the adjectival, which must modify an accompanying substantive, whereas being used alone is being taken substantively. *Ens* as a participle can be used in the plural of the divine Persons like any modifying adjective; *ens* as a substantive can only be used of them in the singular, so as not to multiply the divine act of existence, His essence.[14]

Could anything be clearer or more in accord with the ordinary grammatical meaning of noun and participle as well as with the spontaneous reflection in language of the existential import of being opposed to thing? This explicitly existential significance of being in St. Thomas' mind is brought out even more clearly in numerous other passages. For example:

> Being (*ens*) is nothing else than *that which is*. And hence it is seen to signify both a *thing* (*rem*) by the fact that I say *that which*; and *to be* (*esse*) by the fact that I say *is*. . . . But the composition itself which is implied in that I say *is* [i.e., the judgment of composition, which would be "This thing is"] is not the principal signification but is rather co-signified insofar as being signifies *a thing* having existence (*rem habentem esse*).[15]

> Since in everything which is there must be considered its quiddity, by which it subsists in a determined nature, and its act of existence, in virtue of which it is said of it that it is in act, this name *thing* is imposed on the thing from its quiddity, as

14 *In* I *Sent.*, d. 25, q. 1, a. 4 (ed. Mandonnet).
15 *In* I *Periherm.*, lect. 5, n. 20 (ed. Leon.).

Avicenna says . . . whereas the name *being* or *what is* is imposed from the very act of existence itself.[16]

To be (*esse*) is said to be the act of a being insofar as it is a being, i.e., that by which something is denominated as an actual being in the order of nature.[17]

Being is said to be "a (something) having existence" (*habens esse*).[18]

Being signifies that something properly exists in act.[19]

Every being insofar as it is a being exists in act.[20]

The same existential content is necessarily involved in his analysis of goodness as related to being. Things are good, he says, precisely to the extent that they are beings. Now creatures are beings only by participation because they possess actual existence only by participation rather than by identity with their essence, as God does. But since goodness is rooted formally in the act of existence, the source of all perfection, it follows that creatures are also good only by participation, not by essence. This obviously implies that being means essence conjoined with actual existence.[21] Or again consider the following proof for the convertibility of being and goodness through *esse:*

Therefore the act of existence (*ipsum esse*) verifies the nature of the good. Hence, just as it is impossible that there be a being which does not possess the act of existence, so it is necessary that every being be a good from the very fact that it has existence. . . . And so it follows that the good and being are convertible.[22]

It should be abundantly clear from the above texts that being for St. Thomas habitually means essence conjoined with actual existence. And surely no one would be so temerarious in interpretation of texts as to maintain that when St. Thomas speaks of the act of existence (*esse*) without qualification, as

16 *In* I *Sent.,* d. 8, q. 1, a. 1.
17 *Quodl.* IX, q. 2, a. 3 [3 in old edit.] (ed. Spiazzi, Marietti, 1949).
18 *In* XII *Met.,* lect. 1, n. 2419 (ed. Cathala).
19 I, q. 5, a. 1, ad 1m.
20 I, q. 5, a. 3.
21 *De Ver.,* q. 21, a. 5, ad 6m; q. 21, a. 2.
22 *Ibid.,* q. 21, a. 2.

he does in all these texts, this can be interpreted as signifying also possible existence. In fact, nowhere in St. Thomas have I been able to find a text where he speaks of the possibles as "beings," or even the phrase "possible beings." Rather he repeatedly speaks of the possibles without qualification as "nonbeings" (*non-entia*).[23] Surely this would manifest an amazing technical carelessness of language if he called "nonbeing" that which he really believed should also be properly called "being" according to its most fundamental meaning as object of metaphysics.

But what of those few descriptions of being in St. Thomas that are usually quoted (instead of the above) in support of the traditional position, namely, those in which being, as divided into the ten categories (the object of metaphysics), is said to signify essence or thing as that to which existence belongs or is proper? For example: "It is true that this name *being,* to the extent that (*secundum quod*) it implies a thing to which belongs this particular kind of *esse,* in this way signifies the essence of the thing, and is divided into the ten categories."[24] All that this text and others like it can legitimately be made to say is that being, insofar as it really does include the subject of existence, does to this extent signify essence and so can be divided along the line of essence into the categories. This by no means implies that essence is the *total* content of being in its full metaphysical sense or that the essence signified can be considered prescinding from its accompanying existence. The rest of the above text, in fact, implies just the contrary. Being, it says, is predicated essentially only of God, but of creatures by participation, precisely because it signifies the act of existence, which creatures participate as though accidentally or outside their essence. Never-

---

[23] I, q. 14, a. 9: "Utrum Deus habeat scientiam non entium"; *C. G.,* I, 66.
[24] *Quodl.* II, q. 2, a. 1 [3]. Some of the other texts appealed to are: *De Ente,* c. 1: " . . . ens . . . significat essentiam rei. . . ." But note that the end of the same text presumes essence to be accompanied by *esse:* "Sed essentia dicitur secundum quod per eam et in ea ens habet esse." Cf. also *De Ver.,* q. 21, a. 1, ad 1m: "Ipsa essentia rei absolute considerata sufficit ad hoc quod per eam aliquid dicatur ens." But later on the text specifies that essence here is understood as "essentia creaturae posita," which obviously includes existence. See also I, 48, 2, ad 2m, noting the *prout* and *sic.*

theless, it goes on, because it also implies the subject of existence, it does to that extent also signify the essence itself
as that to which existence belongs. Hence this text, if it proves
anything, proves rather that essence is only an indirectly implied (*importat*) element in the content of being. So, too, the
definition "that whose act is existence" does not imply nor
does the context permit that the "that whose" can be considered in precision from its absolutely primary act and still
be called properly being.[25]

Such is St. Thomas' own understanding of real being: as
the object of metaphysical inquiry it is to be understood as a
substantive and signifies that which is, or essence possessing
its own proper act of existence.[26] This position is clear-cut, in
accord with ordinary language and with the mind's spontaneous natural estimate of what is real, yet rooted in a
profound, fully explicit metaphysical insight into the act of
existence as the act of all acts, the perfection of all perfections, the ultimate wellspring of reality in every truly real
being, that of which every essence is only an intrinsic mode
(*modus essendi*) and from which it draws every bit of substance and reality it can be said to possess as *its* own.

What happened to this interpretation of being after St.
Thomas in his own school? If his followers had fully caught
the primal insight supporting it, it does not seem it would
have been too difficult to pass it down undistorted. Such unfortunately does not seem to have been the case. To trace the
whole story would be a long and tortuous undertaking. A few
sample soundings will indicate the main drift of the current.
Already by the fifteenth century confusion has set in both in
terminology and, it seems, also in doctrine. Dominic of Flan-
ders, author of "the principal synthesis of Thomism before

---

[25] *De nat. generis,* c. 1.

[26] For some of the most clear-cut statements desirable summing up St.
Thomas' position, cf. Maurer's translation, *On Being and Essence* (Toronto,
1949), p. 26, n. 1: "Being (*ens*) is the existing thing (*id quod habet esse*),
including both essence and the act of existing. It is thus complex or
composite"; Klubertanz, *Introduction to the Philosophy of Being,* pp. 24–25;
and above all the masterly chapter of Gilson in *Being and Some Philosophers,*
Chap. V, esp. pp. 174, 187. See also the fine article of J. Vande Wiele, "Le
problème de la vérité ontologique dans la philosophie de s. Thomas," *Rev.
phil. de Louvain,* LII (1954), pp. 521–571, esp. p. 563.

John of St. Thomas," and reflecting, it is claimed, the general school tradition of his time, already has settled on the favorite present-day definition of being as a noun: "that which has an essence to which existence is due" (or belongs?: *competit*). But it is not clear from the texts available to me whether the possibles are included within this meaning or not.[27]

Cajetan, on the other hand, accepts the interpretation that being as a noun signifies essence prescinding (this point is not entirely clear) from existence, but then goes on to dissociate himself from those who claim that this is the sense in which being is understood by St. Thomas in his *De Ente et Essentia* and elsewhere. For the latter, he says, being clearly signifies essence as joined with the act of existence, since this is necessarily implied in St. Thomas' argument for the convertibility of the good and being. Hence the being which the latter is talking about and which is divided into the ten categories is being taken as a participle, not as a noun.[28] Now it is clear that Cajetan is here being faithful to St. Thomas in doctrine, but he has already departed from him in terminology and is promoting confusion by affixing the term "participial" to what is obviously a substantival use of being. It is not too surprising, therefore, though not excusable, that later Thomists, rightly dissatisfied with his terminology in its interpretation of being as a participle, should have wrongly taken over for the object of metaphysics not only the name but the content of the de-existentialized noun use of being which he himself had repudiated.

---

[27] *In Libros Metaphysicae Aristotelis secundum expositionem eiusdem Angeli Doctoris lucidissimae atque utilissimae Quaestiones*, ed. Morelles (Cologne, 1621), IV, q. 2, a. 7 (quoted in L. Mahieu, *Dominique de Flandre: Sa métaphysique* [Paris, 1942], pp. 97–98): "Ens potest accipi dupliciter. Uno modo participaliter ut idem est quod existens et sic ponit in numerum contra substantiam et non praedicatur identice. Alio modo accipitur nominaliter, ut idem est quod habens essentiam cui competit esse per se primo et principaliter."

[28] *In De Ente et Essentia D. Thomae Aquinatis Commentaria,* ed. Laurent (Turin, 1934), c. 4, pp. 88–89. It seems certain there is a misplaced *non* in this text, if self-contradiction is to be avoided: change *non* from 1. 21 to 1. 22 before "est ens nominaliter," on p. 88. See too his lapidary summary of the meaning of *ens,* Proem., fin., p. 20: "Nota quod ens . . . significat id quod habet esse . . . ens ergo ita se habet ad essentiam, quod complectitur in se utrumque, essentiam scilicet et esse."

Writing at about the same time, Sylvester of Ferrara, the other great commentator of the Angelic Doctor, expounds with all the vigor and explicitness that could be desired the identical existential interpretation of being held by Cajetan but in exactly opposite terminology. Some have tried to maintain, he says, that for St. Thomas only being in the participial sense includes actual existence. This is entirely false (*falsissimum est*). Both noun and participle use signify "that which has existence" (*id quod habet esse*). But the noun use signifies primarily the essence, implying (*importat*) secondarily the accompanying act of existence; the participle signifies primarily the act of existence, implying secondarily the accompanying subject or essence. The noun use, therefore, he warns, does not signify essence merely as capable of existence, but as actually united with it, or "under actual existence." He then proceeds to identify being as a noun with being as the object of metaphysics and divided into the ten categories, the reason being that its primary note, essence, allows it to be predicated essentially of all beings, even creatures, whereas the primary note of participial being, existence, allows it to be predicated of creatures only by participation.[29]

There might be room for some technical dispute about the exact meaning of participial for Sylvester, or the appropriateness of "primary signification and secondary implication" as applied to essence and existence within the notion of being. But, all in all, Sylvester's substantival yet existential analysis of being is the most acceptable and closest to St. Thomas of any commentator we have seen. Unfortunately, neither Sylvester's nor Cajetan's interpretation was the one which seems to have gained general acceptance in the later Thomistic tra-

---

[29] "Procedunt ex falso fundamento: scilicet quod *ens,* cum nominaliter sumitur, non dicat esse, sed tantum cum sumitur participialiter. Hoc enim falsissimum est: cum utroque modo, ut superius diximus, significet *id quod habet esse.* . . . Attendendum autem quod non est idem dicere *ens in actu . . .* et *ens participialiter sumptum.* Quia ens actu quod dividit ens, primo et formaliter significat essentiam, sicut et ens quod dividitur: sed significat illam ut est sub esse actualis existentiae; per quod differt ab ente in potentia, quod significat essentiam absque esse actuali. Et ideo ens in actu secundario significat esse" (*Commentaria in Summam Contra Gentiles,* I, 25, n. VIII, 2 [in Leonine edition of St. Thomas, XIII, 79]). Cf. the whole section n. VII–XI; also in I, 38, n. 1.

dition and remains firmly imbedded there to this day. There was another meaning apparently current at the time of Sylvester, which he introduces for the sake of contrast. This he calls being "taken absolutely." It signifies, as its name suggests, essence as prescinding from actual existence. But Sylvester distinguishes it sharply from the existential noun use he has been talking about and makes it clear this is not what St. Thomas means by being.[30] By a strange irony it is precisely this meaning which he rejected (or a close variation of it) that either became confused with or replaced his own interpretation in the school tradition as the almost universally accepted meaning of real being as the object of metaphysics. If tradition be conceived as a stream flowing uncontaminated from an original source, and enriching itself only with what it can transform into its own substance, then surely what stands for Thomistic tradition today as regards this one point must be said to have suffered a notable influx of alien waters somewhere along the line.

What is the source of this gradual and subtle de-existentializing of the notion of being by Thomists, which has left it with the minimum requirement of a mere rational relation of intelligible essence to existence as the only link with its original full-blooded content of actual existence? The most likely explanation that has been proposed is that the majority of Thomists during the period of the decisive formation of the Thomistic tradition, including even the great commentators to some extent, did indeed preserve with admirable fidelity the great technical polemical theses of St. Thomas against their adversaries, the Scotists, the Nominalists, and the Suarezians; but, due in part to their strongly Aristotelian bent, they did not seem to have gotten clearly in focus or even explicitly recognized the all-pervading underlying existentialist perspective of St. Thomas that constitutes the deepest center of his thought. Hence they tended to absorb without even realizing it a considerable amount of the essence-dominated conception of metaphysics and being that was the common patrimony of the non-Thomistic Scholasticism of

---

[30] "Ens enim absolute sumptum significat tantum essentiam tamquam id cui nomen imponitur" (in I, 25, n. XI, 2–3).

their time.[31] Scotus, for example, had already propounded the nonexistentialist interpretation of being as a noun, and the great Scotistic masters elaborated it further.[32] But the fullest and most masterly exposition of the doctrine that the object of metaphysics, real being, is to be interpreted as a noun, signifying "real (i.e., objective, nonfictitious) essence," but prescinding from actual existence and thus including the possibles, is given us by Suarez. He devotes an entire section of one of his *Metaphysical Disputations* to the question, and makes it quite clear that the decisive reason for admitting this interpretation is in order to include the possibles as direct inferiors of the notion of being.[33] As we have said before, this

[31] E.g., the important article of A. P. Monaghan, "The Subject of Metaphysics for Peter of Auvergne," *Mediaeval Studies,* XVI (1954), pp. 118–130, esp. p. 130: "With regard to his relation to St. Thomas, it seems that Peter's doctrine of being as the subject of metaphysics took no cognizance of Aquinas' fundamental view that being is primarily the act of existing. Inasmuch as it failed to incorporate this radical innovation of Thomistic metaphysics, Peter's position is a clear historical indication of the singular lack of favour St. Thomas' doctrine held among his immediate successors. Even the man who received the title of his 'most faithful disciple' did not reflect the most basic tenet of Aquinas' metaphysics. . . . Faithful in general to Aquinas' *Commentary on the Metaphysics,* Peter gives no indication of accepting the properly Thomistic doctrine of being." Cf. esp. the article of Bonnetti cited in n. 9, most telling on this whole point; Gilson, "Cajetan et l'existence," *Tijdschrift voor Philosophie,* XV (1953), 276–286; Huetter, *The Eidetic Existentialism of St. Thomas* (cf. n. 3): "Our historical studies on the question of the possibles have convinced us that the retention of this definition of being reveals an intellectual lag in the penetration of the doctrine of St. Thomas on the concept of being which was brought about by the tremendous influence that the Avicennian speculations have in time past exerted and continue to exert on scholastic thought, even Thomist" (p. 85). Note, too, the contemporary protest of the great Bañez against his own confreres: "Et hoc est quod saepissime Sanctus Thomas clamat et Thomistae nolunt audire, quod esse est actualitas omnis formae et naturae" (reported without reference by Isaac, *Bull. Thom.,* VIII [1952], 574).

[32] "Ens participium significat idem quod existens. . . . Ens nomen . . . significat ens habens essentiam" (*Opus Primum super I Periherm.,* q. 8, n. 10; cf. T. Barth, *De Fundamento Univocationis apud Scotum* [Rome, 1939], p. 28); "Ens, hoc est cui non repugnat esse" (*Opus Oxon.,* IV, d. 8, q. 1, n. 2; ed. Vivès [Paris, 1891], XVII, 7b). Cf. Marc, *L'Idée de l'être,* p. 48.

[33] *Disp. Met.,* II, sect. 4: "*Ens* enim in vi nominis sumptum significat id, quod habet essentiam realem, praescindendo ab actuali existentia" (n. 9); " . . . habens essentiam realem, id est, non fictam, nec chymericam, sed veram et aptam ad realiter existendum" (n. 5); "Dicimus essentiam realem esse, quae in sese nullam involvit repugnantiam, neque est mere conficta per intellectum" (n. 7).

position is quite consistent with the characteristic metaphysical outlook of both Scotus and Suarez, and we have no quarrel with them directly in this paper. But it does not follow that the same position or even a half compromise with it is consistent for Thomists who in the rest of their metaphysical system profess to follow the Angelic Doctor in his original achievement of constructing a metaphysics capable of analyzing the universe of beings not only according to their intelligible essences but also according to their acts of existence.[34]

Enough has been said from the point of view of history and the continuity of tradition. But the mere fact that St. Thomas can be shown to have held a certain position does not necessarily prove it to be true, or the best, or incapable of evolution in order to satisfy compelling theoretical necessities perhaps not fully seen by him. Let us examine briefly, then, some of the deeper intrinsic reasons usually put forward as justifying the inclusion of the possibles under real being and the precision from actual existence.

The first is based on the Aristotelian conception of science as concerned only with essential predicates. Now being in the sense of existent essence cannot be predicated as essential predicate of any being save God. Hence it cannot be the object of the science of metaphysics; otherwise the latter would be dealing with a nonessential or accidental predicate.[35]

This objection can be disposed of quite briefly. It is surprising, to say the least, that Thomists, who elsewhere expound so eloquently the importance and originality of the distinction between essence and existence, should lend any weight to this purely terminological difficulty based on the inadequate Aristotelian categories of essence and accident as exhaustive of reality. St. Thomas himself warns that the substantial act of existence in his theory cannot be fitted into either of these categories. It is neither accident nor essence in the strict sense of the word, but a new *sui generis* principle in the substantial order and distinct from both.[36] The permanent core of truth

---

[34] Cf. the vigorous indictment of modern Scholastics and Thomists on this point by Van Steenberghen, *Ontology*, pp. 42–45.

[35] E.g., Dezza, *Met. Gen.*, p. 25; Gredt, *Elementa*, II, 5.

[36] *Quodl.* XII, a. 5; II, a. 3, ad 2m; *In* IV *Met.*, lect. 2, n. 558.

in the Aristotelian principle is that a science should deal only with necessary and ultimately constitutive, or nonaccidental, predicates. Now if the proper object of metaphysics is precisely existent being as existent, and if the substantial act of existence is according to St. Thomas the most intimate and most fundamentally constitutive element of every real being as long as it remains existent and the object of metaphysics, then the legitimate requirements for a science are met in a genuine, though analogous, way. In other words, the true answer to this difficulty is simply to refuse to accept its premises in a rigid and univocal sense and to insist that the too narrow Aristotelian concept of science be enlarged to make room for the new *sui generis* element of reality brought into focus for the first time by St. Thomas and for the *sui generis* character of the science of metaphysics resulting from the nature of its object.

The next argument is a considerably more serious one, in that its roots extend all the way back to the fountainheads of the *philosophia perennis* through the venerable Platonic-Augustinian tradition. It proceeds thus. The truths of metaphysics, the most ultimate of all sciences, must have the characteristics of absolute necessity and immutability. But the beings accessible to our experience are in their actual existence irremediably contingent and mutable. Therefore the necessary truths of philosophy in general, and above all of metaphysics, can find no solid foundation in this contingent world, but only in a realm of the eternally necessary and immutable essences of things. This is the order of the possibles. The metaphysical order as such, therefore, is the order of the possibles, not of contingent actual existence.[37] Now since metaphysics is by very definition the science of the real as such, if

---

[37] This consideration seems to have had some influence even on Prof. Maritain (*Preface to Metaphysics,* pp. 21–22). For a clear-cut statement of the strong realism of the possibles and the identification of the metaphysical order with them characteristic of much modern Scholasticism, especially in the great Suarezian (and Scotistic) tradition, cf. J. Hontheim, *Institutiones Theodicaeae* (Freiburg, 1893): "Physicum est quod exsistit, metaphysicum est, quod est possibile" (p. 133, n. 1); "Possibile non est omnino nihil, sed ens positivum et reale" (p. 741); "Constat igitur possibilia . . . aliquod esse habere, non quidem actuale, sed . . . esse metaphysicum" (p. 738).

the possibles themselves are not real then metaphysics will find itself in the embarrassing position of being in the last analysis a science of the unreal.

There are two latent premises on which this whole argument rests. The first is that because the world of actual existence around us is contingent and mutable, it cannot bear within itself any necessity or immutability whatever. The second is that only essences in the strict sense can be abstracted. Both of these premises, we believe, are unsound and inconsistent with an integral Thomism, first, because they manifest an inadequate view of reality itself; second, because they fail to take into account the peculiar resources of Thomistic epistemology and metaphysics.

As regards the first proposition, the belief that the existing world of sensible reality is so unstable that it cannot become the object or source of immutable philosophical truth was certainly the profound conviction of Plato, for whom the realm of the ideas alone was the "really real."[38] It also deeply marked the thought of St. Augustine. It is in fact the hidden spring of all his arguments for the existence of God from necessary and eternal truths, whose "reality" and necessity can find no sufficient foundation in contingent existents and hence must be rooted directly in the immutable necessity of the divine mind. But it is precisely one of the most significant advances made by St. Thomas in the history of Christian philosophy that he swung the balance back from this exaggerated Platonic-Augustinian depreciation of the contingent by pointing out the genuine intrinsic necessities (and he does not hesitate to say absolute necessities, though always participated) that lie hidden within the core of even the frailest and most transitory contingent existent. "There is nothing," he says, "so contingent that it does not contain within it something necessary."[39] And he devotes an entire chapter of his *Contra Gentes* (II, 30) to the question: "In what ways can there be absolute necessity within created beings?" It is precisely from this higher estimate of the *intrinsic* in creatures, their intrinsic consistency, intelligibility, dignity, and adequate

---

[38] *Phaedo*, 65–66.
[39] I, q. 86, a. 3.

82   METAPHYSICA

inner resources for action as fully equipped natures, that stem
the radical optimism and rich, positive, humanism so characteristic of his world outlook.[40]

Nor can it be maintained that these necessities lie exclusively, or even primarily (at least as regards the truths of
general metaphysics), on the side of essence. If the act of
existence is the most fundamental common element of all
beings as such, must it not have some common intrinsic
characteristics necessarily accompanying it in whatever being
it is found? The fact is that the great majority of the basic
principles and theses of the Thomistic metaphysical system
contain necessary truths derived from the properties of existing beings considered formally as existent. Thus, for example,
the most fundamental and absolute necessity of all in Thomistic metaphysics is the principle of contradiction taken in its
existential sense, namely, that nothing can simultaneously be
(exist) and not be at the same time. This is because even the
humblest and most short-lived existent being, so long as it
actually exists, even for one moment, and precisely in virtue
of its act of existence, excludes nonbeing with the most absolute necessity, and thus makes it an unconditioned truth for
all time and for all minds that at this moment of time this
particular being was and can in no way be thought not to
have been at the same moment.[41]

The entire analysis of goodness as a transcendental property
of every being is also based formally on the principle that the
act of existence is the root of all perfection and that exactly in
proportion as it possesses an act of actual existence can any
being lay claim to goodness. Possible beings can have no goodness for St. Thomas. What we really desire when we desire a
possible being is its actuality, not its possibility.[42] So, too, the
deduction of the fundamental ontological structure of every
finite being, its composition of essence and existence, is based
on the analysis of the act of existence as common perfection

---

[40] Cf. the great humanistic texts of St. Thomas: *C. G.*, II, 2; IV, 1; III,
69–70; *De Ver.*, q. 5, a. 8; *Sermo V in Dom. 2 Adventu;* also J. Maritain,
"The Humanism of St. Thomas Aquinas," in *Twentieth Century Philosophy,*
ed. D. Runes (New York, 1947), pp. 295–311.
[41] Cf. the lucid exposition in *In IV Met.*, lect. 6, n. 606.
[42] I, q. 5, a. 2, ad 4m; *De Ver.*, q. 21, a. 2.

participated and limited by different essences. Essences themselves, in fact, draw their whole reality and even intelligibility for St. Thomas from their role as modes of existence (*modi essendi*). Furthermore, even if we go beyond the theses peculiar to the Thomistic metaphysical system, is it not true that in any Scholastic metaphysics the analyses of action, change, efficient and final causality must necessarily be founded (whether acknowledged or not) on the characteristics of being as actually existent? For possible essences can neither change nor act nor cause nor be attracted or repelled nor have real compositions or real relations (which all admit can be had only in actual existents).

It cannot be true, then — and here we touch the second latent premise mentioned above — that concrete existents as such are so exclusively particular that they have no common traits among themselves as existent at all. Why, then, cannot these too be disengaged by the mind by some process of abstraction analogous to, but not identical with, the abstraction of essences properly so called? This is precisely the achievement of Thomistic epistemology applied to metaphysics, that it has found a way, by its theory of the special mode of abstraction of the notion of being through the judgment of separation and the reduction of particularities to confused presence, to disengage and retain for intellectual analysis not only the essential but the existential aspects of the real beings that are its object.[43] Thomistic metaphysics, therefore, studies real being (essence-existing) formally as *existent* (that is, under the unifying formal object of the act of existence), which is not at all the same as to say formally as *particular*.[44]

One last difficulty in connection with the above argument can be briefly disposed of. It is the objection that, if metaphysics is based on contingent existents as existent, then none of its propositions can be stated as unconditional absolute

---

[43] Cf. R. J. Henle, S.J., "Existentialism and the Judgment," *Proc. Amer. Cath. Phil. Assoc.*, XXI (1946), 40–52; Klubertanz, *Introd. to Phil. of Being*, Chap. II; L. B. Geiger, O.P., "Abstraction et séparation d'après S. Thomas," *Rev. des sc. phil. et théol.*, XXXI (1947), 3–40.

[44] Cf. G. Phelan, "A Note on the Formal Object of Metaphysics," *The New Scholasticism*, XVIII (1944), 197–201; Van Steenberghen, *Ontology*, p. 42.

truths but must always be prefixed by the condition: *"If any-thing exists,* then it must be good, etc., etc." This is absolutely correct. But the objection seems to overlook the fact that if there is one condition about whose verification the metaphysician need not worry it is the proposition, "Something exists." The very fact that any metaphysician existentially puts such a question to himself is the absolutely unconditioned guarantee that at least one being exists, himself. And once he knows that one being exists, he can prove that some being must always of necessity exist. Such an objection, instead of weakening, only illuminates more deeply the nature and validity of an existence-centered metaphysics.

The conclusion of the foregoing analysis is that it is quite possible to construct a general metaphysics the main principles and theses of which can be established with absolute certainty directly from the analysis of beings as actually existent, with no need of recourse to the possibles to guarantee this certitude. In fact, it is difficult to see how any sound metaphysics which does not start off with the existence of God as already given by faith or intuition, but accepts its responsibility for providing an absolutely certain base for proving His existence, can possibly establish the certainty of its own basic theses by recourse to the possibles. Is it not evident that the very objectivity of the possibles themselves depends entirely on the prior certainty of the existence of God as already established by independently valid metaphysical principles? This is by no means to deny, it cannot too strongly be asserted, that the recourse to the possibles (and the divine will) becomes absolutely necessary when the metaphysician wishes to discover, not whether or not there is necessity in contingent things, but what is the ultimate source whence they derive these various necessities really within them, but whose presence they show themselves unable to explain of themselves.

There remains the last and perhaps the strongest argument for the reality of the possibles, that drawn from the direct analysis of the nature of the possibles in themselves and their objective foundation in God. It reasons thus. First of all, the possibles are endowed with positive intelligibility, each distinct from the other, hence from mere nonbeing. Second, the constitutive notes of each coalesce into a self-consistent intelligible unit. This unit is founded on the most real of all realities, the divine essence seen by the divine intellect as really and existentially imitable in this particular way. Hence this intelligible unit is seen as objectively capable of actual existence outside the divine mind, if the divine will wished to confer such actual existence on it. Such an intelligible unit cannot be classed among mere beings of reason, which of their very nature do not have the *per se* unity of a genuine essence and are incapable of actual subsistence outside of the mind actually thinking them. In sum, that which in its objective intelligibility is distinguishable from, and irreducible to, pure nonbeing, as well as to mere beings of reason, must necessarily be identified with real being in some proper and intrinsic sense.

This argument is admittedly impressive and on outward appearance seems foolproof in its logical rigor. In fact, however, its conclusion goes beyond the content of its premises, with the help of a subtle and elusive, but nonetheless illicit, transition from thought to reality. Aside from the necessary, immutable, and objectively founded intelligibility of the possibles,[45] what exactly does it prove? Simply this: that the *idea*

---

[45] The necessary, immutable, and objectively founded *intelligibility* of the possibles we accept as rigorously and adequately established by the traditional Thomistic analysis. We also recognize it as an extremely important and absolutely necessary truth in order to safeguard the wisdom of God in creating, His providence in governing the universe, the permanence of ethical law based on permanent essences, etc., lest we flounder helpless in a compassless relativism and empiricism. The whole great tradition of Christian exemplarism fits in here, but interpreted precisely as an exemplarism of divine *ideas* only, which acquire formally distinct intelligibility only in the divine mind and exclusively as the result of its infinitely fecund, artistically inventive activity, which does not find them somehow ready-made in His essence (what could that possibly mean ontologically?) but literally "invents," "excogitates" them, using the infinitely simple plenitude of *Esse* that is His essence as supreme *analogical* model or norm, so that all His "inventions" will be only so many diversely limited modes (or "variations on the theme") of the one great central perfection of His own act of existence. (St. Thomas deliberately uses the terms "rationes quasi excogitatas" [*De Pot.*, q. 1, a. 5, ad 11m] and "adinvenit, ut ita dicam" [*De Ver.*, q. 3, a. 2, ad 6m]. *Adinvenio* in his vocabulary is the precise term he uses to signify not "discover" — *invenio* — but "invent" or "make up" logical relations: cf. *Lexicon of St. Thomas*, Defarrari.) The Scotistic and Suarezian theories, which refuse to found the possibles formally in the divine intellect but somehow in the divine essence itself naturally prior to the intellect's activity on it, are only the logical consequences of their realism of the possibles.

content or *intelligibility* of a possible is not the same as that of
pure nonbeing or of a being-of-reason; or it is not the same to
think of a possible as to *think* of nonbeing or an *ens rationis.*
Quite true. But it does not follow that *what* is being thought
about thereby acquires any ontological status of its own as
opposed to ontological or extramental nonbeing. Otherwise
one would have proved too much, and "he who proves too
much proves nothing." One would also have proved that, from
the mere fact that one being-of-reason is intelligibly distinct
from another and from nonbeing (e.g., $\sqrt{-1}$, $\sqrt{-2}$, or any
two positive relations of reason), it therefore follows that the
same beings-of-reason are really opposed to ontological nonbeing and hence must be called somehow real beings — a conclusion repudiated by everyone. It would also follow that just
because one thought about nonbeing with a definite actual act
of the mind, it would therefore ensue that nonbeing itself was
somehow real just because it was the object of a real thought.

In other words, we are here face to face with the ultimate
abyss between the order of pure thought and the order of the
ontologically real, the real in itself, the "really real." This
abyss cannot be bridged by intellect alone but only by will;
only love can call up being out of nonbeing. What we are
asserting here is what seems to us the absolutely primary
condition of any thoroughgoing and fully conscious realism
of being: that to be a pure *esse intentionale,* or object of
thought, in any intellect, even the divine, confers no proper or
intrinsic reality of its own whatsoever on the object. In other
words, the "being" or "existence" of a thought object or
"intentional being" is not a "to be" but a "to-be-thought,"
not a "to-be-real" but a "to-be-really-thought by a real act of
a real mind." The reality resides entirely in the real act of
the mind thinking, not in the object of this thought.[46]

There is admittedly a genuine mystery involved here, how

---

[46] Cf. St. Thomas, *C. G.,* IV, 11: " . . . esse intentionis intellectae consistit
in ipso intelligi"; also the conclusion of Hawkins' analysis of possibility in *Being
and Becoming,* p. 109: "A passing mention is all that is deserved by the
attempt to attribute some sort of reality to the possible by saying that it
exists in those minds which can conceive it. . . . To say that a thing exists
in thought is only a misleading way of saying that the thought of it exists;
it confers no reality on the contents of the thought."

the mind can spin an endless thought progeny out of its own substance, so to speak, without adding in the slightest bit to the real multiplicity of the universe. This order of *esse intentionale* is one that desperately needs rigorous ontological analysis by Thomists and has not yet received anything like the attention it deserves. This paper will have been well worth the effort if it at least has the effect of stimulating further research into this obscure and neglected area. But no theory of the intentional order can lead to anything but further confusion unless it preserves inviolate the absolute irreducibility of the "to-be-real" and the "to-be-thought."

This means, of course, that when the terms "being," "existence," "real," and the like are applied to the intentional order, as indeed they must since we have no more ultimate terms of reference, they at once take on a new distinct meaning, irreducible by any intrinsic analogy to their primary and proper meaning, just as the orders themselves are irreducible to any common denominator. There is an extrinsic link of dependence, however, between the two meanings, just as between the two orders, which permits the extension of the same term from one to the other according to the laws of the analogy of extrinsic attribution (not proper proportionality) but with a radical shift in intrinsic signification. Thus an object of thought can be called "a being," or "real," not because it is a real being in itself, but because it is thought by a real being, and, in the case of a possible, has an intelligible relation to the real order.

Why is it so necessary to insist that possibles can only have an *esse intentionale?* In order to safeguard the two most important truths of all: first, the absolute simplicity of God's entire essence, His "real being," which allows no real multiplicity within Him whatsoever, not even real relations (save those between the three divine Persons); and second, the doctrine of strict creation, which asserts the production of all finite beings entirely and unqualifiedly out of nothing, with no shred of pre-existing reality of their own at all. There is no more unequivocal expression of the common doctrine on this point than that of Suarez himself, when he says: "We must lay it down at the very start that the essence of the creature . . . before it is produced by God, possesses within itself no true real existence, and, in this sense, such an essence deprived of its existential being (*esse existentiae*) is not even a thing at all but absolutely nothing." It is a little disconcerting, however, to recall that some thirty disputations earlier the same author has told us that the possibles have a "real essence" which is directly and properly included in real being as the object of metaphysics, the science of the real precisely as real![47]

If all this is true, how then do the possibles differ at all from those other intentional beings called beings-of-reason? From the point of view of their intrinsic reality, not a whit. The difference is solely in their intelligible content. This is thought up by the divine mind precisely as an exemplar or blueprint (guaranteed to work) of one way in which He *could* (intellect and will together) imitate, in the real order, if He so wished, the supremely real subsistent act of existence that is His own essence. Hence the possible has as an inseparable part of its very intelligibility a set of relations (rational, not real) toward the real, one of analogous imitation of the uncreated Real, its model, the other of potential exemplary ordination toward a created real terminus. These intelligible relations, not possessed by the *entia rationis,* distinguish the possible in its intelligible content from the latter and permit it to be called "real" by a special kind of extrinsic denomination or extrinsic attribution, which means: "that which is not real in itself but is intelligibly ordered to the real." It is possible in this way, if one so insists, to give a valid interpretation to the traditional classification of the possibles among real beings as opposed to beings-of-reason, but only on the condition that it be explicitly recognized that real covers two different and irreducible meanings, one primary, proper, and absolute, the other secondary, improper, and denominated by relation only, and that it is not a single meaning intrinsically verified in both actuals and possibles. However, it would be much clearer, more accurate, and more in accord with the strong meaning of real as opposed to idea in the modern languages, we think, to divide being first into two primary

---

[47] *Disp. Met.,* XXXI, sect. 2, n. 1; compare II, sect. 4.

orders, real being and intentional being, and then subdivide the latter into its main classes, possible beings and beings-of-reason.[48]

Finally, if real being as the object of metaphysics signifies directly and properly only existent being, how can the possibles come at all under the science of metaphysics, as indeed they should? The answer is very simple. They come under it in precisely the same way that their intelligibility is related to real being. Their intelligibility has intentional existence entirely in and through the reality of God, His essence and His act of thought, and can only be validly postulated and analyzed by us through the mediation of the divine reality, as a necessary consequence of the divine attributes. Therefore they enter necessarily into the science of metaphysics and are studied by it, not directly in themselves, but indirectly through its primary object, existing being, as inseparably linked with it by a relation of necessary intelligibility — a quasi projection of the Supreme Being's own necessary intelligibility as existent, intelligent, and all-powerful.[49]

In conclusion, we invite our fellow American Catholic philosophers, to whose rapidly growing maturity and competence

---

[48] The author had already been teaching this theory for several years when he found practically the identical terminology being used independently by Fr. Huetter in his thesis on the possibles in St. Thomas (n. 3): "The 'id quod' [of the *id quod est*], if it is an object which does not exist extramentally, has only intentional existence in the mind. Such mental or intentional beings are so called being only by an analogy of improper proportionality or by extrinsic denomination inasmuch as they are divested of true reality" (p. 82). Also: "It is our earnest conviction that the habit of calling the possibles real is a relic from a metaphysical tradition which is not that of St. Thomas" (p. 368).

A similar position is proposed by the well-known French metaphysician, J. Isaac, O.P., for years an intrepidly consistent champion of existential Thomism: " . . . la notion d'être possible ne serait pas obtenue par une division bipartite de l'être appelé *réel* (par opposition à l'être de raison), mais par opposition directe à l'être actuel; l'idée 'd'être réel (soit actuel, soit possible),' si traditionnelle qu'elle soit, n'est-t-elle pas quelque peu platonicienne? N'y a-t-il pas plus qu'une possibilité, une véritable implication ou connotation d'existence (*consignificat*, précise S. Thomas . . .) dans le 'id quod est' ou le 'hoc habens esse' de S. Thomas?" (*Bulletin thomiste*, VIII [1952], 490.) Cajetan also holds for two distinct meanings of real (not two classes fitting under one meaning), one proper, the other improper (*Comm. in De Ente*, c. 4, a. 6, n. 59; ed. Laurent, p. 92).

[49] Cf. Van Steenberghen, *Ontology*, pp. 44–45.

in philosophical thought this whole volume is intended as a testimony and an incentive, to test critically and explore further the conclusions of this paper, which we have tried to show are only the inherent logical consequences of a fully self-conscious and consistent existential Thomism in the most authentic tradition of St. Thomas himself. These conclusions are:

1. Being as the object of metaphysics should mean, and did mean for St. Thomas, being taken as a noun, signifying existing essence precisely as existent, with all the intelligible conditions and consequences necessarily connected with it.

2. Real being in its proper sense is strictly convertible with existent being. The possibles, therefore, cannot properly be called real being nor fit into a common class of real being which is the direct object of metaphysics. They can be called beings only in a secondary, nonproper sense, strictly irreducible to the primary proper sense by any intrinsic analogy of proper proportionality, but related to it and dependent on it by a kind of extrinsic denomination or, better, analogy of extrinsic attribution. The possibles can also be called real in the same way by extrinsic denomination, but it would be more accurate to divide being into two primary classes, real and intentional, and then subdivide the second into possibles and beings-of-reason.

3. The possibles enter into the scope of metaphysics not as direct objects but only indirectly through their necessary intelligible connection with the direct object, existent being, as a projection of the latter's own intelligibility.

In one word, the Supremely Real has as its proper name, "He Who is." Hence nothing else can be called "really real" unless it, too, bear the family name, "that which is."

Fordham University
New York City

Professor Scheltens and the Proof
of God's Existence

BY FRANCIS X. MEEHAN

Extremely interesting if somewhat disquieting to the complacent is the provocative analysis by G. Scheltens (Vaalbeek-Louvain) of the present status of the proof for God's existence in Neo-Scholastic philosophy.[1] It exposes the underlying intellectual ferment that has agitated the mass of thinkers in this recrudescent period of Scholasticism from the moment when in 1888 (not ten years after Leo XIII's *Aeterni Patris*) M. A. DeMargerie addressed the International Scientific Congress of Catholics at Paris and, to the scandal and consternation of his hearers, questioned the analytic character of the principle of causality.[2] Because of the importance of the subject it would seem fitting and desirable to present to American readers for critical appraisal Professor Scheltens' exposition of this half century's controversy with an evaluation of the major elements of his own interpretation of it. This paper, then, shall take the form of a presentation of the controversy so thoroughly reviewed by Scheltens, and the solution he proposes (which he represents as being that of the foremost Neo-Scholastics of the day) followed by some critical comments occasioned thereby.

The point of departure for Scheltens' study is a critique of what is called the "traditional" proof of God's existence. It is

---

[1] G. Scheltens, O.F.M., "La Preuve de l'existence de Dieu dans la Philosophie néoscolastique," *Franciscan Studies,* Vol. XIV, n. 3, pp. 293–309.

[2] M. A. DeMargerie, "Le principe de causalité est-il un proposition analytique ou une proposition synthétique 'a priori'?" *Congrès scientifique des Catholiques tenu à Paris en 1888* (Paris, 1889), t. I, pp. 2, 76, 288 ff.

clear that by "traditional" proof is not meant that derived by
modern Scholastic philosophers from the great masters of the
Middle Ages (for the critique and the development of thought
that follows upon it consist for him indeed in a return to, and
a better grasp of, the fundamental metaphysical ideas of these
medieval doctors). Rather by "traditional" proof he means the
demonstration which until twenty years ago had been (mis-
takenly) regarded as the unadulterated heritage of medieval
ancestors though in reality it has roots no deeper than the
Wolfian rationalism of the late eighteenth century. Its structure is familiar. It can be reduced to the simple syllogistic
form:

> What is contingent is caused
> @ the world is contingent
> therefore the world is caused

The major here is what has been regarded as a general
a priori principle — that of causality — which was regarded
as the hinge and center of gravity of the proof of God's existence; the minor, but a simple affirmation of the contingency
of the existent world which scarcely merited attention. The
two premises traditionally (in the same sense of the term)
have been given in turn their separate groundings and only
thereafter compared or related to one another. Successive
examination of each reveals their faulty and inadequate structure according to Scheltens.

The major:
The statement of the major— that is, the principle of causality and its more generalized expression, the principle of
sufficient reason — became the subject of interminable controversy focusing on the question whether each principle was
an analytic judgment or a synthetic *a priori* one. Until the
end of the nineteenth century, the purely analytic character
of these principles was generally admitted among Scholastic
philosophers of that era. The existence of synthetic *a priori*
judgments was simply rejected and the Kantian question as
to how synthetic *a priori* judgments were possible was tabbed
as a false problem. Still there were apparently insurmountable
difficulties attending the acceptance of the principle as purely

analytic that demanded attention and required resolution. How, it was asked, could a purely analytical judgment enrich our knowledge (the old Kantian conundrum)? If the principle of causality were purely analytic, what then (presuming that there would be thereby no enrichment of knowledge) could it add to the minor of the syllogism? If the mere affirmation of the contingency of the world could not lead us to the affirmation of God's existence without reliance on some principle, could a proposition that was analytic be of any avail in conducting us further toward that affirmation? It was at this juncture and in support of this criticism that DeMargerie came forward with his attack and strongly denounced the *petitio principii* that he was convinced was always implied in every effort to reduce the principle of causality to the principle of contradiction and voiced the viewpoint that it was rather a synthetic *a priori* principle which by definition was irreducible. For a time the controversy smoldered only to flare out anew twenty years later (1912) when M. P. Laminne defended precisely the same thesis[3] subscribed to thereafter in great numbers by metaphysicians of note, philosophers such as P. Descoqs, J. de Vries, L. Fuetscher, J. Geyser, J. Hessen, J. Santeler, F. Sawicki, to mention only the more influential.[4]

In declaring the principle to be synthetic, nothing was thereby resolved. Rather did new problems arise. So long as there was acceptance of its analytic character, the principle of causality, properly speaking, required no foundation — for a principle whose predicate is implied in the notion of the

---

[3] J. Laminne, "Le principe de contradiction et le principe de causalité," *Rev. néoscol. philos.*, 19 (1912), pp. 453, 488.

[4] Cf. P. Picard (colleague of P. Descoqs), *Le Problème critique fondamental;* J. de Vries, *Denken und Sein* (Freiburg [Germ.], 1937), and "Geschichtliches zum Streit um die metaphysischen Prinzipien, *Scholastik,* 6 (1937), pp. 196–221; L. Fuetscher, *Die ersten Seins — und Denkprinzipien* (Innsbruck, 1930); M. J. Geyser, *Erkenntnistheorie* (Munster, 1922), *Das Prinzip vom Zureichenden Grunde, eine logisch-ontologische Untersuchung* (Regensburg, 1929), *Das Gesetz der Ursache* (München, 1933); J. Hessen, *Das Kausalprinzip* (Augsburg, 1928); J. Santeler, *Intuition und Wahrheiterkenntnis* (Innsbruck, 1934); F. Sawicki, "Das Irrationale in den Grundlagen der Erkenntnis und die Gottesbeweises," *Philosophisches Jahrbuch,* 44 (1931), pp. 410–418.

subject is self-evident. Once declare, however, the principle to be synthetic and the problem of its founding immediately arises and on this point there seems to be no agreement or satisfactory solution.

Some sought it in the analysis of our experience of causality — especially the conscious experience of causal influence in the subject's own acts; still others fell back on the immediate evidence of the principle in question. The latter position was the easier and was successively defended by M. DeMargerie, M. J. Laminne, and J. de Vries. In their view the comparisons of the concepts "contingent" and "caused" are such that we see immediately that the second must be attributed to the first even though the content of the predicate concept is in no way contained in the thought content of the subject concept. In the mind of Professor Scheltens there seems to be something quite arbitrary in such an appeal to evidence.

The Neo-Scholastics who attempted the other way — i.e., the analysis of the experience of causality — scarcely fared better in their efforts. Their argument comes down to this: I know myself as the cause of my own acts, thoughts, volitions, movements, and the like; but if, they say, one can uncover by an analysis of one's own effects the formal reason why they can be labeled "effects," why they can be said to be "caused," then one can thereby arrive at a justifiable basis for the principle of causality. For it would be possible then to say that where the same formal reason presents itself there would have to be causality.

A detailed evaluation of this approach is scarcely possible here but by way of criticism one might note the flagrant extrapolation already alluded to. The terms "causality" and "contingency" are not univocal. Each science deals with a different type of causality. It is especially important to distinguish intramundane causality from transcendental or metaphysical causality.

The minor:
While the foundation of the major proved to be a matter of such disagreement among the Scholastic philosophers, there was an accord that was practically unanimous in the proof

of the minor. All these philosophers readily admitted the contingency of the world and for the same reasons. Unfortunately, however, the unanimity does not seem to be a sufficient guarantee of the sound basis of their view.

The examination, then, of the so-called traditional argument for God's existence would in Professor Scheltens' view appear to lead us to a conclusion that is at least uncertain if not dubious, and this stalemate is due, he feels, to a superficial use of the terms "sufficient reason" and "contingency." The contingent, they said, is what lacks in itself its sufficient reason for being. The question is, however, when and under what conditions could we say of the world that it lacks its own *raison d'être?* The answer is simple. There is only one way of pointing up the contingency of the world, and that is to show that it is positively inconceivable, i.e., that it becomes contradictory without God.

These philosophers however were not of this mind. It is difficult to see how they could affirm the contingency of the world before uncovering the latent contradiction of which we speak. Still less understandable is the fact that DeMargerie, Laminne, Geyser, Fuetscher, and others would assert the contingency of the world and yet declare this contradiction did not exist. In this event it is a puzzle to know just what they understand by contingency. Is it possible to attribute to the notion of contingency even a purely negative sense, i.e., that the contingent is what *has not* its *raison d'être* and yet not see that this insufficiency postulates an exigency, a void that requires filling? Had these philosophers reflected more deeply on the meaning of contingency, Professor Scheltens affirms, they could not have failed to see the impossibility of their attempt and might have spared themselves much time and discussion.

The examination of the "traditional" proof of God's existence has convinced him then of basic structural flaws. God's existence cannot, he feels, be the conclusion of a syllogism whose major (the abstract general principle of causality) and minor (the affirmation of the contingency of the world) are first separately proved and only thereafter compared. For him the major and minor cannot be separated: they are not exterior to one another. He is convinced that the proof of the minor leads immediately to the affirmation of God. This comes down to saying that recourse to a general principle after proof of the world's contingency is superfluous.

The difficulty, he maintains, we are confronted with in the proof of God's existence does not consist (as is generally believed) in the foundation of the general principle of causality. It resides rather in the question, how bring to light the contingency of the world? The entire proof then is situated on the level of the analysis of concrete reality. There is only one thing to do: by reflection on the world of experience we must show the inner contradiction implied in the conception of this world apart from its total dependence on the Transcendent Being. The important question then is: how does reflection on the concrete world of our experience reveal to us the insufficiency of this world without God? — the same question originally raised, but now more precisely formulated through the enrichment derived from the experience and appraisal of the abortive attempt. The effort to answer this question reveals two distinct approaches each of which has its ardent defenders — one by way of synthesis (typified in the thought of P. J. Maréchal), the other by way of analysis of the concrete real (represented by DeRaeymaeker, Geiger, *et al.*).

The synthetic method — P. J. Maréchal:
For Maréchal, the discovery of the world's dependence upon God is a result of an *a priori* synthesis — a synthesis, specifically, of an *a posteriori given* appearing as a brute, isolated fact, and a natural and *a priori* tendency of human intelligence. The human mind, according to Maréchal, is not an inert, static tablet on which things come to be written, but an active tendency, an orientation, a dynamism that can have for its final term only the Infinite. But with good reason does it seem that Maréchal has been reproached by his critics with basing his demonstration on a *petitio principii*. Actually must not one already be assured of the existence of God before affirming the existence of a natural tendency toward Him?

The analytic method:
It is Professor Scheltens' position that it is beings them-

selves that reveal their transcendent source. If we wish to
bring to light the causal relation of the world to God we must
discover it in being itself. Being does not present itself to us
as a brute or isolated fact or given to be afterward informed
of its origin by our own intellectual finality; rather is it the
very thing which communicates to us the secret of its ultimate
basis. Consequently, it is rather by analysis than by synthesis
that the relation of the world to God becomes manifest. Let
us not deceive ourselves however. This is not to say that the
analysis of finite being will uncover God at its center as one
discovers a stone or pit within the fruit. The analysis of being
never leads us to an intuition of God.

Still, God must be present in some way in the world of
experience. But under what form does the Absolute reveal
Himself? Not, certainly, immediately under the form of a transcendent infinite but under the veil of a *basic* and *mysterious*
unity englobing all beings in a transcendental synthesis.

It is in judgment as affirmation that we seize being as existent. But an affirmation never bears uniquely on an isolated
given but also on the absolute, on the totality of being.

Take an example: Peter is a man. This judgment has as term
not only Peter insofar as he is a man. Its meaning can be transformed thus: the totality of being is such that the existence
of Peter as man finds an ineffaceable place there, is written
there in indelible characters. The reality of Peter then is af-
firmed as being in harmony with all the rest and the rest is
in harmony with Peter.

Every judgment posits then a fundamental unity of all
beings, fundamental because it is not superadded to beings
but lies within being itself.

But if on the one hand the being of particular beings cannot explain the unity and if on the other, being does without
question unify, it must be that in particular being we do not
reach the ultimate basis of being. Beyond particular beings
then there must be a unique and transcendent source whence
all particular beings emanate. The unity of particular beings
cannot be in the last analysis immanent, it must be conceived
as transcendent.

The transcendental synthesis of particular beings must then

be conceived as the reflection of a unique and transcendent source; it is the way we move toward God.

This evolution of thought that we have noted as taking place in the bosom of Neo-Scholastic philosophy must be characterized (as Scheltens has said in his introduction) as a return to fundamental ideas of the metaphysics of the Middle Ages.

Criticism. There can be no doubt but what Professor Scheltens has made a penetrating study of the present status of the proof of God's existence among continental Neo-Scholastics and has offered a stimulating solution to the seeming impasse. There is so much that commends itself in this work that one hesitates to address oneself to the task of criticism in the limitations of a paper of this nature lest it appear that by the forced concentration on amphibolous or ambivalent matter, general approbation of the spirit and tenor of the study, and genuine appreciation of the scholarship therein revealed be overlooked. In reluctant risk of such an impression we shall perforce restrict ourselves to some phases only of the study that seem to call especially for comment, some having to do with the historical, some with the personally interpretative and constructive section of the article in the hope that a fairer appraisal might in consequence be made.

Considerations relative to the criticism of the major of the "traditional" proof:

The first remarks, of a merely suggestive kind, will focus on the controversy centering about the principle of causality: (1) its character, (2) its formulation, (3) the possible "enrichment" of knowledge deriving therefrom, and (4) the question of intramundane versus metaphysical causality.

1. As to the character of the principle of causality. In reflection on the controversy concerning the analytic character of the principle in question this fact stands out. The completeness of understanding about analytic propositions appears to have been lost sight of. If by an analytic proposition is meant solely a proposition the content of whose predicate term is contained in the thought content of the subject term, i.e., one in which the predicate enters into the definition of the

subject, then with good reason is the analytic character of the principle of causality challenged and denied. For "being-caused" is not of the definition of that which is caused. St. Thomas surely was quite definite and unmistakable on this point.[5] Yet it would be untrue to assume he thereby denied its analytic character. His was a broader understanding of analytic judgments (or propositions *per se* known). He followed Aristotle in this matter and proposed what, in a better sense, can be called the "traditional" teaching of the Stagirite. An analytic judgment (or one *per se* known) would be any proposition, known immediately, not by some medium extrinsic to the terms in which it is expressed, but through "the proper knowledge of these terms" themselves,[6] and such would include not only those wherein the predicate enters into the definition of the subject, but also those wherein the subject enters into the definition of the predicate, i.e., wherein the predicate is a proper accident of the subject.[7] And with respect to this enlarged view, this much can be said that St. Thomas would certainly regard the principle of causality as an analytic proposition of this second variety, and he does so on sound ground.[8] It would be somewhat arbitrary and quite unhistorical to disregard this kind of analytic proposition in discussing the matter. Possibly this second mode was what DeMargerie, Laminne, and deVries called a "synthetic *a priori*" proposition, having immediacy of evidence, necessity and universality. If so, though their terminology might be considered to be unhappily chosen, they were nearer to the truth than those who sought to defend its analytic character in the narrower sense. It seems unfortunate that the broader meaning of analytic judgments held by Aristotle and St. Thomas was not retained or was lost to view. At least the retention might have sharpened issues.

---

[5] *S. T.* I, 44, 1, 1m: " . . . habitudo ad causam non intret definitionem entis quod est causatum."

[6] *In I Post. Anal.*, 6, Vivès, Vol. XXII, p. 120b: " . . . non per aliquod medium extrinsecum cognoscuntur sed per propriam cognitionem terminorum."

[7] Cf. *ibid.*, 9, p. 126a; *In II De Anima,* 14, Pirotta edit. n. 401. For a more extended explanation see also F. Meehan, *Efficient Causality in Aristotle and St. Thomas* (Washington, D. C.: Catholic University Press, 1940), c. 12, "Necessity of Cause," *passim,* especially p. 333 ff. and notes.

[8] Cf. Meehan, *op. cit.,* pp. 366–367.

2. Insight might be gained into the immediacy of evidence, and therefore, the necessity of truth and the reason for regarding it as analytic (in this broader aspect) if one looks to the significance of the various formulations used by St. Thomas in expressing the principle of causality. Whether one is confronted in the concrete entitative order with existents that once were not and have begun to be, or with beings that are in motion (and therefore are having a passive potentiality actualized), or with contingent beings (in St. Thomas' sense of the term — *"possibile esse et non esse,"* with a potency, therefore, to nonbeing and a consequent innate indifference to existence signalized by a material thing's susceptibility of another form), or with a composite being (with always the ultimate and radical composition of essence and existence), then one has to deal in every case with a being that must be caused, that cannot not be caused. Universalized then we have a variety of formulas expressing the same need: "omne quod non semper fuit, si esse incipiat, indiget aliquo quod sit ei causa essendi";[9] "in quocumque enim est motus illud movetur";[10] "omne quod est possibile esse et non esse habet causam, quia in se consideratum ad utrumlibet se habet";[11] "omnis compositio indiget aliquo componente . . . componens autem est causa efficiens compositi."[12] In the last analysis each of these is true and truly necessary, for in every instance their subjects, through the imperfection and lack revealed in each, proclaim themselves to be participated existents, and participated existents are caused existents. To deny this is to deny an acceptable and intelligible *raison d'être*. They would surely not have it of themselves, for inceptive being, passively actuated being, contingent being, composite being are all innately and intrinsically indigent beings. To deny them a cause that alone complements their indigence is to allow no assignable reason for existence; this is to make them a contradiction in terms and hence inconceivable. We would be

9 St. Thomas, *Comp. Theol.*, I, c. 6, Vivès, XXVII, p. 3b.

10 St. Thomas, *In III De Anima*, 2, Pirotta edit., n. 592; *In III Phy.*, 4, Vivès, XXII, p. 392b.

11 St. Thomas, *C. G.*, II, 15, *Praeterea*; I, 16, *Amplius*.

12 *Ibid.*, I, 18, *Amplius*.

confronted with a temporally inceptive being without an inceptor, a moved without a mover, a contingent existent (one therefore indifferent to existence) unaccountably determined to exist, a composite (ultimately of potency and act, essence and existence) without an efficiently unifying composer, a participant in existence without an imparter of existence. It is like denying to a begotten being a begetter, to a derived being a source of derivation. It would miss the point to charge that there is a begging of the question in all this. One is not surreptitiously assuming the existence of the cause in these instances and then saying that the effect is necessarily related to it. One is simply noting the undeniable fact of indigence in the confronted given and affirming its requirement of another. The terms that designate this indigence and inadequacy are *post-factum* labels, not *pre-factum* assumptions that prejudge the case. To say that every effect requires a cause would be sheer presumption and pure tautology if by effect we meant with anterior insistence something that is effected or produced by another. But to label something as an effect, something, therefore, which requires a cause, posterior to discovering why by its insufficiency it must be a term of causal action is no prejudgment, no begging of the question. This is the approach that was St. Thomas' and must be recognized in all his formulations of causal necessity, even to the ultimate expression in terms of participation to which the others can be reduced, viz., "Ex eo quod aliquid est ens per participationem sequitur quod sit causatam ab alio."[13] The reason why inceptive beings, moved beings, contingent beings, composite beings, even necessary beings that have not the reason for their necessity in themselves are all produced and therefore terms of causal action lies ultimately in their being beings-by-participation that bespeak a necessary relation of dependence in which they all stand with respect to an efficient cause that in the last analysis is uncaused, that exists *per se* in unparticipated fashion. The principle of causality in this full-blown expression does seem to lead inexorably to the

---

[13] St. Thomas, *S. T.,* I, 44, 1 c: "Si enim aliquid invenitur in aliquo per participationem, necesse est quod causetur in ipso ab eo cui essentialiter convenit." Cf. *ibid.,* 44, 1, 1m.

First Cause, God. That is perhaps why St. Thomas, while conceding the truth of the proposition that "the first cause which is God does not enter into the essence of created things" could still go on to say: "Nevertheless the existence (esse) that is present to created things cannot be understood save as derived from the divine existence (as we cannot understand a proper effect save as owing to its proper cause)."[14] Being caused is something that though not entering into the essence of the effect flows necessarily therefrom; and being-caused-by-God follows necessarily from the nature of this "contingent" world. Scheltens is perfectly right in saying that if the world is the work of God, He must somehow be revealed therein; he is perfectly wise in insisting that the analysis of the world's contingency holds the key to the question of God's existence for it alone lays bare along with the evidence of communication of being and goodness, the deficiency and limitation of the same in the beings of the world and therefore the ineradicable mark of total dependence. "Thus saith the Lord that created thee . . . and formed thee . . . 'Thou art mine'" (Isa. 43:1). God's seal must be on His work. The seal reveals the sealer, but always through efficient (if not, in addition, through exemplary) causality. Hence the importance of the principle. It is an irreplaceable way to Him. It is basic to the proof of His existence (as also to the deeper knowledge of something of His nature). It is fundamental to the *quinque viae*. If it is not necessary and evident and certain, then nothing is, and no *a posteriori* argument is of any value. One might just as well abandon all effort at intelligent discourse.

3. These last observations touch upon an objection that is raised against the acceptance of the principle of causality as analytic. It is asked, in that case what enrichment of knowledge can it bring? (More specifically what can it add to the minor in the argument for God's existence?) The questions seem to imply a strange understanding of analytic propositions and their place in demonstrations, a strange interpretation of

---

[14] St. Thomas, *De Pot.*, 3, 5, 1m: " . . . licet causa prima, quae Deus est, non intret essentiam rerum creatarum; tamen esse, quod rebus creatis inest, non potest intelligi nisi ut deductum ab esse divino; sicut nec proprius effectus potest nisi ut deductus a causa propria."

enrichment. Enrichment of knowledge (an obvious metaphor) can only be construed as advancement, and/or perfection of knowledge, its widening and deepening. It can be understood then both extensively and intensively. We grow in knowledge by coming to know more things and by coming to know better what we already know. Would anyone deny to the first principles of being (and of thought) such a function of enrichment with respect to knowledge? Surely we do not come to know these principles and then have done with them as though they shed no additional or continuous light on subsequent knowledge nor helped in the gathering and perfecting of that knowledge? Such a view would betray an utter ignorance of the part they play in all demonstration as conceived by Aristotle. The indemonstrables must ever be resorted to in every argumentation. They are as the same sun that ever enriches our ever changing lives, and surely as important for our intellectual life. But more specifically, is not the principle of causality behind every investigation of nature that seeks to lay bare the causes of phenomena? Does it not ever guide us to a deeper knowledge of the cause from its effects? Does it not help us to know more causes and therefore more *being* and does it not enable us to know these causes and beings better (and knowing them better to know better their effects)? There is hardly impoverishment in such a principle. It is surely this world that we investigate but by the principle of causality we are led to the knowledge of its otherworldly cause, that cause's beauty and wisdom and power and majesty, its supreme sovereignty and utter dominion of all beings; and the continued use of its light can bring us ever more enriched knowledge and awe in the knowledge of all that this Transcendent Cause does, of all that His power extends to, of all that His wisdom devises and His beauty contrives. An expanding universe (in any sense in which it can be said to expand) cannot but bring us, through the principle of causality, a better knowledge of its infinitely expansive Source. It is a truism to state that the effect cannot be greater than the cause and the greater the effect the greater the cause. Such natural corollaries of the principle of causality surely enrich our knowledge of the material universe, relate it to God, and enlighten us considerably on the extent and fecundity of divine causality.

4. This matter touches on the objection raised in Humean fashion against the transition to extra- or supra-mundane causality from the experience solely of intramundane causality. While it is true that causality — and this holds good for efficient — cannot be regarded as univocal, still it can never be thought of as utterly equivocal. For one to know that causality is present of whatever sort, it is not necessary that the cause as well as the effect fall within the purview of our observations and sense experience. Enough that we come to know a being as derived for us to posit at least the existence of its cause. Nor need this positing stop at earthly limits if such limits do not hold the adequate explanation of the phenomenon. Analogical, to be sure, cause is, but there is an irreducible denominator proportionally realized in every causation — the dependentiality of the effect with respect to it. And this warrants on occasion our passing to a supramundane cause where nothing else satisfies the quest for intelligibility.

Considerations relative to the criticism of the minor of the "traditional" proof:

Professor Scheltens sounds a salient note in stressing the "contingency" of the world as the crux of the argument and is perfectly wise in interpreting "contingency" in the deeper meaning of the term that reposes it on the principles of contradiction and sufficient reason (though as shall be noted — one cannot get away from it — it is mediately through the principle of causality that this is done). It brings out the radical insufficiency of the contingent, its unintelligibility, its inconceivability, apart from a cause. Any other understanding of it must be regarded as superficial. Surely that is so when the contingent is equated with everything-that-begins-to-be. The "ratio" of temporal beginning is not, *de facto,* philosophically demonstrable for everything in the world or for the universe as a whole as Scheltens observes; nor is this necessary to establish the caused character of the cosmos. Were it so, God's existence would have to wait upon the proof of temporal inception and that is yet to be proved beyond question, as far as science is concerned (though there is more and more evidence along those lines). St. Thomas did it the hard way but it was the only way for him at his time. He sought to prove the world was produced in its total being, indeed was created, even on the assumption that it was eternal. He stands pat by his arguments for the created character of the world,[15] even though he concedes that its begun-character is something that we hold "by faith alone" and can be proved "by no demonstration."[16] This required then a deeper understanding of what we call contingency — one that prescinded from temporal beginnings and endings. This deeper understanding is reached in the knowledge of beings as participated, in the recognition of their composition of essence and existence. Nor would it be a valid objection to state that such a recognition is based upon "a typically rationalist presupposition" that would imply a perfect equation between human knowledge and the essences of beings. There is no Thomistic claim to know perfectly what the essences of beings are, only the insistence that we can know what they are not; and with sound reason can it be said they are not their own existence.

Professor Scheltens' positive position:

As one passes to the constructive part of Professor Scheltens' study the following two points stand out that seem to call for special comment (though the comments must be necessarily brief, expressive only of questions raised, not of answers given conclusively); they have to do with: (1) his understanding of the nature of the "proof" and (2) the means used to establish the world's contingency.

1. It seems quite clear from his explicit statements that Professor Scheltens regards the "proof" for God's existence as a "monstration" and not a demonstration properly speaking.[17] Demonstration, he feels, is confined to the proof of the minor alone of the "traditional" syllogistic form (i.e., the

---

[15] St. Thomas, *S. T.*, I, 44–45.

[16] *Ibid.*, 46, 2 c: "Respondeo dicendum quod mundum non semper fuisse sola fide tenetur et demonstrative probari non potest"; cf. I, 32, 1 c.

[17] *Loc. cit.*, p. 301. See also p. 308: "L'existence de Dieu n'est donc pas démonstrée à proprement parler, on ne saurait faire que *montrer* sa présence" (italics his).

world is contingent) and once this is done one is led immediately to the affirmation of God for then "le recours à une
principe général devient superflu" (p. 301). One wonders if
this is actually so or even possible. He has expressed his
variant of the proof in the form at least of a hypothetical syllogism (*ponendo ponens*), that would run: "If the world is
conceivable only in dependence on God then God must be
for the world to exist" (p. 299); but the world presents
itself as such (and this is what is meant in the last analysis
by calling it contingent); therefore God must be. Here we
have an extremely compact, highly concentrated form of reasoning, but a form of reasoning nevertheless; and a syllogistic
form it is, with major and minor and conclusion. (It would
indeed be very easy to cast it into the form of a simple cate-
goric syllogism rather than a partially hypothetical one.)[18]
The liaison between antecedent and consequent of the conditional major is evident beyond dispute and the inexorable
necessity of the conclusion follows from the positing of the
antecedent in the minor. Clearly is it seen why the certitude
of the conclusion hinges on the establishing of the truth of
the posited minor, the antecedent of the conditional major.
But as to the nature of the argument there seems to be no
reason for reluctance in calling it a demonstration in the strict
sense of the term — a *demonstratio quia,* to be sure, not a
demonstratio propter quid; it is a demonstration of fact, not
of "reasoned fact." Beyond this, however, we might raise the
question with respect to it: Are we to understand that "recourse to a general principle" is not involved here? To be
sure, if by "recourse" is meant a second appeal to a general
principle after one is made, then that would be superfluous.
But if the impression were made that no appeal at all is
present, or is required, that would be misleading, indeed erroneous. Telescoped into the compressed antecedent of the
conditional major are the prime principles which cannot be
disregarded. If we are to ask what is it that is inconceivable,
the answer must be the denial of a cause to that which re-

---

[18] Every being whose uncaused existence would render it inconceivable as
existent requires a cause; but the world is such an existent; therefore it
requires a cause.

quires a cause (the implied acceptance, here, and application of the principle of causality — some existents, at least, require a cause and would be inconceivable without one). And if we further ask what beings require a cause, the answer must be, all that do not have a *raison d'être* in and of themselves (the implied acceptance and use of the principle of sufficient reason). The establishing therefore of the condition's antecedent (which is what the minor seeks to do) rests definitely on recourse to the general principle of sufficient reason by way of the principle of causality (the latter offering the sufficient reason for a being that would otherwise lack being). And both are made reducible to the principle of contradiction. Professor Scheltens' understanding of the concept of sufficient reason and its corresponding principle involves this reduction. There are existents (and we shall call them contingent) whose uncaused and unconditioned existence (whose existence without a cause) would render them unintelligible, contradictions in terms; or, to express it positively, there are existents whose dependent condition and therefore caused existence would alone make them conceivable as existing.

2. And how is the world shown to be a congeries of such contingent beings? It seems that Professor Scheltens' criticism on this point of the Maréchalian method of synthesis is well taken. The contingency of the world is better grounded on the analysis of contingent beings themselves than on a synthetic *a priori* activity of the knowing subject. It is more reasonable to suppose that it is particular beings themselves that should betray their own want and reveal their derived natures. But does the analysis of the concrete real bring this home to us in the way in which Professor Scheltens suggests in the form and under the veil of "a basic and mysterious unity that englobes all beings in a transcendental synthesis" (p. 304)? And if so, is this basic and mysterious unity shown for certain in the light either of the theory of judgment here presented by Scheltens or a theory of knowledge (Platonic, Augustinian, Bonaventurian) that would fix the cognition of finite things in *rationibus aeternis?* This last question does not admit of an unqualified and unchallengeable "Yes." Attractive and intriguing though these theories may be, suggestive though

they are of truths that we only glimpse and have not fully exploited, still, in their present state they are at least somewhat aporetic and inceptive and do not, it seems, afford the assured ground that is sought to bring to clear light the world's necessary relation to God. As to the basic and mysterious unity that Professor Scheltens professes to see, one wonders whether he means by this a real ontological bond that extramentally unites them, or a simple logical oneness of all beings under the unitary concept of "being."

If the former, that would signify surely no more than that the aggregate beings of our experience are not disgregate but form *a* cosmos, one world, compacted into a single universe with all entities united only accidentally (for they do not form one substantial being) through mutual relationships of co-ordination and subordination one to another.[19] While all this is true, does it not suppose as already established (as do all ordered relationships) the existence of a final cause, in this case, an ultimate one, accounting for the ontological bond?[20] (In this connection, too, is it not something of an extension of the transcendental character of being and its convertibility with oneness — *ens et unum convertuntur* — to imply that all beings taken collectively are one, and not merely that each and every being, taken singly, is one? Is this interpretation contained in, and allowable to, the expression: *omne ens est unum?*)

If on the other hand we are merely gathering all the inferiors of being under its unitary concept as we make individual men one under the concept of man, then the unity is not real but logical and it would be less of a unity than is the case with man, for being is not univocal. It would simply mean that the reality connoted by the "ratio" of being is realized proportionately in all its inferiors. The unification comes about solely by the activity of the mind.

Nevertheless the elements of a solution are to be found it

---

[19] St. Thomas, *De Pot.*, 3, 16, 1m: " . . . sicut Deus est unus, ita et unum produxit, non solum quia unumquodque in se est unum, sed etiam quia omnia quodammodo sunt unum perfectum." Note the qualification *quodammodo*.

[20] *Ibid.*, 2m: " . . . creatura assimilatur Deo in unitate, in quantum unaquaeque in se una est, et in quantum omnes unum sunt unitate ordinis."

seems in what the mind does see of unity amid diversity of beings. They are beings by all that they are, by all that they have. Its reality applies as readily to the differences as to the likenesses (which makes being transcendental and analogical). It is to be noted, however, that regardless of how different they are (and they are different by their essences and all their accidental accretions), still these beings *are* (i.e., exist) and their differences *are* (for we are speaking of the existent world) and they all are *beings* or *of being* by a connatural ordination to a common act of existence. And is it not this act of existence, shared in by all beings' infinite diversifications, that points to a single cause of their total being? Existence is common to all the particularized beings of this plural universe and what properly constitutes them as different from each other cannot be the source of this common attribute. We must look for this source in an Existent, supreme and unique, of whom alone other existents are the proper effect. Multitude is traceable to unity, particularized existents, to one universal font of existence.

It is along this line, we submit, suggested by St. Thomas in several places (notably in *De Potentia*, 3, 5c; in *Contra Gentiles*, 2, 15; more briefly in *Summa Theologica*, I, 44, 1 c) that we must look for the evidence of the world's dependence on God for its existence, and from it, for His existence. It seems the simpler and safer way. There must be an argument *for* participated existence (and each one of the five ways brings this out) before there is an argument *from* participated existence. No being of the world is the adequate reason for its own existence nor — and it would be on that same account — for the existence of any other. There must be One who alone can say with all its implication: "I am he who *is*" (Exod. 3:14). True, there is more to being than existence. True too, that all participated perfections, absolute and relative, must be accounted for. Geiger has made the point in a powerful polemic that we cannot limit ourselves to the perfection of sheer existence, that we are looking for a universal cause of being in all its amplitude (and this is to be found only in a Being with all its plenitude), that we must avoid the error that Avicenna fell into of ascribing pure *esse* and nothing more to this cause.[21] St. Thomas did not miss out on these points and he succeeded in avoiding the error of Avicenna. There cannot be existence alone, but only the existence of some essence, nor can any other perfection or essence be actual apart from the act of existence. Whatever, then, of other perfection there is, since it *is* only by existence, is due to the universal cause of existence who is at once the total cause of being. It is the world as existent that we must account for. But God has left His mark upon it. We see Him to be sure *per speculum, in aenigmate,* in the mirror of finite beings. These give dark, but definite indications of their own dearth and need of Him. He is not a *deus recens* that by definition eludes us. Transcendent to the world, He is nevertheless immanent in it, near to every being in the "now" of time, "by His power, by His presence, by His essence," and this is not without its evidence. His conservation of all beings in existence, the prolongation of creation, reveals it. His countenance is ever reflected on the face of the deep. "Abyssus abyssum invocat" (Ps. 41:7). And "one depth makes answer to the other" (Knox translation of the same), the one speaking forth of its emptiness, "In him, we live and move and have our *being*" (Acts 17:28), the other responding from His fullness, "I am the God, who *Is*" (Exod. 3:14).

St. John's Seminary
Brighton, Mass.

---

[21] Cf. *La Participation dans la Philosophie de S. Thomas d'Aquin,* especially pp. 191–216.

Part Three NATURALIA

ON THE MATHEMATICAL APPROACH TO NATURE

BY VINCENT EDWARD SMITH

Although the objects of mathematical knowledge reside only in the mobile world, they do not depend on motion to be mathematically understood.[1] Such freedom from motion invests mathematics with unusual strength. For to the extent that an object enjoys an immobile status, it cannot be other than it is; hence the necessity in mathematical sciences.[2] In proportion as the mathematician leaves motion outside his science, he makes no reference to act and potency[3] which, because they are variously intermixed in the mobile world, often rule out simple "yes" and "no" answers to our questions; hence, in part at least, the clarity and precision of mathematical knowledge. Moreover, since mathematics cannot consider the final cause, directing things to established ends, it acquires a liberty to construct that makes it an ally of the modern ambition to understand nature through that constructive enterprise which is controlled experiment.

But while there is strength in mathematics through abstraction from motion, from the same source come notable weaknesses. The failure to consider motion means a lack of contact with nature and with that capital distinction between what is by nature and what is by human art;[4] hence, the frequent confusion in modern mathematics between the real or objective order on the one hand and the logical or man-made order on

---

[1] *In Boeth. de Trin.*, V, 1; 3, ed. Wyser.
[2] *Ibid.*, V, 1.
[3] *Summa contra Gentiles*, I, 82.
[4] *In II Phys.*, 1, n. 299, ed. Angeli-Pirotta.

113

the other. The deliverance from act and potency, while favoring clarity and distinctness, denies to mathematics an insight into those nuances which make our world a hierarchy, and the resulting outlook upon the real is univocal and equalitarian. Last, at least for present purposes, the ignoring of final causes abolishes in our logic that crucial difference in the real between the essential or natural (*per se*) and the incidental (*per accidens*).[5]

Because mathematics ignores the mobile or physical, it ignores a datum that is quite obvious in human experience and supremely important in our scientific struggle to understand our world. Nothing, not even being, is known more explicitly to our intellect than the mobile. It is motion that first strikes our senses, evokes our attention, and arouses that wonder which leads in time to science. Motion is so well known that in terms of it we test whether things are real or make-believe.

Yet motion is not simply obvious. It is also our vehicle to the natures of things, and to the distinctions of one thing from another. Cotton, for instance, can simulate snow, and on the basis of looks alone — what Whitehead has called "visual immediacy" — the two substances cannot be distinguished from each other. Thus learning their differences for the first time, a child must attend to their mobile qualities, by feeling them, pulling each apart and pressing each together, fingering their texture, discerning their temperature and their dryness or wetness, watching the one burn when ignited by a match while the other melts or simply puts out the fire. By such mobile properties of things we know their respective natures.

By the test of motion, an animal is pronounced living or dead. Our days and years are regimented by the motion of the solar system. By adverting to a matter that has now this set of mobile properties and now a different set, the mind discovers substantial change and, through such change, the reality of substance itself. It is from motion too that the first scientific notion of causality is formed, and so it is quite consistent that a merely mathematical approach to nature, ignor-

---

[5] *Ibid.*, 8, nn. 425–433.

ing motion as such, would also in time surrender its interest in causes.

But motion cannot be ignored with impunity, and a discipline that proceeds to explore nature without the equipment to grasp motion is bound to turn up with an irrational report. To exalt the mathematical technique into a physical instrument able to treat the mobile as such is to miss the truly physical or mobile. Because it neglects motion, mathematics relinquishes a crucial fact about nature.

For this, of course, mathematics is not to be reprehended; in ignoring motion, it is only obeying the limits that make it a distinct and even unique science of the real world. Yet in evaluating the various systems of modern physics which all employ a mathematical approach to nature, it is important to underscore in bold type that the most salient fact about our universe, its motions, resists any reduction to mathematical categories.

However, it would seem as though mathematics does take motion into account after all. It is common, even in elementary geometry, to speak of a line as generated by a moving point or of a plane as produced by a moving line or of a solid as the locus of a moving plane. Yet common as these expressions may be, they are only scaffolds to aid our imagination, and as the concepts of mathematical science are built, the temporary and extrinsic supports in reaching them must be dismantled. Points, for instance, are not moved from place to place, and indeed, in the mathematical order, there is no reference to place at all. Point p cannot go from, say, A to B. At B, there is no longer the same point but a new and different one. At A, p was not a distinct point; it coincided with A. In short, the position of a point is included in its very definition or essence, and it cannot be changed short of changing the whole reality of the point in question. Points have no potency to move elsewhere, as though an "elsewhere" were distinct from the point that is now in it.[6]

Pure mathematics is thus out of communion with the physi-

---

[6] That there is no reference to place in mathematics, cf. *In II Met.*, 10, n. 2339, ed. Cathala.

cal, natural, mobile as such; and applied mathematics, e.g., modern physics, can be physically significant only to the extent that priority is given to the nonmathematical component in the discipline. If mathematics does not allude to the potential, it cannot define motion, and a consecutive, truly scientific approach to the physical order should first define what motion is at the pre-experimental and premetrical level where motion is first encountered. This means a purely physical analysis without measurement, without experiment, and without any preconceived hypotheses. In short, the resources for formulating the definition of motion have not improved since Aristotle's time, since they are human reason and human experience.

The mathematical assault upon motion in modern times has led to a number of misunderstandings which a prior physical analysis of nature could have avoided. Consider the old problem, mentioned as late as Newton, of a sailor on a moving ship. At rest in the ship, the sailor is said to be moving with the velocity of the ship. If the ship is moving forward at a speed of five knots and the sailor is walking aft at the same rate, the sailor is immobile with respect to the earth. If the earth is spinning in its diurnal motion, then the ship and the sailor and everything else on our globe are in a state of perpetual movement, and all motion and rest become merely relative. So at least it would seem from a merely mathematical description of the motions in our universe. Mathematically, the composition of velocities in relative motions can be worked out at least in principle.

But does the mathematical report on motion really yield insight into the physical situation? No, not where the mathematical physics is applied without a prior analysis of nature at a purely physical level. The sailor, moving backward with the ship's forward velocity, is performing a motion natural to him. He is in a motion according to his nature. That he is walking on a ship is incidental (*per accidens*). A fish swimming in the ocean is also undergoing a natural movement; that it is also caught up in the diurnal motion of the earth is incidental.

The distinction between essential and incidental causality is thus not mathematically significant, although physically it is quite meaningful, and hence the study of nature in purely mathematical terms overlooks a distinction quite critical in our investigation of the universe. The mathematical approach to nature was fated of its nature to at least a Galilean type of relativity where a ship can be considered as moving with respect to the earth or the earth with respect to the ship and where, no matter which alternative is chosen, the results come out the same. Einstein was only pushing forward a weakness of modern mathematical physics when he proposed his theory of relativity on the ground that the immobile in our world cannot be mathematically established. A discipline that cannot study the mobile, as such, cannot make scientific sense out of the contrary reality of the immobile, and besides, to miss the distinction between the essential and the incidental is to forbid any differentiation between the absolute and the relative in the first place.

Such an analysis, if true, is not an indictment of mathematical physics in its genuine meaning. The only conclusion here authorized is that the study of nature by measurement cannot, under its own power, proceed realistically but requires a prior physical analysis to achieve a truly physical perspective of definition and distinction. The distinction between the essential and the incidental, in the case of the sailor walking on a ship, cannot be made by measurement, but once made through physical analysis, it makes sense of the measurement itself. Subordinated in a manner like this to a prior physical analysis, the mathematical techniques of modern physics assume a meaning, find a completion, and yield results at variance with the typically relativistic outlook of a purely mathematical physics.

Relativity theory is one of the two contemporary systems of physics that have caused perplexity within a method that cannot define motion nor distinguish between the natural and the incidental. The other present-day theory that has proved unsettling in modern physics is quantum mechanics, and the philosophical problem which has emerged in the quantum context is that of indeterminism or chance.

Now from the purely physical point of view, a chance event is contrary to the natural intentions or purposes of the nature it befalls, and chance comes about because of the intersecting of two essential lines of causality.[7] In the classical example, one man is digging for water at the same spot where another has buried a treasure. The first cuts across the line of causality initiated by the second and finds a treasure instead. Each man had an essential line of causation which he was following, but the two lines collided with one another. The first man's discovery of the treasure would be said to be by chance or luck or, in the more technical expression, *per accidens.*

That quantum physics has somehow raised the problem of chance is too well known to warrant further elaboration. The Bohr atom, the Heisenberg principle, the de Broglie matter waves, Planck's quantum explanation of black-body radiation, Einstein's theory of the photoelectric phenomenon, Compton's experiments on X-ray scattering, together with the Schroedinger-Born synthesis of wave equations — all have conspired to favor the view that nature, in its microscopic dimensions, is indeterminate, that all laws are statistical, and that the order in macroscopic experience is only one of a chance aggregate arising from a favorable probability ratio. Without entering in any detail upon the various experimental and theoretical stages of the growth of wave mechanics, it suffices here to note that quantum physics employs a language of indeterminism, disorder, and chance.

But how can chance have a truly scientific definition and how can chance be discerned in nature without a previous truly physical analysis of the mobile world? If mathematics is unequipped to distinguish the essential or natural from the incidental, it cannot even raise, much less resolve, the problem of chance.

There is a natural order between the man and his walking but only an incidental or chancelike reference between walking and a ship. Hence, a metrical approach to nature, failing to discern ordered motion from what is disordered or *per accidens* even at a macroscopic level, cannot properly discern chance. Order and disorder have meaning only within a physical frame of reference where the reality of nature is taken into account,

---

[7] *In II Phys.,* 9, n. 442.

where order is seen as flowing from nature, and where disorder is the unnatural or, more exactly, the antinatural.

This verdict is upheld by a consideration of final causality; for it is only the reality of final causes that can yield an understanding of disorder no less than order in our cosmos. Nature intends one thing, and something else interferes. There are two essential lines of causality, and they intersect. Lightning, for instance, tends to be neutralized and strikes downward toward the earth. This is its causal order. On the other hand, a cow, following its own causal nature, is grazing in a pasture. As the two causal chains cross one another, the lightning strikes the cow and kills it. There is order in the activities of both the lightning and the cow, but there is no order between the two series of motions. What has a final cause is ordered, what lacks such a cause is chance. To put the essential and the incidental — the walking of the sailor and its purely extrinsic relation to the ship, the activities of the cow and its extrinsic connection with lightning — to put the natural and the accidental on the same plane is to ignore an important distinction for rendering an account of nature, of its various motions, of its orders, and of its disorders.

Where the distinction between the *per se* and the *per accidens* is overlooked, either the incidental is reduced to the essential as in relativity mechanics or the essential is reduced to the incidental as in quantum theory. By its commitment to a mathematical report on nature, mathematical physics cannot retain both divisions of motions or events.

Emerging within an atmosphere of mathematical physics, the whole contemporary problem of determinism and predictability has remained a pseudo-problem. The history of modern determinism has an important chapter in the often-quoted dictum of Laplace that an intellect great enough to take in all of the present states of physical things could make an exact prediction of the future states of such entities for any time of interest. But even with the privilege of such present knowledge, the human mind could not make the predictions envisioned by Laplace. And the reason is that there is no intrinsic connectedness between all the realities of our universe.

A leaf, turning brown, may be blowing back and forth in the autumnal wind, but such local motion is incidental to the discoloration of the leaf. That a worm may have fastened itself to the underside of the leaf is also incidental to the discoloration process. There is no essential, and hence scientific, relation between the change of color and the change of place on the part of the leaf, and the presence of the worm on the leaf is likewise extrinsic and incidental to both of the other motions. There is no scientific predictability involving the three processes taken together, the change of color, the local motion of the leaf, and the local motion of the worm, because there is no essential relation between the three events in reality.

Strict determinism could prevail only where there would be an intrinsic connectedness between all of the factors and forces of a given system, but there is certainly no such relation between all things in nature. Hence, chance cannot be merely a result of human ignorance. Because the incidental is real, the future cannot be predicted in a Laplacian way even with a Laplacian knowledge of the present.

Parenthetically, it might be appropriate to remark here that chance is not detected by a merely mathematical count and that, by number alone, there would surely be more cases of the incidental in our cosmos than of the natural and the essential. Hence, on a basis of merely mathematical ratios, it might be concluded that this is a predominantly chance or incidental universe and that order, within it, is a rather rare statistical exception. But chance is not established by a mere count. Only by contrasting the essential and the incidental within a purely physical context can chance be detected and defined.

All of this reasoning, if correct, is not intended to belittle mathematical physics. The only contention here is that such a physics cannot stand alone and that, for special reasons, it cannot form the first approach of man to a scientific reduction of nature. A philosophical physics is indispensable not merely as a critic sitting in judgment upon sciences that are previously established but as a beacon going before the sciences in the order of learning and discovery. The general study of nature, disengaging the definitions of nature itself, of the four causes, of motion and the infinite, of place and time, should antedate mathematical physics in the logical and hence curricular order. So conceived, the philosophy of nature provides the large architecture within which empiriological findings can be interpreted with a fuller and richer meaning than they now can claim.

Thus, a purely mathematical physics is not able to define what motion is, but within a perspective provided by a purely physical definition of motion, measurements of speed, velocity, and acceleration assume a fuller significance. The notion of nature, foreign to the mathematical approach but a beginning point for philosophical physics, leads to a distinction between the essential and the incidental, and in such a framework, the mathematical physicist can then interpret his measurements to put them into accord with the full physical situation and not merely with the indifference of quantity.

Or, to take the more complicated question of place. Quantity alone can never answer the question *where?* but only the question *how much?* To the question, "Where is the sun?" the reply cannot be simply, "Ninety-three million miles." Such an answer makes no sense. But if it is answered that the sun is ninety-three million miles from the earth, a physical meaning begins to emerge.

In kindred fashion, all of the mathematical physicist's means of telling time have no significance until it is first determined what time is.

Such are a few examples, at a quite elementary level, of how the philosopher can, from a purely physical point of view, supply categories that enable mathematical physics to be not only physical but also truly scientific. The function of the mathematical technique of studying our universe is not to constitute our knowledge of the physical world but to enlarge and enrich a knowledge begun, both chronologically and logically, with purely physical considerations.

At the introductory level of mathematical physics, where simple measurements are made of distance, weight, and time, it is easy enough to agree that there is no conflict between a purely physical analysis of mobile being and the mathematical measurement of trajectories. However, at the more sophisticated stages of modern physics, the precise relationship between the physical situation and our measurements becomes dim and difficult.

But to complicate a principle does not change the principle. Moreover, our inability to apply distinctions made at a general level does not mean that in principle these distinctions are not applicable. Finally, the structure of matter as analyzed by Aristotle and Aquinas, while according a priority to a purely physical study of nature,[8] has ample room for all of the supplementary knowledge of our cosmos which the techniques of mathematical physics can supply.

For material substance receives its accidents in a certain order of priority and posteriority. First comes quantity, the medium by which all other accidents inhere in their material subjects. Then comes quality, inhering through quantity in material substance.[9] Finally, there are the motions of matter providing our deepest insight into the mobile world because they are the final causes of the structure — substance plus quantity plus quality — which precedes.[10] If matter exists in order to operate, then from its motions should come the strongest light upon its nature.

This is a reason why a consideration of nature must begin with a study not of quantity but of motion. The motions of things, in the order of final causality, explain why this or that material substance owns the structure which analysis reveals. A carnivorous animal, for instance, has sharp teeth. With a foreknowledge of function intended by nature and apparent to our experience, the anatomy of teeth is not merely a study of geometry but a meaningful physical knowledge in the light of what is truly first in causing — the final cause. Barring this reference to end or purpose, the only alternative viewpoint is mechanism, where the relation between the sharp teeth and the chewing of meat must be viewed as a matter of chance.

---

[8] For St. Thomas' notions of the relation between a purely physical approach to nature and a mathematical approach like that employed in the *De Coelo*, cf. his pedagogical order for the study of the physical world in *In I Phys.*, 1, n. 7.

[9] *In Boeth. de Trin.*, V, 3; *In II Phys.*, 3, n. 332.

[10] Cf. my *St. Thomas on the Object of Geometry* (Milwaukee, 1954), pp. 20–21.

Once again the *per accidens* is confused with the *per se*.

Equipped with a knowledge that there is a motion specific to each kind of subject in the physical world, the mind can supplement that knowledge by a study of the qualities, quantities, and substances of things as preparations for the motions that finalize the previous structures. A quality, like sharpness, is a disposition toward the final cause in the case of carnivorous teeth, and such a quality is obviously prepared for by the quantities involved. Hence, by reference to the motion, the quality of the sharp teeth can be better understood from a physical point of view, and in turn, by a relation to quality, the quantity involved becomes more intelligible.

An interesting study of the relations of quality and quantity occurs in connection with color which is visible in the region of the spectrum from 3900 to 7800 angstrom units. Each color has its own specific frequency or wave length, but neither of these quantities, obviously, is color. The blind man can know both of them and still be ignorant of color as such. Wave length or frequency are the quantitative dispositions associated with color and specific to each part of the spectrum. Knowledge of color in both its qualitative or formal and quantitative or material aspects yields a more or less complete knowledge of what color is.

As motion sheds light on quality and quality on physical quantity, so quantitative knowledge of nature can enrich our knowledge of physical substance. Indeed, when dealing with the microworld where direct observation of motion and of quality is closed off to us because of the weakness of our senses, quantitative results, even though interlarded with the uncertainties of our theories, are the only means available for the study of material substance.

But apart from the theoretical haze surrounding the microworld, it should not be a scandal that some sort of quantitative measurements remains our only resource to get at nature. For quantity, the closest of all material accidents to substance, yields, in the hierarchy of structure described above, a considerable vision of the differences between one kind of thing and another.[11] Even a simple black and white drawing

---

[11] *In VII Phys.*, 5, n. 1848.

of a rabbit, with the dimensions corresponding more or less to the original, is sufficient to identify the rabbit and to differentiate it from other types of rodents, not to mention such other animals as cats or elephants. Here again is an example quite simple, but once more the complication of a principle, as in quantum or relativity mechanics, does not change the principle itself. There is, for instance, something specific about the charge on an electron and its mass; and even where there is indeterminism, as in quantum mechanics, the degree of such indeterminism is specific to the particle in question in function of its mass. This can be seen by consulting the de Broglie equation where the wave length or "probability of a particle" is inversely proportional to the mass ($\lambda = \frac{h}{mv}$). Since atoms of different elements have different masses, they each have a different degree of indeterminism, and the same is true of subatomic particles. In the very practice of atomic physics today, quantity has been a useful device for identifying substances and discriminating them from each other. In the Aristotelian language, substances are prepared by their quantities for their qualitative constitution and eventually for the mobile ends which show up in the sensible universe.

Yet without guidance from a discipline that distinguishes in principle the essential and the incidental events of nature, mathematical physics must regard our world to be absolutely determined in relativity mechanics or to be absolutely chance-like as in quantum theory. The concept of final causality enables us to avoid both extremes in obedience to full human experience which finds both in reality.

Order in the macroscopic world, as the final cause of events in the smaller regions of matter, is evidence that the microscopic means of attaining macroscopic order is somehow ordered also, even though it may be opaque to us. Heirs of a nineteenth-century belief that the macroscopic universe is merely a mechanical sum of microscopic processes and particles, our present assault upon atoms and their parts tends to understand the macroscopic in terms of the microscopic rather than the reverse. As a result, the common-sense world of colors and sounds and tangible qualities is often shouldered aside as an illusion, and atoms and their parts assume more reality than what is directly experienced.

Once more it appears that the failure to advert to the final cause has blurred the distinction between the natural and the incidental and has leveled off all reality into the same univocal plane where larger things are viewed as mechanical aggregates of smaller ones and where, from the failure of this mechanical ambition as in quantum theory, there emerges a crisis. It is the macroscopic world of direct experience which, as a final cause, renders the microworld intelligible.

The structure of the physical universe — substance, plus quantity, plus quality, plus the motions of matter — enables us to approach a truly physical understanding of one of the most elusive entities in modern physics, that of energy. Energy is most familiar in its mathematical symbolism, $E = \frac{1}{2}mv^2$ or $E = mc^2$. But such equations, while making for the precision of knowledge, do not of themselves have truly physical meaning. Energy is commonly called the power to do work, and work in turn is defined as the force exerted upon a particle times the distance through which the particle is moved. But force is almost as obscure to the mind as energy. Hence, it may be said that while energy remains a useful concept for mathematical physics, its physical reality remains extremely ill defined. Is energy a substance? or an accident? If it is real at all, how does it relate to the categories? Is it possibly some new kind of entity not capable of being encompassed by the usual division of material reality into substance and the nine accidents?

In approaching this problem, it should be remembered that energy is a highly theoretical concept whose meaning is established less by insight into its nature than by the metrical results to which it leads. But like all successful constructs in empiriological analysis, the idea of energy must involve at least an oblique and indirect communion with the real. Otherwise, there could be no reason for the remarkable fruitfulness of the concept of energy in modern physics. What then is the physical basis for the idea of energy?

Energy may well enable us to measure the dispositions of

matter where things are to execute this or that motion in the order of final causality and hence require material preparations, like the sharpness of teeth in the preceding example of carnivorous animals. Each kind of reaction in atomic physics requires specific energies to set it going. In the fission of Uranium 235, to take an example, the bombarding neutrons must possess a specific velocity and hence a specific energy in order to achieve a nuclear reaction. Traveling too slow, the neutrons will be captured, and moving too fast, they will pass through the target atoms. The stream of neutrons must possess just the right amount of energy if the smashing of the uranium in question is to be accomplished.

It may be doubted whether energy is anything but a name to describe a combination of mass and velocity. Certainly it would not appear that the neutrons approaching a target have energy as something distinct from their mass and their motion. Energy cannot be measured without being spent, spent on an instrument or in the matter like uranium which the moving neutrons affect. In the uranium, operating intrinsically within the material to be subjected to fission, the neutrons at the proper velocity dispose the matter toward the new form that atom-smashing is to bring to be.

Or, consider the photoelectric effect as ingeniously explained by Einstein. In this phenomenon, a light particle strikes a conducting surface in such a fashion that an electron with a definite energy is emitted. However, the energy of the incident particle is greater than the energy of the emitted electron. The difference, according to Einstein, is supplied by the work done in dislodging the electron from the surface.

Once more, it may be questioned whether the incident particle no less than the emitted electron has energy as a distinct possession. There are two masses and there are two velocities, but the energy cannot be detected until it is spent. The expenditure of energy in the photoelectric effect is in the form of the work done in freeing the electron from its original position in a metallic surface. This work or energy, as measured in terms of mass and the square of velocity, may once again be regarded as a disposition of the matter to its new form which is the end of the whole process. As in the case of the uranium nucleus, the energy required for disposing the matter to a new form is specific to the raw material in question.

If these examples are accepted and if they are truly typical, then energy is in the order of matter's dispositions to form and is not a subsisting reality much less the basic stuff of the whole universe. Knowledge of energies supplements the philosopher's knowledge of form by presenting a report on the material dispositions that prepare form, while the knowledge of form confers upon the empiriological analysis of energy that richest of all physical knowledge which comes to us from our study of ends.

The modern physicist does not study substantial change. But he does study, whether he admits it or not, the dispositions of matter in the order of quantity and certain of its qualitative determinations. In the usual nomenclature, the philosopher studies the final causes, where he can, and the scientist studies matter's preparations for the attainment of its ends. There is no more conflict here than there is between the destiny of a journey and its beginning, but where the end is not studied first, the beginning cannot make any sense. Where end or purpose is overlooked, energy descends into a univocal and neutral world, incapable of physical definition and fated to that purely mathematical account which cannot distinguish the essential from the incidental.

To all of this reasoning, it might be retorted that the modern physicist is not merely a mathematician but a mathematical physicist. In this respect, he would seem to escape the strictures of a purely mathematical approach to the real. To such an objection, it should be replied that the modern physicist is interested only in those facets of the physical world that he can measure and that the only reality that can be measured is that of quantity. In short, the applications of mathematics must carry with them all of the shortcomings of mathematics. The precision of mathematical physics does not compensate for the failure of such a physics to bear upon truly physical reality.

By the techniques of modern mathematical physics alone, our study of nature will always ignore the most basic fact about nature — its motions — and since motion alone enables us to raise the problem of final causes and to make the important distinction between the essential and the incidental, the mathematical approach to nature, unsupported by a previous and purely physical analysis, is unsuited to answer the most basic questions that man asks about his cosmic home and his own place within it.

However, in the light of a truly physical science of our universe, with its concern especially for final causality, the mathematical approach to nature can find a meaning that the present mechanical temper of modern man refuses to seek. Such an integrated study can enlarge philosophy with new fact and enhance modern science with a meaningful perspective. Moreover, such a union is necessary if philosophy is not to grow barren and science is not to be blind.

University of Notre Dame
Notre Dame, Ind.

THE ASSIMILATION OF THE NEW TO THE OLD IN THE PHILOSOPHY OF NATURE

BY LEO A. FOLEY, S.M.

Within the comparatively short lifetime of the American Catholic Philosophical Association, we have seen scholastic philosophy gradually assuming its place in public life. We have seen it come out of the seminary classroom and become a respectable and respected force in American thought. We have made our weight felt most strongly in natural theology, metaphysics, ethics, and aesthetics. We have also begun to become respected in our philosophy of nature. Much of this is due to factors beyond our control: to the breakdown of scientific as well as philosophical mechanism; to the re-emphasis upon reality as it is, rather than the pseudo-reality of symbolism; to the Aristotelian reasoning that has come back with some of the developments of relativity and quantum mechanics. Yet, the great reason for the respect paid Scholastic cosmology is the patient work of Scholastic cosmologists. The pioneers in this field have had the courage not only to go into the sciences, but to reinvestigate the great thinkers and writers in the philosophy of nature. Thus, we have seen a welcome and overdue concentration upon *all* the works of Aristotle, all the pertinent works of St. Albert the Great, and all the works of St. Thomas.

Yet, when we take time to review the work done, we begin to realize some of the force of the pithy Latin dictum: *Nil factum si quid agendum*. We cannot rest on our laurels because of what has been done. The sciences will make progress, and we must evaluate and assimilate their conclusions. Assimilation is the key, not only because no one has ever had

129

the last word in philosophy, but also because assimilation is the acceptance of truth based upon evaluation in the light of proven principles. We have the proven principles in Scholastic cosmology, as this article will attempt to show. Perhaps we can see this best by looking at several problems in the relations between cosmology and the sciences. The problems will be two: (1) content; and (2) the epistemology and method involved. Much work has been done in these, but the door to their investigation has only been opened.

When we compare the modern sciences, with their many subdivisions, subdevelopments, and specialties, to Aristotelian and Scholastic science, the over-all impression is the development from the extremely simple to the extremely complex. It is like comparing the simple mechanics of the inclined plane and simple machines to the intricacies of quantum mechanics and molecular chemistry. However, the main points in physics and chemistry, from Thales to Einstein, hinge about two main problems: (1) the mechanics of moving bodies and bodies at rest; and (2) the intrinsic structure of bodies.

In seeking the Aristotelian answer to these problems, we discover a good amount of sound scientific principle in the works of the *Physics* and *De Coelo*. To give several examples, one discovers the Newtonian law of inertia expressly stated in the *Physics*.[1] Not only that, one discovers that Aristotle was more universal and more accurate in its presentation than was Newton. Aristotle's presentation was more accurate because he based it upon potency and act. Body-at-rest is a being in potency to local motion. Body-in-motion is the actualization of the potency, and as equally a natural state of a body as a body at rest. A body in motion resists any tendency to change its motion, and is only worn down, so to speak, by something more forceful than itself. Aristotle's consideration is also more universal than Newton's. Newton considered the uniform motion of a body to be rectilinear. Aristotle considered it to be natural according to the circumstances under which it is moving. If it is falling toward the earth, then and only then is natural motion rectilinear. Otherwise, it is motion in the line of least resistance, a principle which is intrinsic

---

[1] *Physics*, Bk. IV, Ch. 8; 215a19 ff.

to the General Relativity Theory of Albert Einstein. Furthermore, since Aristotle considers motion from the point of view
of natural motion and motion by constraint, he necessarily
introduces the concept of tendency, or appetition, into the
question; that is, he has teleology in all and every motion,
which is more universal than Newton's simple mechanistic
notion of it.

From his studies of the character and velocities of moving
bodies, most particularly falling bodies, Aristotle was to advance his theories of the law of displacement,[2] the fullness of
the universe,[3] and the structure of the universe.[4] In connection
with the second two propositions, it is interesting to notice
that Galileo Galilei, in his *Dialogues Concerning Two New
Sciences,* mentions Aristotle no less than fifteen times, and
uses Aristotle as a starting place for his own theories. As a
matter of fact, he differs with Aristotle concerning the rate of
falling bodies, not so much as to the fact that they actually fall
at different rates of speed, but that, according to Aristotle, they
tend to fall at the same rate of speed, and would really do so
in a vacuum. He also differs with Aristotle in the question of
the geocentric universe, but he had behind him the acceptance
of the Copernican theories, which, although geometrically
consistent, were scientifically inaccurate. It is interesting to
note, though, that Galileo uses Aristotelian reasoning in all
cases, and was unpopular because he could use Aristotle
against the rather reactionary seventeenth-century Aristotelians.

Aristotle's reasoning in favor of the geocentric universe was
that all gravitational movement is radial with respect to the
center of the earth. Therefore, the center of the earth is the
universal center of gravity.[5] This reasoning is as sound as can
be, and strictly speaking has never been modified until
Einstein was to advance the concept of local gravitational
fields. Copernicus never answered Aristotle properly, while
Galileo, Brahe, Kepler, Newton, and Cavendish suppose his
reasoning in their theories of the motions and orbits of planets

---

[2] *Ibid.,* Bk. II, Ch. 7 and 8; 213b30 ff.
[3] *Ibid.*
[4] *Ibid.,* Bk. III, Ch. 4–8; 202b30 ff.
[5] *De Coelo,* Bk. II, Ch. 13 and 14; 295b20 ff.

and satellites. The reason why they could base themselves upon Aristotelian reasoning and yet differ in Aristotelian content is because of the telescopic and spectroscopic evidence that the universe is so much larger than supposed by Aristotle that the differences in the mutual attraction of bodies toward one another and toward a center of gravity would be too minute to be measured.

A third factor in the physical consideration of the universe is that of the possible infinity of the universe.[6] After rejecting a metaphysical infinity on the basis of substance and accidents, and having dismissed the Pythagorean mathematical infinity (in a manner indicative of some knowledge of infinitesimals and of prime numbers closely resembling the reasoning of Jacob Cantor), Aristotle takes the stand that the universe is finite in its dimensions. His reasoning is twofold: (1) were the universe infinite, it would fall apart of its own weight. Note that this possible fragmentation of the universe is implicit in our expanding universe theories. (2) Were the universe infinite in mass, it would have to be held together by an infinite force. Were that the case, bodies would either be infinitely in motion or infinitely at rest. Now again, this type of reasoning is used to confirm the geometrical interpretations of the distribution of matter in Einstein's General Relativity Theory.

If we may digress for a moment, the point behind this association of physical principles then and now is to note that although Aristotle, as a matter of fact, was frequently wrong in the content of his science, his reasoning is correct. This, in turn, might well suggest to us that in Aristotle we have the philosopher of science. At least, we can agree that Aristotle is not called the Father of Western Science in vain.

Aristotle also considered the intrinsic structure of bodies. In so doing, he was attempting to explain the operations of the universe in terms of the proper operations of the bodies in the universe. Since motion is an accident, then we must find the ultimate explanation in substance. Yet, since substance, *per se,* is indifferent to a given bodily structure, we must turn to the bodily structure of things to explain their

---

6 *Physics,* Bk. III, Ch. 4–8; 202b30 ff; cf. *De Coelo,* Bk. I, Ch. 7; 274a30.

characteristic and proper operations and changes.

Aristotle had his choice between two prevalent theories:[7] (1) various atomic theories; and (2) theories involving elements. The difficulty with the atomic theories of such as Democritus and Leucippus was their failure to explain differentiation. The atoms postulated were either homogeneous or differentiated with natural affinities. If these atoms were homogeneous, no mere aggregation, whether geometric or chaotic, would explain differentiation in the result. Differentiation does not come from nondifferentiation. If the atoms were differentiated already, that, in turn, had to be explained. In either case, the fact of physical and chemical composition had to be thrown back into the possibility or potentiality to be so combined. The answer must always be in terms of potency and act, or matter and form. Yet, these are answers remote to the immediate problem, which is one of structure. Consequently, the only remaining theory is that of elements.

So much is explicit in Aristotle. Also explicit is the Aristotelian concept of minimal parts. Every body is, in theory, infinitely divisible, since every actual division leaves a remainder, which, insofar as it is quantified, is, in turn, divisible. Nevertheless, to hold the entire structure together, there must be minimal parts. The inference is that these really existing simple bodies that we call elements are composed of minimal parts containing the characteristics and properties of the element. This is essentially the same as Dalton's theory of atoms.

Aristotle's reduction of terrene elements to four is the result of two physical principles that he maintained and used: the law of displacement and the specific gravities of bodies.[8] Aristotle maintained that there are only two forms of natural motion, the rotational motion of the celestial bodies, and gravitation. (It is somewhat enlightening to realize that long before the possibilities of space flight and its consequent "weightlessness" of bodies in space could be considered, Aristotle would hold that a conditioned "free fall" is the most natural motion of a body.) Aristotle then noticed that the only

---

[7] *De Coelo*, Bk. III, Ch. 3–6; 302a10 ff.
[8] *Ibid.*, Bk. III, Ch. 2; 300a20 ff.

way to explain that less heavy bodies went upward was to suppose that they were pushed upward by heavier bodies descending.[9] Consequently, he postulated a varied composition of an absolutely light element (fire), a relatively light element (air), a relatively heavy element (water), and an absolutely heavy element, (earth). In this way, together with the motion of propelled bodies, Aristotle was able to prove that there is neither a total nor a partial vacuum in the universe.

In this elementary-atomic theory, Aristotle explained the intrinsic characteristics and tendencies of bodies. There is the further fact that energy proceeds from bodies. It proceeds from bodies as a whole, and must be in the minimal parts. Consequently, the only inference is that these minimal parts must be energetic in themselves. Now, of course, Aristotle knew nothing about nuclear physics. Furthermore, although he did speculate about the velocity rate of falling bodies, and may have considered the increment of energy, he knew nothing about the formula: $E = mc^2$. Nevertheless, we are safe in concluding that his whole theory about the properties and activities of bodies supposes a kinetic-atomic theory.

Even in the field of measurement, Aristotle has given us relativity. Not only has he expressed the intermeasurement of time through space (and *vice versa*),[10] but the whole weight of his cosmology and physics has denied the possibility of an absolute time and an absolute space.

All of the above should lead us to the conclusion that in our own cosmology we have nothing to fear from scientific discoveries. We are on safe grounds, because the essential problems of the sciences have been investigated by Aristotle. He has given us the principles of a philosophy of nature that have been thoroughly developed by St. Albert and St. Thomas.

It is inevitably somewhat of a shock to hear a physicist state that the ultimate particles are "probability waves that are unpredictable but which obey the laws of mathematics." A difficulty about such a statement is that people philosophize about it. They take it at its face value, and proceed to confuse the objective with the subjective. They come to a completely

---

[9] *Physics*, Bk. IV, Ch. 7 and 8; 213b30 ff.
[10] *Ibid.*, Bk. IV, Ch. 12; 220b15.

symbolical world, and then fall back upon "the God of Spinoza" to get them out of it. Upon such epistemological developments have been built the philosophy of Kant and the philosophy of Mach, which have terminated in the philosophical tenets of Jeans and Eddington, on the one hand, and Einstein, on the other. "The fallacy of the bifurcation of nature" is the expression used by Whitehead to castigate such confusion of the objective and subjective.

In Scholasticism we have no fear of such statements if (1) we know what the physicist means when he advances them, and (2) if we know our Scholastic epistemology. We might do well to analyze that statement to see exactly what it does mean, and to see, thereby, how our scholastic epistemology is the best tool in facing some of the problems of the philosophy of nature.

When the physicist speaks about "probability waves," he means that they are particles, but that it is easier to treat them as though they were waves, for they have wave characteristics. (We might note here that this is only a form of the analogy of attribution, except that the physicist calls it "projection.") The "probability" factor does not mean any doubt whether or not they exist. It means we cannot tell the exact position of them. If light is a radiation, it consists of photons. We cannot state where an individual photon is, because by the time we state the fact, it is over 186,000 miles elsewhere. Nevertheless, we know that light *is*. Since we cannot tell the position of the photons, we fall back upon the statistics of average distribution, and thus the particles "obey" (that is, are most accurately described by) mathematical laws. We may compare the above problem to a person in a crowd. I know that a friend of mine is at this moment in a theater. I do not know exactly where he is in that crowd, nor how he will react to the plot of the play. Consequently, I have to apply average distribution statistics to him, so to speak. I have to suppose that he will laugh at certain jokes, follow the plot, react psychologically to the situations, and if the play is a good one, he will terminate in a "catharsis of the emotions."

When we analyze the above examples further, we discover that there is a legitimate place for both certitude and opinion (or "probability"). The certitude is metaphysical. Light is. Yet, there is room for doubt, first about the nature of light, and second about the position of the individual photons. It may seem strange that we may speak about the same thing with metaphysical certitude, in one aspect, and with only physical opinion in another. Nevertheless, such is the case. Furthermore, we can have metaphysical certitude, physical certitude, and physical opinion about the same thing. I am metaphysically certain about an individual man. He exists. I am also physically certain of his essence. Furthermore, I know that he will react to startling stimuli. Nevertheless I can only guess as to his reaction when someone shouts "Fire!" in a crowded theater.

There are two reasons why such is the case. The first is that when we consider the contingent as the contingent, we can only arrive at a probable conclusion. In order to attain certitude, we must be able to compare one element of the judgment against a universal.[11] In order to have that, we must have the distributed middle, that is to say, a commensurate universal, which means that we must have an understanding of at least the generic nature of the object, and we must keep our judgments within the area of that nature. We can say that since a dog is alive, he is mortal. However, we can never predict whether or not the dog is going to dash in front of a speeding automobile. In the latter case, we have to fall back upon some such generalization as that he has been trained not to go into the streets. We then act according to normal expectancy. The second reason why we cannot expect certitude is that sometimes we must devise a generalization by way of a hypothesis that requires confirmation. This is the scientific method, advanced by Aristotle for a logical consideration of those problems which defy certitude and which offer only probable conclusions. We have to our great advantage not only the logic of certitude, in the *Prior Analytics* and the *Posterior Analytics,* but also the logic of probabilities and opinion, in the *Topics.*

The fact that there are such differences in conclusions should make us realize exactly what we mean by the three

___
[11] *Posterior Analytics,* Bk. I, Ch. 24; 85a13 ff.

degrees of abstraction.[12] Above all, they do not mean remote-
ness from reality. They mean the special attitude under which
we consider reality. There is only one of them that is removed
from reality, and that is some of the speculative developments
of mathematics in the second degree of abstraction. More important than that, though, is that the three degrees give us
the proper relationships of disciplines within philosophy and
between philosophy and the sciences. Thus, from the point of
view of ultimate principles, we can consider a body within
the first degree of abstraction and within the third degree. The
mass of the body and its spatial and numerical relations with
other bodies gives us the suggestions of consideration within
the second degree.

A second factor of consideration, and often not considered
sufficiently, is the distinction between total abstraction and
formal abstraction.[13] Both are tools in philosophy, whereas the
physical sciences, taking a specialized stance as they do, make
use of formal abstraction. Thus, a body taken from the aspect
of total abstraction must be considered as *ens mobile*, from
the ultimate principles of *ens mobile*. In formal abstraction,
physics will consider mass and energy, chemistry, the molecular structure, etc. Both types of abstraction are quite proper
from the nature of truth, which resides in the intellect analyzing and synthesizing.

There remains a word to be said about the second degree
of abstraction. The best and most concise consideration of
this is to be found in St. Thomas' commentary on Boethius'
De Trinitate.[14] What is important is the distinction that St.
Thomas makes in the consideration of *ens quantum* from the
point of view of its continuity and from the point of view
of discreteness. The continuum is the basis of geometries. The
discrete is the basis of number calculations. In this distinction
we have the essence of a philosophy of mathematics, and in
this we must keep clearly before our minds that (1) mathematics, as such, exists only in the mind, and (2) that in its
applications to reality it must be adjusted according to the

---

[12] St. Thomas, *In Boet. De Trinitate Commentarium*, q. V, a. 1–4.
[13] *S. T.*, I, q. 75, a. 1 ad 1.
[14] *In Boet. De Trinitate Commentarium*, q. V, a. 2–4.

nature of reality. It is unfortunate that this Aristotelian and Thomistic principle had to await the Special Relativity Theory of Albert Einstein for confirmation. Had we Scholastics developed this Thomistic philosophy of mathematics, we would scarcely have good scientists giving unreal pictures of the universe because their philosophy is nonformal mathematics. We would all know that the space-time continuum is common sense, as real as a timetable, and not a sort of fourth-dimensional world interlaced with our three-dimensional universe after the manner of water permeating a sponge. We would realize that curved space is a valid geometrical development, descriptive of a characteristic distribution of three-dimensional matter.

Mention has been made above of Aristotle as the founder of the scientific method. Whether or not he was the founder is an obscure point in history. As far as we know, he was actually the first philosopher to write it up as a scientific method of investigation. So much is said about the scientific method today. A good deal must be said about it because it is necessarily the logic of contingency. Its elevation to the ultimate by the English school is because of the failure of Scholastics to develop the wealth of Aristotle, St. Albert, and St. Thomas, after the death of the latter two.

To return to the opening note of this article, when we state that truth is never stagnant, is always to be valued, persists to give the principles of proper interpretation of new discoveries, we may well be thankful that we have had the opportunity to be part of a newer, living development of Scholasticism. Yet, we are at the beginning, especially in the philosophy of nature. Our research, although it has covered a number of years, still faces the future.

There are many problems that we must face in the interpretation of new discoveries. Again, however, we are most fortunate in having the three great philosophers of nature, Aristotle, St. Albert, and St. Thomas. In their works we find three things. The first, and perhaps most important, is their willingness to assimilate every sound discovery. It is to be noted that Aristotle incorporated, from his predecessors, everything sound that he could accept according to the evidence.

Aristotle would be completely at home today in the new science and the new instruments. We can most certainly say the same of St. Albert and St. Thomas.

Second, the fundamental problems of science are usually intricate variations on a few basic truths. Some of the content, but all of the value of these has been developed philosophically by the Aristotelians. We could do well to base our future research in a continued, thorough, and penetrating investigation of the works of Aristotle, St. Albert, and St. Thomas.

Third, we have the epistemology and the method. Yet, we could do well to review and reinvestigate the whole question of demonstration, certitude, and opinion.

At any event, and always, our spirit of investigation could well be the Pauline advice to the Philippians: ". . . whatever things are true, whatever honorable, whatever just, whatever holy, whatever lovable, whatever of good repute, if there be any virtue, or anything worthy of praise, think upon these things" (Phil. 4:7, 8).

Marist Seminary
Washington, D. C.

In Seipsa Subsistere

An Examination of St. Bonaventure's Doctrine on the Substantiality of the Soul

BY IGNATIUS BRADY, O.F.M.

Though deeply penetrated by the seraphic spirit of St. Bonaventure, in his own estimation the *Breviloquium* is not meant to be a full presentation of doctrine. It is *aliquid breve in summa de veritate theologiae . . . in quo summatim non omnia sed aliqua magis opportuna [tanguntur]*.[1] Later than the *Commentary on the Sentences*,[2] it does not necessarily contain the fullest or best exposé of the Saint's theology, nor does it represent an evolution of his thought. Scholars claim therefore that the *Commentary* should not be explained by the *Breviloquium*, but on the contrary that the *Breviloquium* can be properly understood only in the broader treatment of the larger work.[3]

As a result we may legitimately ask whether the *locus classicus* for St. Bonaventure's doctrine on man and the soul lies precisely in those few brief chapters of the *Breviloquium* which consider creation. In these, in keeping with the gen-

---

[1] *Breviloquium*, Prol. § 6, n. 5; in *Tria Opuscula* (ed. 5, Ad Cl. Aquas, 1938), p. 29.

[2] The *Commentary on the Sentences* is dated 1250–1252. The *Breviloquium* is evidently prior to Bonaventure's election as Minister General (February 2, 1257), since the Troyes manuscript 1891 is dated that year. For the chronology of St. Bonaventure, cf. E. Longpré, art. "Bonaventure (saint)," DHGE, IX, 741–788, and also in *Catholicisme*, II, col. 123 ff.; and G. Abate, "Per la storia e la cronologia di S. Bonaventura, O. Min. (c. 1217–1274)," *Miscellanea Francescana*, 49 (1949), 534–568; 50 (1950), 97–130.

[3] Cf. G. Tavard, "La théologie d'après le Breviloque de saint Bonaventure," *L'Année théologique*, 10 (1949), 201–214; and *Transiency and Permanence: the Nature of Theology according to Saint Bonaventure* (Franciscan Institute, 1954), pp. 112–113.

141

eral starting point of the whole work, God as First Principle,[4] the author considers the soul, the body, the *totum coniunctum*, in terms of man's final end. The soul is a *forma beatificabilis;* but since in the present condition of man it will be separated from the body at death, it is also a *hoc aliquid*, with substantiality in itself. Therefore, it would seem, substantiality is given the soul primarily to assure its immortality. Such is the conclusion that has been drawn repeatedly. Yet we would submit that a study of the *Sentences* reveals an aspect often neglected, that (abstracting from the spiritual operations of intellect and will) substantiality is given immediately in view of the union with the body, though ultimately in view of beatitude.[5]

A handbook of theology, the *Breviloquium* calls into service the data of philosophy to the extent that such knowledge helps to fashion a "ladder" which while resting on the earth will reach up to heaven (Prol. § 3, 2). It does not pretend to be a philosophical work or to make any contribution to philosophy. The chapters on man, then, present a theologian's analysis of the ultimate purpose of human nature and its component parts.

Why the soul must be considered a form that is a being, living, intelligent, and endowed with liberty, the philosopher will have to explain in his own fashion. For the theologian, the basic reason must be sought in the First Principle to which as efficient, exemplar, and final cause all things are related. Since that Principle is most blessed and most benevolent, He communicates His beatitude to creatures: not, indeed, to the purely spiritual alone, which are close to him by

---

[4] *Breviloquium,* Prol. § 6, n. 6 (p. 29): "In assignatione rationum in omnibus quae in hoc toto opusculo vel tractatulo continentur, conatus sum rationem sumere a primo principio . . . ut merito ista scientia appareat una esse et ordinata."

[5] The *Commentary* corroborates the nexus between beatitude, substantiality, and immortality in at least two passages (II *Sent.,* d. 19, a. 1, q. 1; ed. minor, II, p. 472a; d. 26, q. 4, ad 1, p. 661b). However, there is no mention of separation (e.g., in the proof drawn for immortality *ex fine hominis*). Beatitude in the plan of God, as we shall see, was for the whole man: primarily for the soul, and by redundance for the body; therefore the soul would have to be an immortal substance as the subject of happiness.

nature, but to that also which is corporeal and far from God. It is a law of the Godhead, to quote pseudo-Dionysius, that the lowest is brought to the highest through that which is between. Corporeal nature then is to come to beatitude through a spirit which is conjoined to it, the human soul. Thus it is that God created the soul as *beatificabilis* in itself, i.e., as possessing a natural aptitude for happiness in intellect and will.[6] But because material creation is called to beatitude through the spiritual, the soul is created as a principle capable of being united to matter: it must therefore be a form.

Now, since "the end, which is beatitude, implies the necessity of certain conditions on the part of the soul itself as ordained to that end," the soul must be more than a form. To be capable of true happiness, which is permanent and unending, it must be immortal and incorruptible. The body, however, to which it is united is mortal; consequently, the soul must be so united to the body that it can also be separated from it and continue to exist apart from the body: *ac per hoc non tantum forma est, verum etiam hoc aliquid.* It must be a substance in its own right, in view of its own immortality.[7]

Thus far the *Breviloquium*. The union of soul and body is such that the whole man will be brought to beatitude. Since at death the body is dissolved and must wait the future resurrection to be united once again to the soul for full reward or punishment, the soul must live on and be the pledge of future reunion. It must therefore have the ability to survive the body; and this ability is found in the very substantiality of the soul, whereby it is a singular and individuated substance. Substantiality is thus the guarantee of separability, incorruption, and immortality.

This text has been often used, and rightly so, by expositors of the anthropology of St. Bonaventure. It is one facet of his thought, the approach he used when as a pure theologian he

---

[6] This too brief statement of the *Breviloquium* must be supplemented by the distinction of the *Sentences* between the natural aptitude found in human nature and the supernatural disposition added by grace (II *Sent.*, d. 19, a. 3, q. 1; *ed. cit.*, p. 483b).

[7] *Breviloquium*, p. II, c. 9 (*ed. cit.*, pp. 82–84).

wrote the *Breviloquium*. Is it, however, of such importance as to provide the interpretation of those questions of the *Commentary* which concern the substantiality of the soul? Are we justified in saying that the substantiality of the soul and its aptitude to exist apart are two points of view that are practically inseparable for St. Bonaventure?[8] Or that the chief characteristics of Bonaventure's conception of the soul "are an earnest desire to safeguard immortality and substantiality, or (what is more nearly correct) to stress the substantiality of the soul in order to assure is immortality?"[9]

We readily submit that there is basis for such a relationship in St. Bonaventure's own words. Yet we also suggest that this is neither the complete nor the primary reason for substantiality, and that therefore the *Breviloquium* does not contain the controlling text. On the contrary, such a rapport between substantiality and immortality has led to a faulty interpretation of the doctrine and of a fundamental formula of the *Commentary: nata est [anima] per se et in se subsistere.* It is not correct to render this as *für sich selber existieren kann* or as *son aptitude à subsister à part,* if we mean thereby the soul's existence separate from the body, for we thus divorce subsistence from any nexus with the soul's role as form and perfection of the body.[10] On the other hand, to

---

[8] Cf. C. M. O'Donnell, *The Psychology of St. Bonaventure and St. Thomas* (Washington, 1937), p. 36: "In the doctrine of St. Bonaventure the soul is in itself a complete substance and this is a guarantee that it will continue in existence after its separation from the body." Also E. Gilson, *La philosophie de saint Bonaventure,* ed. I, p. 306; ed. 2, p. 257: "En même temps que la composition de matière et de forme explique la mutabilité de l'âme humaine, elle fonde aux yeux de saint Bonaventure sa substantialité et garantit ainsi son aptitude à subsister à part; les deux points de vue lui semblent pratiquement inseparables, et il lui arrive de nous les proposer simultanément: cum planum sit animam rationalem posse pati et agere et mutari ab una proprietate in aliam et *in se ipsa subsistere"* (II *Sent.,* d. 17, a. 1, q. 2, resp.; *ed. cit.,* p. 426a).

[9] A. C. Pegis, *St. Thomas and the Problem of the Soul in the Thirteenth Century* (Toronto, 1934), p. 32. Cf. E. Gilson, op. cit., p. 324 (ed. 2, p. 272): "Dans son essence même, elle reste avant tout pour lui (S. Bonaventure) cette substance spirituelle dont la composition hylémorphique assure la subsistance, l'indépendance à l'égard du corps et l'immortalité."

[10] E. Lutz, *Die Psychologie Bonaventuras nach den Quellen dargestellt* (BGPTMA, VI, Heft 4–5; Münster, 1909), p. 18: "Obwohl die Seele ein 'hoc aliquid' ist und darum für sich selber existieren kann, sahen wir schon

translate the formula as "by itself" is acceptable if it is meant to mark a distinction to "by another" (e.g., *per ipsum compositum*), but not if it means "apart from, or separate from the body."[11]

By this we do not deny that the substantiality of the soul does assure its survival or independence of the body or the composite, but simply affirm that this is not St. Bonaventure's first meaning of *in seipsa subsistere*. A careful analysis of certain questions, on the other hand, of the second book of the *Sentences* will yield a new viewpoint, that a primary reason for substantiality is not separability and immortality but the very relation of the soul to the body. The questions to which we would appeal are those which concern the formation of the first man in body and soul, the fall of Adam from the state of original justice, and the consequences of that fall for the nature of man.[12] Admittedly scriptural and theological in content, they do not seem to have been hitherto exploited for the psychology of the Seraphic Doctor. Yet, unless they are carefully studied, it is doubtful whether the full doctrine on man and particularly the relation of soul and body may be grasped.

Ignorance of original sin, St. Bonaventure emphasized more than once, has prevented the philosophers from understanding fully the nature and present state of man. Relying on reason alone, they have concluded that his present condition is his original status, whereas the theologian knows he must distinguish three states in which human nature may exist: that of innocence, the present condition of man (*status miseriae; status naturae lapsae*), and the state of glory (or eternal misery) to come.[13] In each of these the nature of man is fundamentally the same: *eadem naturalia secundum substantiam;* with some important accidental differences in capacity, power,

---

im Vorausgehenden, ist sie dennoch mit dem Körper verbunden, etc." E. Gilson, in note 8, *supra*.

[11] Cf. A. C. Pegis, *op. cit.*, p. 37; the interpretation *ibid.* is correct.

[12] Cf. II *Sent.*, d. 17–18; d. 19, a. 2–3; d. 30–31. The former deal with the soul and body of Adam; the latter with original sin. To these must be added some very relevant questions of the fourth book, on the resurrection.

[13] *Ibid.*, d. 30, a. 1, q. 1 (*ed. min.*, p. 737b); d. 17, a. 2, q. 3 (p. 438b). Cf. E. Gilson, *op. cit.*, pp. 102–103; ed. 2, p. 87 ff.

knowledge, etc.[14] Thus, the union of soul and body is essentially the same in each state, though the body possesses different conditions of being. That this has definite bearing on the problem of substantiality is apparent.

In the original state of man, St. Bonaventure is careful to distinguish the creation of Adam, the gift of original justice, and the later gift of sanctifying grace; and by emphasizing the natural priority of human nature to the gift of original justice he is able to achieve certain clarifications of our problem.[15] He is thus led to hold that death is unnatural and penal in character, even though in his present state man must die for natural reasons.

In the creation of man, the soul was of course made immortal by nature, given the sustaining hand of God.[16] The body of Adam, however, considered in itself apart from original justice, was created in a state of indifference: it possessed no necessity requiring its permanence, nor on the other hand was it necessarily subject to corruption.[17] In this state of changeableness there was a natural aptitude for immortality, both in the intrinsic harmony between soul and body and between the well-balanced elements of the body, and in the ability to ward off any attack from without.[18] This poten-

---

[14] II *Sent.*, d. 24, p. 1, a. 1, q. 2, ad 2 (*ed. cit.*, p. 574); and d. 23, a. 2, q. 3 (pp. 564–565); IV *Sent.*, d. 49, p. 2, sect. 1, a. 1, q. 2 (*ed. cit.*, IV, p. 999), and a. 2, q. 1 (p. 1000).

[15] In considering the doctrine of St. Bonaventure here, we do well to keep it within the larger framework of the historical development of the teaching on original sin among the Scholastics. Many of his positions differ widely from those of St. Thomas, Duns Scotus, etc. Cf. I. Brady, "The Relation between Sin and Death according to Mediaeval Theologians," *Studia Mariana*, VII (1950), 50–80.

[16] II *Sent.*, d. 17, a. 1, q. 1, ad 5 (*ed. cit.*, p. 424): "Anima, etsi de sui natura sit ad permanendum idonea, nunquam permaneret nisi conservaretur per gratuitam Dei influentiam." See also II, d. 19, a. 1, q. 1, ad 1 (p. 472b).

[17] *Ibid.*, d. 19, a. 2, q. 2, ad 4 (p. 481): "Corpus Adae, antequam peccaret, nec habebat necessitatem ad permanendum nec necessitatem ad corrumpendum; sed postquam homo peccavit, corpus eius subiectum fuit necessitati moriendi." II, d. 32, a. 3, q. 2 (p. 798): "Ipsum Adam [Deus] instituit in statu mutabilitatis, in quo scilicet posset effici mortalis et immortalis." This seems to go back to St. Anselm, *Cur Deus Homo*, II, xi (*PL* 158, 410CD): "Non mortalitatem ad puram sed ad corruptam hominis naturam pertinere . . . Non ergo pertinet ad sinceritatem humanae naturae corruptibilitas sive incorruptibilitas."

[18] II *Sent.*, d. 19, a. 3, q. 1 (II, p. 483 ff.); *Breviloquium*, II, c. 10, n. 1 (*ed. cit.*, p. 86 ff.).

tiality would be actualized by the disposition effected by original justice. But there was also a natural aptitude for mortality in the very fact that the body was made up of heterogeneous parts, a possibility of death because of the defectibility inherent in such parts. To this extent human nature has always been mortal, *secundum naturalem aptitudinem*.[19]

To human nature in creation God added that gift called natural or original justice, and after an interval the further gift of sanctifying grace.[20] Original justice, residing primarily in the *liberum arbitrium*, gave the soul the power to rule the body and keep all in right order to God.[21] Thereby man as such was rendered immortal, by reason of the *potentia corporis regitiva* (or *contentiva*) which is either part of or the result of original justice.[22]

This condition of immortality was thus the result of a combination of natural aptitudes on the part of Adam and a higher help, the actual disposition, given him by God. The soul was immortal in itself because it was a spiritual substance. In addition, original justice bestowed the power to rule, contain, support, and preserve the body by actualizing the latter's natural aptitude for immortality, and thereby continuing the union as permanent. From without, the tree of life provided a means of replenishing the *humidum radicale* of the body; and the rule of divine providence conserved man in himself and protected him from dangers without.[23]

---

[19] IV *Sent.*, d. 43, a. 1, q. 4, ad 3 (*ed. cit.*, pp. 879–880); III *Sent.*, d. 16, a. 1, q. 3 (*ed. cit.*, pp. 344–345).

[20] II *Sent.*, d. 29, a. 2, q. 2 (*ed. cit.*, p. 725 ff.). This position differs widely from that of St. Thomas; cf. I. Brady, *art. cit.*, 70–73.

[21] II *Sent.*, d. 19, a. 3, q. 1, resp. (p. 484a): "Et ideo datum fuit illi animae donum gratiae, per quam posset corpori praesidere et illud regere et elementa quasi in quadam amicitia custodire, et hoc, quamdiu vellet, suo auctori subiacere." Cf. *ibid.*, d. 31, a. 1, q. 2 (p. 767).

[22] *Ibid.*, d. 19, a. 3, q. 2, resp. (p. 486b): "Immortale autem dicitur quod est aptum natum sive potens non mori; immortalitas igitur idem est quod potentia sive aptitudo ad non moriendum. Et haec potentia ad non moriendum non est aliud quam potentia animae in regendo et continuando corpus, ut nunquam deficiat nec ab ea separetur. Haec autem potentia consequitur ipsum liberum arbitrium et ei conformatur. Unde sicut in statu innocentiae homo poterat peccare et non peccare, sic anima poterat corpus continere et non continere et homo poterat mori et non mori."

[23] II *Sent.*, d. 17, a. 2, q. 3, resp. (p. 438b); *Breviloquium*, II, c. 10, n. 6

The union was meant to be permanent in character, for it was according to the nature of the component parts, soul and body.[24] Therefore in the *status naturae institutae,* the substantiality and immortality of the soul were primarily designed for its union with the body, to be, so to speak, the "backbone," the support, of the union.[25]

Had Adam remained in innocence, his soul could have preserved his body from any corruption. But his status was conditional on his obedience. His fall resulted instead in the complete *deordinatio* of soul and body, though it did not indeed produce any essential change in his human nature. He fell from grace and from the order of nature into the order of divine justice, and rightly merited the punishments of God.[26] These were felt first in the powers of the soul, and chiefly in the will (or *liberum arbitrium*) as the seat of original justice. The first effect was the loss of sanctifying grace and of justice. To the latter was coupled the loss of the *virtus contentiva,* the power to uphold the body in being. Rebellion followed on the part of the body, which was now necessarily subject to corruption and death, because it was left to its own natural course. The mortality inherent in it by reason of heterogeneous composition was no longer restrained, and death was the ultimate consequence.[27]

However, while death is to this degree natural to man, St. Bonaventure dwells rather on its penal character. Death would not have entered human history had Adam remained faithful; but when man's will rebelled, death came as a natural punishment. Though natural, it is for all that a punish-

---

(*ed. cit.,* pp. 89–90). On the *lignum vitae,* cf. II *Sent.,* d. 19, a. 2, q. 2 (p. 481); *ibid.,* dub. 4 (p. 489b).

[24] II *Sent.,* d. 18, a. 2, q. 2, ad 5 (p. 464a): "Spiritus enim, qui naturaliter coniungitur corpori, nunquam natus est a corpore separari nisi propter poenam peccati."

[25] *Ibid.,* d. 1, p. 2, a. 3, q. 2, ad 4 (p. 43b): "Anima rationalis *eo ipso* quod nata est perficere corpus sic perfectum et ordinatum per naturam ad immortalitatem, *est immortalis.*

[26] *Breviloquium,* III, c. 4, n. 2 (*ed. cit.,* p. 104).

[27] II *Sent.,* d. 19, a. 2, q. 1, ad 1–2 (p. 479); IV *Sent.,* d. 43, a. 1, q. 4, ad 3 (pp. 879–880).

ment, the principal temporal punishment of original sin.[28]
Death is not natural in the sense that it is demanded by the
very essence and nature of man or of the union of soul and
body. The union is natural; the separation, on the other hand,
militates against nature and is thus unnatural.[29] The permanence of such a union is intended by the nature of things;
the separation is something supervening the tendencies or
natural appetite of human nature. Consequently, were it not
for the *de facto* punishment of sin and the loss of original
justice, the soul would and could (though not of its own
power alone) remain forever united to the body, since it is by
nature made for permanent union.[30]

Not all power over the body has been lost by the soul.
Certainly, from the beginning the soul was the natural perfection of the human body, the *forma completiva,* giving being
and life, conservation and growth to the body; it was and is
as well the mover of the body through the organs. It would
seem likewise that the will of itself, perhaps as natural, had
and retains some power over the body (whereas as delibera-
tive, in the *liberum arbitrium,* it possessed but now has lost
the *vis regitiva* of original justice). This natural power, however, is not such as to keep man from suffering and from
eventual death.[31] But the source and seat of this power is the
soul as substance. On the other hand, the loss of original
justice has not caused the body complete loss of the inner

---

[28] II *Sent.,* d. 33, a. 2, q. 2, ad 3 (p. 819a); III *Sent.,* d. 15, a. 1, q. 2 (p. 326).

[29] II *Sent.,* d. 1, p. 2, a. 2, q. 2, ad 4 (p. 43b) :"Quod anima separatur,
hoc est in poenam peccati." II *Sent.,* d. 18, a. 2, q. 2, resp. (p. 462b): "Videmus
animam, quantumcumque bonam, nolle a corpore separari . . . quod mirum
esset, si ad corpus naturalem aptitudinem et inclinationem non haberet sicut
ad suum sodalem, non sicut ad carcerem."

[30] II *Sent.,* d. 18, a. 2, q. 2, ad 5 (p. 464): "Spiritus enim, qui naturaliter
coniungitur corpori, nunquam natus est a corpore separari nisi propter poenam
peccati." We would again call attention to the fact that this explanation is not
followed by St. Thomas or Duns Scotus. The latter is indeed more at odds
with Saint Bonaventure than is Saint Thomas. Cf. I. Brady, *art. cit.,* 77–78.

[31] There is some lack of clarity in St. Bonaventure's position here. In fallen
man, he writes, the body is no longer under the will, but is subject only to
the *virtus naturalis* of the soul (II *Sent.,* d. 19, a. 2, q. 1, ad 1; p. 479). Yet we
do in our present state possess a *vis regitiva* both on the part of nature and
of the ruling will, though in respect to both we are amenable to suffering
(III *Sent.,* d. 16, a. 1, q. 3 [p. 345]).

harmony and equality of its elements: there still remains an *aequalitas diminuta,* insufficient however to survive its own intrinsic defects.[32]

Neither soul nor body is therefore capable of itself of perpetuating the union. Yet the separation that takes place at death contravenes the very essence of the soul. To be separated, to exist apart from the body, is a punishment; and though it may immediately enter the realms of beatitude, its true *esse naturae* is lacking to it.[33] Unless we admit this, then we must conclude that the union of soul and body is preternatural, beyond nature, and prejudicial to the soul, whereas the separation would be a welcome reward and relief; neither of which is true.[34] Substantiality, therefore, can hardly be designed primarily for such a preternatural condition.

Because the separation of soul and body is thus penal in character and beyond the intention of nature, it is not final or lasting. In the decrees of God, the union of an immortal soul with the body is intended to be perpetual; if it is interrupted because of sin, it must once more be resumed to fulfill the justice of God. The resurrection must therefore take place for all men, to provide for the reward or punishment of all, according to the demands of divine justice. It likewise fulfills, as St. Bonaventure clearly stresses, the divine plan that the union of soul and body be perpetual.

By reason of this decree and plan of God, the body has received through its union with the immortal soul not only the necessity of dying (because of original sin in the soul) but also an *ordinatio* and possibility for incorruption and unending life.[35] While this does not imply that by the union

---

[32] II *Sent.,* d. 19, a. 2, q. 1, ad 2 (p. 479b); d. 17, a. 2, q. 3, resp. (p. 438b).

[33] III *Sent.,* d. 5, a. 2, q. 3, ad 6 (p. 131b); IV *Sent.* d. 49, p. 2, s. 1, a. 1, q. 1, fund. 4 (p. 996b); ad 6 (p. 998a).

[34] III *Sent.,* d. 5, a. 2, q. 3, resp. (p. 130b): "Alioquin [i.e., if separated soul were a person] sequerentur praedicta inconvenientia, videlicet quod unio esset *praeternaturalis* et separatio non esset poenalis; iterum, quod unio esset in animae praeiudicium et *separatio in praemium;* quorum quodlibet falsum est." See also *ibid.,* d. 22, q. 1, resp. (p. 443b): "Nec anima separata est persona, nec homo est anima sua, nec verius est homo cum moritur quam cum vivit, quantum ad esse naturae, licet fortassis possit augeri in eo esse gratiae."

[35] IV *Sent.,* d. 43, a. 1, q. 2, resp. (p. 874b): "Corpus unitur animae immortali

the body has received any intrinsic disposition of incorrupti-
bility, by this *ordinatio* the body does preserve such an identity, no matter how much it may be mixed with other elements
after death, that it can be distinguished and separated once
more by the wisdom and power of God and reunited to the
same soul.[36] That soul, on the other hand, retains throughout
its separation a desire or appetite for its body.[37]

Finally, in the actual resurrection the soul and body will
be completely and lastingly united, whether for glory or for
eternal damnation.[38] The soul will regain forever the *potentia
contentiva,* and thus perpetuate the union. If the soul is in
glory, its beatitude overflows to the body which is now made
incorruptible and glorified. If the soul is already assigned to
the torments of hell, its body, now immortal, is reunited to it
to suffer with it without being consumed. The whole man is
glorified; or the whole man suffers in hell. And thus is fulfilled
the purpose of substantiality.

Such a doctrine is beyond the ken of the philosopher; it is
Christian theology. Yet is that approach less theological which
stresses the nexus between substantiality and separation? We
cannot avoid the teachings of theology if we would achieve
a full understanding of man, his origin, his nature, his destiny.
Nor shall we know St. Bonaventure's total doctrine on man
unless we take into account his teaching on all the states or
conditions in which human nature can be found.

---

per naturam et mortuae per culpam in ipsa unione; et ideo necessitatem con-
trahit ad moriendum et possibilitatem ad semper vivendum, quae secundum
ordinem divinae providentiae ad actum semper debet prodire, exigente hoc
nihilominus merito vel demerito et etiam divino iudicio." *Ibid.,* ad 5 (p. 875):
"Remuneratio non est tota ratio quare fit resurrectio, sed divinae ordinationis
decretum, qui, coniungendo animam immortalem corpori, per hoc decrevit illud
corpus perpetuo vivificari. Si ergo divinum decretum non potest infirmari,
necesse est illud corpus animae revivificari . . . Ratione cuius decreti corpus
humanum dicitur ordinari et possibilitatem habere ad incorruptionem, quamvis
in sui natura nihil habeat plus de incorruptibilitate quam alia corpora mixta."

[36] *Ibid.,* d. 43, a. 1, q. 5 (p. 883); II *Sent.,* d. 30, a. 3, q. 2, resp. (p. 758b).

[37] IV *Sent.,* d. 43, a. 1, q. 5, ad 6 (pp. 883b–884a): "Propter colligantiam et
coniunctionem quam habuit ad illud corpus . . . anima habet ordinationem et
appetitum, per quem ordinatur ad illud corpus, quantumcumque aliis con-
formetur; sed corpus habet ordinationem ratione divinae providentiae."

[38] Details of this doctrine will be found in IV *Sent.,* d. 43, a. 1 (p. 872 ff.);
d. 44, a. 1 (p. 897 ff.); and d. 49, p. 2, sect. 1, a. 1 (p. 996 ff.).

In such a comprehensive view it becomes evident that the substantiality of the soul, besides assuring the soul's capacity for purely spiritual acts while it is united to the body, is intended by nature, by the plan of God, to function primarily in the union of soul and body, not primarily in the "preternatural" state of separation after death. *In seipsa subsistere*, therefore, does not mean existence outside the body, but primarily an existence in the body which is not intrinsically dependent on or "founded in" the body or the composite.

Franciscan Institute
St. Bonaventure, N. Y.

St. Thomas and the Unity of Man

BY ANTON C. PEGIS

"Quid igitur aliud agimus cum studemus esse sapientes, nisi quanta possumus alacritate, ad id quod mente contigimus totam animam nostram quodammodo colligamus, et ponamus ibi, atque stabiliter infigamus" (St. Augustine, *De Libero Arbitrio,* II, XVI. 41 [PL 32, col. 1263]).

The purpose of the present paper is to examine St. Thomas' doctrine of the unity of man, and especially the unity of human nature. In its intention, this Thomistic doctrine is disarmingly simple and straightforward; so much so, that it is a puzzle to understand why the doctrine found so little acceptance in St. Thomas' own day and since that day. What is even more puzzling, the Thomistic doctrine on the unity of man, which its author presents as Aristotelian, is unknown within the history of Aristotelianism before St. Thomas. To complicate matters still further, the Thomistic doctrine on the unity of man's nature is intended by its author to be an answer to a classic Aristotelian dilemma voiced in the twelfth century by the great Averroës. In this situation, because St. Thomas has understated his own original and even revolutionary contribution to Aristotelian psychology, we are in danger of taking as an obvious doctrine something which, had he not existed, the prior history of Aristotelianism would have declared an impossibility. And yet, what the history of Aristotelianism considered impossible, St. Thomas made quite possible. That is why, to appreciate the meaning of St. Thomas' teaching on man, we must make some effort to surround it with the circumstances and the considerations that gave it its historical meaning and made it to be a revolutionary philosophical creation.

I

Let us, at the outset, locate ourselves within the problem of the nature of man as seen within the perspective of history. At the risk of simplifying history, let me suggest for purposes of location that the notion of man has gone through two important phases within Christian thought. The first may be called the religious phase and, more specifically, the Augustinian phase. The second may be called the philosophical phase and, more specifically, the Aristotelian phase.

Up to the thirteenth century, the prevailing notion of the nature and unity of man could be traced to St. Augustine. St. Augustine had more than once defined man as a soul using a body. What is important in man is the soul. St. Augustine did not deny that soul and body belonged together; in fact, he thought it insane that anyone should think otherwise; but, nevertheless, it is a fact that St. Augustine was concerned to stress the superiority of the soul over the body. In other words, granted that soul and body belonged together, St. Augustine wanted to be sure that the body was the servant of the soul, just as the soul should be the servant of God. What he did not set out to explain was how and why soul and body belonged together as parts making up the whole that we call man. In his writings, St. Augustine frequently has said that the body is the instrument of the soul. But he has not explained why the soul should have or need such an instrument. This question, which deals with the structure of man, did not engage the attention of St. Augustine and did not receive an answer from him.[1]

In the thirteenth century, Christian thinkers came face to face with a new situation. Having meditated on what St. Augustine and his disciples had to say about man, they began reading a new treatise on the nature of man. This treatise was written by Aristotle; it was called in Latin the *De Anima*, and it began to circulate in the Latin world at the turn of the

---

[1] See the references in E. Gilson, *History of Christian Philosophy in the Middle Ages* (New York: Random House, 1955), p. 593, note 27.

thirteenth century. In this treatise, Aristotle was occupied
with the question that St. Augustine had not considered. He
began with the idea that man is a *besouled body*.[2] In other
words, man is a body; but, as distinguished from other bodies,
he is a living body; furthermore, as distinguished from other
living bodies, he is a body living with a rational life. It is not
difficult to see that Aristotle's view of man is strongly biological, just as the view of St. Augustine is strongly moral and
spiritual.

Aristotle approaches man as a physical substance, living in
a world of physical substances. Man is the highest physical
substance on earth, since he exists and lives through the highest form in nature. To say that he is a besouled body is not
to demean or belittle him; it is to say exactly what he is
in his very being and constitution. Nor does the conception
of man as a besouled body mean to say that what is important
in man is that he is a body; for the question of what is important in man is a question of the inner finality and purpose
of his whole being. We have an idea of the Aristotelian answer
to this question from the *Ethics*. To be living with a rational
life is for man, even as a besouled body, to be aiming at something universal and eternal and divine. In short, if we look
at the inner purpose of man, we can see that the whole of
his being serves, or should serve, the good of the reason. *That*
is highest in man. But, even so, considered merely in his
nature and structure, in the reality that he is, man is a besouled body.

In principle, St. Thomas accepted both St. Augustine and
Aristotle. The Thomistic notion of man in its fullness was born
of the fusion of the Augustinian man, who examined his nature as a religious moralist, and the Aristotelian man, who
examined his nature as a metaphysical psychologist. In psychology, Aristotle taught St. Thomas what man is; or, more
correctly, how to examine and express philosophically what
man is. St. Augustine taught St. Thomas what man is for. It
will solve no problem to say that on the nature of man St.
Thomas was both an Augustinian and an Aristotelian. Quite
the contrary, this is a paradox, whose meaning depends on its

---

[2] *De Anima,* II, 1.412a 11 ff.

possibility. How can a thinker successfully follow both Augustine and Aristotle on the nature of man? The answer to this question depends on what St. Thomas did in the presence of the psychology of Aristotle.

II

The simplicity of St. Thomas' attitude toward Aristotle is nowhere more apparent than in an early text in which he points out that the ancients handed down two views on the relations between soul and body.[3] These are the views of Plato and Aristotle.

According to the Platonic view, the soul is joined to the body as one complete being to another. This would mean that man is in some sense the union of two beings. To avoid the difficulties involved in saying that man is the union of two beings (for how can two beings, with two natures, unite to constitute one being with one nature?), Plato said that man is a soul wearing a body. Of course, it would further follow from this position that the soul by itself is the whole man, carrying the body as some sort of accidental attachment. St. Thomas, as is well known, does not think much of this position. If the position were true, the body would be joined to the soul accidentally, and hence the name *man* would at best mean something accidentally one.[4]

The Aristotelian opinion on the union of soul and body St. Thomas reports as follows. "The second opinion is that of Aristotle, *which all the moderns follow,* namely, that the soul is joined to the body as form to matter. Therefore the soul is not by itself a certain nature; it is a part of human nature."[5] If we can believe it, St. Thomas is telling us a great deal in these words. He is telling us that all the moderns, which presumably means the theologians and philosophers of the thirteenth century, followed Aristotle; they did not follow Plato. It does not require much knowledge of the thirteenth century to realize that St. Thomas' contemporaries did not

---

[3] *In III Sent.,* d. 5, q. 3, a. 2; ed. M. F. Moos (Paris: P. Lethielleux, 1933), pp. 206–207.

[4] *Ibid.,* p. 207.

[5] *Ibid.*

agree with one another or with him either in interpreting or evaluating the psychology of Aristotle. Even when, in some sense, they all said that the soul is related to the body as form to matter, they did not agree on what they meant by this formula. What, then, can be in St. Thomas' mind?

As far as I can see, there is only one answer possible to this question. The moderns, St. Thomas' contemporaries, began to understand from Aristotle's *De Anima* and *Metaphysics* the meaning of saying that a given being is *one* substance or *one* being. In the case of a composite being, you could not say that it was made up of two whole or complete beings, since this would be philosophical nonsense. How could you hold that soul and body belong together essentially, if you really thought that they belonged together as two beings belonged together? For you could never so put two beings together as to get one being out of them. Soul and body therefore belong together as parts within one being: their nature is to be such parts. What is more, as parts they are unintelligible except in relation to one another and in completion through one another. St. Thomas' contemporaries, therefore, regardless of their differences, were all Aristotelian in the sense of recognizing that, if man is one being in his very being and nature, soul and body are parts that are not only in themselves incomplete but also intended in their very nature to be completed by one another.

If, in what I have just said, I am merely rehearsing well-known doctrine, I beg to add that I have also been walking on very controversial and dangerous ground. Indeed, we have only to look a little more closely at this conception of soul and body as parts intended for one another in order to see that we are in the presence of a veritable dilemma. At first glance, it might not seem so. You might think it a simple matter to recognize that, if soul and body belong together within the unity of man, they are parts; and furthermore, if they are parts, they must have some inner relation to one another. For parts are not parts except in relation to very definite other parts, and soul and body are parts in relation to one another within the unity of man. This sounds so simple, that I sometimes have the illusion that I understand it. Having understood it, I have the further illusion that it is evidently true and that there can be no question about it. These two illusions lead me to a third. This doctrine of soul and body as parts within the unity of man St. Thomas found in Aristotle, so that he was fully justified in defending the doctrine as both true and Aristotelian. But after this third illusion the spell is broken. We may agree with St. Thomas that his contemporaries in general saw the necessity of considering soul and body as parts. But the great and stormy figure of Averroës rises before us at this point to warn that Brother Thomas is proposing a doctrine on the unity of man that no Aristotelian commentator before him had ever entertained either as Aristotelian or even as philosophically possible. And the more we think of the Averroistic interpretation of Aristotle, the more we see that my illusions were, if not genuine illusions, at least dangerous and hasty simplifications. There is nothing easy or simple about saying that the soul of man is the form of the body, making one substance with it. Far from it. Indeed, the classic question among Aristotelian commentators has always been whether it can be said that an intellectual substance is the form of matter.

III

We are now standing with St. Thomas and Averroës in the presence of Aristotle. Both of them were absolutely convinced of their respective interpretations of Aristotle; unfortunately for us, they were not only convinced, they were also diametrically opposed. He who agrees with St. Thomas must have ample and convincing reasons for disagreeing with Averroës. Averroës is no mean adversary, and we must walk carefully when we disagree with him. This is especially the case when we disagree with him on the interpretation of his master Aristotle.

Now, fortunately for us, some things are simple in the present problem. In its barest essentials, the question of interpreting the psychology of Aristotle, so far as St. Thomas and Averroës are concerned, reduces itself to admitting and harmonizing three points of doctrine that Aristotle seems to make in the *De Anima*. I say "seems to make" because Averroës and St. Thomas are not agreed that he does. These points are the following: (1) In the first chapter of the Second Book of the *De Anima* Aristotle lays down what he calls a common definition of the soul. He writes: "If we must say something common for every soul, it is this: the soul is the first entelechy of a physical, organic body." Here is, then, a universal statement by Aristotle on the soul. As universal, it applies to all souls, so that presumably we can say of every soul that it is the entelechy or form of an organic body. In Chapters Four and Five of the Third Book of the *De Anima,* Aristotle goes on to make two further points. (2) In Chapter Four he refers to the intellect as *part* of the soul, and (3) in Chapter Five he says that when the intellect is *separated,* it is its pure self, and is alone immortal and eternal.[6] The dilemma facing all Aristotelian commentators is how to put these three statements of Aristotle together in a coherent doctrine. To repeat: Aristotle has given us what is apparently a universal definition of the soul: the soul is the form of an organic body. Then he has said that the intellect is part of the soul. Finally, he has said that it is separate. How do we put these three points together? What is a soul that has an intellect as part of itself, which intellect is yet separate? To this question Averroës and St. Thomas have given such opposed answers that you begin to wonder whether they are talking about the same Aristotle. Consider, first, the answer of Averroës.

The whole position of Averroës in relation to Aristotle hinges on one basic issue. That issue is the proportion that must exist between form and matter in composite substances. Form and matter are related to one another as part to part within the unity of the composite substance. Since form and matter are parts, they must have the nature to become completed in one another and by one another. To say this is, for Averroës at least, to say that a form of matter must be realized in matter. In other words, for Averroës a form *of* matter is a form *in* matter: it is what he calls an immersed form, in other words, a form that is purely and simply material.[7] This is a

---

[6] *De Anima,* II, 1.412a 5, a 19–21, b 4–6; III, 4.429a 10–14, a 22–23; III, 5.430a 22–23. Cf. also I, 1.402b 5–8.

[7] Averroës, *Commentarium Magnum in Aristotelis de Anima Libros,* III, t.c. 4, ed. F. S. Crawford (Cambridge, Mass.: The Mediaeval Academy of America, 1953), pp. 383[6]–384[33], 385[62]–386[105].

cardinal principle in Averroës. It governs his whole interpretation of Aristotle on the three points that we have just outlined
from the *De Anima*. For Averroës, Aristotle cannot mean the
definition of the soul to be a universal one, since, if he did, he
would have to hold that there was an intellectual soul that was
the form of matter. To Averroës this would be a contradiction
in terms. An intellectual substance is an immaterial one.
Hence, if the definition of the soul in the Second Book of the
De Anima were universal, Aristotle would be saying that there
is an immaterial substance that is the form of matter. Now if,
following Averroës, we hold that a form of matter is a form
in matter — an immersed form — then there cannot be an
immaterial form of matter. There is only one way out of the
difficulty when the problem is so defined, and Aristotle's definition of the soul cannot be universal since it cannot include the
intellect. The intellect is *separate* from the soul in the sense
that it is not a constitutive part of the soul that is the form of
matter.[8]

In brief, then, the position of Averroës really says that there
can be no such thing as an *intellectual* soul. To say *soul* is to
say a form of matter, in other words, something material; to
say *intellect* is to say something immaterial, in other words,
something that in its very reality is separate from matter. To
this let us add a historical commentary. If Averroës is right
in his position, he effectively ruined the doctrine of St. Thomas
Aquinas, including its very possibility, and he did so many
years before the Angelic Doctor became an illustrious Dominican master in Paris.

At the very least, we can grant to Averroës that his position
is clear cut and consistent. It rests on a single principle. To
repeat, the position of Averroës is this: *there cannot be an
intellectual form of matter*. That which is form of matter is
itself purely material, and that which is intellectual is in its
very being separate from matter. The principle underlying this
position is the doctrine that matter and form are proportioned
to one another.[9] If Averroës denies that anything intellectual

---

[8] *Ibid.*, II, t.c. 7; III, t.c. 4 and 5; *ed. cit.*, pp. 138[11-21], 386[80-92], 396[277-]
397[298].

[9] Note, especially, *ibid.*, III, t.c. 4; *ed. cit.*, pp. 385[76]–386[86].

can be the form of matter, that is because for him a form of matter is either a body or a form in a body, in other words, something mixed and immersed in matter. This in turn means that a form of matter is so proportioned to the matter whose form it is that it is wholly realized within the potentiality of that matter. A form of matter exists by the being of the material substance whose form it is. When that substance is corrupted, so is the form. In short, as Averroës understands it, the proportion between matter and form is so complete that in its very existence every form of matter, by the fact of being such a form, is something corporeal and corruptible.

We know, of course, that Averroës does not stand alone as an interpreter of Aristotle on this point. Many centuries before him his ancient predecessor, the Greek Alexander of Aphrodisias, had argued that the intellect by which the soul knows is part of the soul; but having argued thus, Alexander then went on to infer that this intellect, being part of a soul that is the form of matter and hence corruptible, is itself corruptible.[10] In other words, as a commentator of Aristotle,

---

[10] The Aristotelian doctrine of matter and form rules the position of Alexander with remarkable strictness. Every body is composed of matter and form (Alexander of Aphrodisias, περὶ ψυχῆς [ed. Ivo Bruns, Berlin: George Reimer, 1887], p. 90$^{14-16}$). In the animal, soul and body are as matter and form (p. 12$^{5-6}$). The soul is the form of the body, moreover, because it can do nothing without the body: there is no activity of the soul without bodily movement; and hence the soul belongs to the body and is inseparable from it (p. 12$^{7-22}$). But the soul is not a body. Though inseparable, in itself the soul is non-bodily and immobile (p. 17$^{9-10}$). Those who say that the soul is the form of the body and yet make the soul to be a body (e.g., fire or air) are mistaken; for form is another nature from matter (p. 19$^{21-24}$). Since, then, the soul is the inseparable form of the body, it (as much of it as is the form of a corruptible body) is corrupted with the body (p. 21$^{22-24}$).

Alexander follows this conclusion to its last consequence — to the dismay of Averroës. He distinguishes the reason or intellect with which we are born from the practical and speculative intellects that we acquire from experience and training (pp. 81$^{23-25}$, 80^{40}–81^{10}, 81$^{10-11}$, 81$^{20-22}$, 82$^{1-3}$). The intellect with which we are born Alexander calls potential, material, receptive, physical (pp. 81$^{23-25}$, 81$^{26-29}$). The material intellect is free of all things, being all *potentially* (p. 84^{22}). It is therefore an aptitude to receive intelligibles, being like an unwritten slate — "or rather the unwrittenness of the slate" (p. 84$^{24-26}$); it is not like the slate itself (p. 84^{26}). Why not? Because the slate is a being, "whereas the *unwritten* in the soul is what is called the material intellect, or the aptitude to be written on" (pp. 84^{25}–85^{1}). The material intellect is receptivity, but not a subject, being nothing in act (p. 85$^{1-5}$).

The cause of the development and perfection of the material intellect is the

Alexander held that the intellect by which the soul knows is corruptible because it is part of the soul. On the other hand, Averroës, having decided that the intellect is an immaterial power since it is capable of knowing the immaterial and the universal, could not make the intellect a part of the soul because of its very immateriality. Alexander and Averroës differ, therefore, on whether the intellect by which the soul knows is a part of the soul. They do not differ on the principle that, if it is a part, it is corruptible. Alexander said that it is a part and therefore corruptible; Averroës said that it is not corruptible and therefore not a part.[11] On the central issue, Alexander and Averroës are in full agreement; for both of them, there cannot be an intellectual form of matter.

IV

Perhaps, at this point, we may remark how extraordinary was the problem confronting St. Thomas Aquinas. That is why we can only express astonishment at his assurance in the presence of Averroës. For, if anything is clear to St. Thomas, it is the proposition that there *can* be an intellectual form of matter. To him, the obvious and straightforward interpretation of the *De Anima* requires us to say that such was in fact the view of Aristotle himself.[12] But there is more.

---

agent intellect (p. 88[17-24]). It is the first good and the first intelligible, the cause of the goodness and intelligibility for others (p. 89[1-5]). It is the first cause, and on this account an agent, being the cause of all intelligibles (p. 89[11]). The agent intellect is separate, impassible, unmixed, being without matter (p. 85[12]). Aristotle showed that it was the first cause (p. 89[18-19]). The agent intellect is nobler than our material intellect which is corrupted with the corruption of the soul. Though present in us, the agent intellect is separate, "from the outside," and incorruptible (p. 90[20]).

This position of Alexander helps to explain both the dismay of Averroës and also the necessity of a metaphysical revolution in the Aristotelian notion of form.

[11]For Averroës' vigorous critique of Alexander, see *Comm. Magnum in A. de Anima*, III, t.c. 5; *ed. cit.*, p. 393[196] ff. For the famous "O Alexander," see III, t.c. 14; *ed. cit.*, p. 431[84] ff.

[12] See *De Unitate Intellectus*, I; ed. L. Keeler (Romae: apud Aedes Pont. Univ. Gregorianae, 1936), ¶50, p. 33. St. Thomas reaches this conclusion after systematically examining, in *De Unitate Intellectus*, I, the coherence of Aristotle's doctrine on the notion of an individual intellectual soul. From this follows the notion of Averroës as the "corruptor" and the "perversor" of Peripateticism (*De Unitate Intellectus*, II, V; ed. L. Keeler, ¶59, p. 38; ¶121, pp. 77–78).

Not only does St. Thomas think that he can meet the main Averroistic position; he also holds that Averroës failed on the very point which, no less than St. Thomas after him, Averroës had been concerned to uphold and defend. For, to do him justice, Averroës had not intended to deny the perfectly obvious fact that there are individual human beings, composed of soul and body, endowed with an intellect, and performing acts of both sense life *and* intellectual life. Individual human beings exist. Within the unity of one life, each human being sees and thinks, feels and understands, desires and chooses. One and the same being is the author of these operations. Now, as appears clearly enough to anyone who reads the *Great Commentary* on the *De Anima*, Averroës did not intend to deny this common fact.[13] He meant to explain it. And yet, as St. Thomas was quick to point out, Averroës was forced by his own doctrine to render this fact impossible.[14] For if the intellect by which man is supposed to think is not part of the soul that is part of him, then man himself is not doing any thinking. Perhaps there is thinking going on in him if we suppose (as Averroës supposed) that some separate thinking intellect is somehow present to him and even in him.[15] But the fact remains. If the intellect is not part of him so that *he* is using it as *his* power, then he is not doing any thinking. In short, whatever other considerations may be on Averroës' side, a hard fact makes that position untenable. Individual human beings do include an intellect as part of themselves. Perhaps this fact will prove difficult to understand, and even more difficult to explain. But, be that as it may, Averroës' own doctrine is untenable by as much as its premise is the impossibility of what is an actual fact.

Now explaining the fact is, admittedly, much more difficult than merely recognizing it. But the circumstance that Averroës explained the fact away should throw some light on the precise point at issue. Indeed, the more we reflect on Averroës' posi-

---

[13] See, for example, the conclusion of the long development in *Comm. Magnum in A. de Anima*, III, t.c. 36; *ed. cit.*, p. 500[611-616].

[14] *De Unitate Intellectus*, IV; *ed. cit.*, ¶96–98, pp. 61–65.

[15] Against Averroistic *continuatio*, St. Thomas has a relentless criticism in *De Unitate Intellectus*, III; *ed. cit.*, ¶63–66, pp. 40–42.

tion, the more it becomes clear that St. Thomas found in him
an ally as well as an opponent. For if there is any doctrine
that characterizes the Thomistic view of man, it is the notion
that there is only one substantial form in man. But from the
very beginning of his teaching career, St. Thomas had read in
the *De Substantia Orbis* of Averroës the principle: *one substance, one substantial form;* and though St. Thomas considered this principle Aristotelian, he knew it from Averroës
at a time when he had not yet separated Aristotle from the
history of his commentators.[16]

But the principle that there is only one substantial form for
each substance composed of matter and form would seem to
strengthen the position of Averroës. Form is the act of its
matter. For matter to be a substance means for it to be actualized by a form; so much so, that both matter and form
have reality only in and through the corporeal substance whose
principles they are. In that case, how can there be an intellectual form of matter?

We are thus face to face with the issue posed for St. Thomas
by Averroës. The issue can be put in two successive questions, which, taken together, constitute the historical dimensions of the problem of the unity of man. How is it possible
that there be an intellectual form of matter? Assuming that
we can successfully answer this question, a second question
remains. What is the internal *why* of a composite substance,
man, having an intellectual form? It is not enough to stop with
the first question. The second question is of decisive importance in the opposition between Averroës and St. Thomas. The
question really concerns the proportion of form to matter in a
composite substance. Form and matter are parts, which have
one another as co-parts. That is why they form a whole being,
that is to say, a being with a single internally coherent nature.
What is the whole, the coherent nature, that soul and body
constitute? If we answer: *man,* we are naming the whole, we
are not explaining it. Supposing, therefore, that we can escape

---

[16] Averroës, *Sermo de Substantia Orbis,* cap. I (*Averrois Cordubensis . . .*
vol. IX, Venetiis apud Iuntas, 1573, fol. 3 vb).— St. Thomas cites the *De
Substantia Orbis* at least as early as *In II Sent.,* d. 3, q. 1, a. 4 (ed. P.
Mandonnet, Paris: P. Lethielleux, 1929), p. 97. St. Thomas' caution on Aristotle may be seen from *In II Sent.,* d. 17, q. 2, a. 1; ed. cit., pp. 422–428.

from Averroës on the first question; in other words, supposing
that we can successfully show how there can be an intellectual
form of matter, we must still show the *proportion* between the
intellectual form and its matter in order to meet and overcome
the position of Averroës at its most crucial point. For, and the
consideration is not unimportant, to escape from Averroës
without explaining the proportion between form and matter in
man is not to escape at all. Proportion is what drives Averroës
to say that every form of matter is immersed, corporeal and
corruptible. Anyone who says that the principle of proportion
does not make impossible an immaterial form of matter must
explain (1) how this is possible, and also and especially (2)
how the principle of proportion is maintained in this situation.

V

To keep our discussion within bounds, we shall first violate
Averroës' interpretation of the idea of proportion between
form and matter. This will enable us to see how, in St. Thomas'
eyes, an intellectual or immaterial form of matter is possible.
We shall then show how and under what conditions, in spite of
Averroës, there can be a proportion between an intellectual
form and the matter whose form it is.

Concerning the first of the two points I shall be brief, since
this part of St. Thomas' doctrine is generally well known. In a
late tract against the Parisian Averroists, the *De Unitate Intellectus*, St. Thomas had more than one opportunity to discuss
how the intellectual soul was essentially united to the body of
man and yet how it had a power, the intellect, that functioned
separately, that is, without using or needing to use a corporeal
organ. The Averroists, following the straight Averroistic position, thought that St. Thomas could not have it both ways. If
he said that the human soul is essentially joined to the body,
he should also say that all its powers act through bodily
organs: this, after all, is the Averroistic rock of proportion.
On the other hand, if St. Thomas said that the intellect of man
does not need and is not joined to a bodily organ, then he
should say that the soul itself is as separated from the body
as its intellect. In short, join the soul to the body, and you join
the intellect to a bodily organ; separate the intellect from a

bodily organ, and you must separate the soul itself from the body.[17] This is the dilemma propounded by the Averroists for anyone who defended the view that there is an intellectual form of matter.

At first glance, St. Thomas' position in the presence of this dilemma seems highly vulnerable. Notice, for example, the following: "We do not say that the human soul is the form of the body according to its intellectual power. In the teaching of Aristotle, this power is not the act of any organ. Hence, as far as the intellectual power is concerned, it remains that it is immaterial."[18] The issue lies here. How can a soul essentially joined to matter have a power that transcends matter? St. Thomas is aware of this question. Having just said that a soul joined to matter can have a power transcending matter, he goes on, quite deliberately, to pose and to answer the Averroistic objection:

> If it be objected that a power of the soul cannot be more immaterial and simple than its essence, the argument of the objector would indeed be a valid one if the essence of the human soul were in such wise the form of matter that it existed, not through its own being, but through the being of the composite. Such is the case with other forms, which in themselves have neither being nor an operation in which matter does not share, and which on this account are said to be immersed in matter. But the human soul exists through its own being; and matter shares in this being up to a point without completely enveloping it, because the dignity of such a form transcends the capacity of matter. And that is why nothing prevents the soul from having an operation or a power beyond the reach of matter.[19]

Both as doctrine and as anti-Averroistic polemic this paragraph is decisive. May I paraphrase it? It is objected to St. Thomas that there cannot be a form of matter with an immaterial power. Why not? Because a form of matter is, in its essence, itself material; this is the consequence of its being a

---

[17] See Siger of Brabant, *Quaestiones de Anima Intellectiva*, III, especially the five arguments Siger uses against St. Albert and St. Thomas, and the position he reaches that soul and body are one *in opere*, not in being (in P. Mandonnet, *Siger de Brabant*, 2nd ed., Vol. 2 [Louvain: Institut Supérieur de Philosophie, 1908], pp. 152–153, 154–155, 156, *ad ultimum*).

[18] *De Unitate Intellectus*, III; *ed. cit.*, ¶83, p. 52.

[19] *Op. cit.*, III; *ed. cit.*, ¶84, p. 53.

form of matter. We are, as you can see, in straight Averroism. The argument, St. Thomas replies, holds good in the case of all forms of matter except the human soul. Whereas these forms exist by the actuality of their composites, the human soul does not depend on the human composite for its being. On the contrary, the human soul has its own being within itself, and the body shares in this being. Hence, whereas in all other composites, being belongs first to the composite and then to the form, in the case of man being belongs first to soul and then to the composite. And finally, since the soul is immaterial in its very being, there is no reason why it cannot have an immaterial power and immaterial operations. That is to say, there is every intrinsic reason why an *immaterial* form joined to matter can have *immaterial* operations through an *immaterial* power.

But a question remains, and it is a formidable one. Why is an immaterial form joined to matter? Granted that the human soul is an immaterial and intellectual substance in its own right; granted that, when such a substance is essentially joined to matter as its form, it does not lose its intellectual nature or power and does not become "immersed," even so, the question remains: what is the purpose of the union? Can we, in our understanding of them, so understand soul and body together that we can see the proportion between an intellectual substance and matter, between the immaterial and the material? If we cannot do this, all we have explained is how it is that, since being in the human composite derives from the soul to the composite, and not *vice versa,* an immaterial soul retains its immateriality even as form of matter. Yet, for all we have explained, man might remain for us a philosophical monstrosity.

VI

The easier part of the internal why of the human composite is to state it correctly — I mean, to state the doctrine of St. Thomas Aquinas faithfully. There should be no hesitation on this point since St. Thomas has given at least one direct statement of the peculiar relations of soul to body. Like his contemporaries, St. Thomas knew and said that the soul is both an intellectual substance in its own right and also a form of matter. But St. Thomas did not stop with saying that the soul is a substance and a form. For if one and the same soul is, and this in its very nature, both substance and form, then the soul must be *a substance as a form*.[20] And this is what St. Thomas says, and it is in this notion that we must seek the proportion between soul and body and the meaning of human nature.

Yet the point that St. Thomas is making is an elusive one. What is a spiritual substance which as substance — that is, in its very substantiality — is the form of the body in the constitution of man? Such is in St. Thomas' eyes the human soul. It is a substance, but it is part of man; though a substance, it is not in itself a whole being. The soul is, therefore, not a substance *and* a form, but a substance *as* a form, a substance whose spiritual nature is essentially suited to informing matter. And it is in the soul that the reason for this union is to be found; whatever the human body is, this it is for the sake of, and in view of, the human soul. It is in the soul, therefore, that we must find St. Thomas' answer to our question. Averroës had not been able to see how a form of matter can have an intellect as one of its powers. St. Thomas' answer to this difficulty is astonishing — and to the point. The point can be put in the form of a question. This is a question that needs to be answered by anyone who considers the why of the union of soul and body. The question is this. How does it happen that the soul, which is an immaterial and intellectual substance, has *lesser* than intellectual powers? The angels are intellectual substances, and they have only intellectual powers, the intellect and will. The human soul is an intellectual substance, it has an intellect and a will, but *in addition* it has the whole range of sensible powers. Why should the human soul, being itself intellectual, have powers *in addition to* the intellect and the will? Nor can we say that this is so because the soul is joined to the body; for the union of the soul to the body is a consequence of the soul's nature, and not the cause. *Because* the soul has sensible powers, *therefore* it is joined to the body.

---

[20] The classic and unique Thomistic text on this point is *Q. D. De Anima*, I.

That is St. Thomas' doctrine.[21] We cannot explain the soul by the body; we must explain the body by the soul. And the human soul is a remarkable phenomenon — a spiritual substance, intellectual in nature and purpose, and yet possessing in its intellectual nature both intellectual powers and powers of sense life needing bodily organs for their operation. Unless we are willing to abandon man as a monstrosity, we must try to understand why an intellectual substance has, in addition to the intellect, powers lesser than the intellect.

When St. Thomas' point is put in this way, his view of man becomes somewhat more tangible. The crux of the matter lies in seeing that, though man has powers in addition to the intellect, he is not *more* than intellectual. The unity of human nature hinges on this point. If we say that man is spiritual and corporeal, immaterial and material, or that he has intellectual and sensible powers (all of which would in a sense be true of man), we can easily reduce man to a patchwork quilt of two natures. Yet if, though spiritual and material, he has one nature, whole and intelligible, what is the value of the "and" when we say "intellectual *and* sensible" powers? No, though man is a composite being, we must not make him or his nature a compound being. If all the powers of man are rooted in the soul; if, furthermore, one and the same intellectual soul has within its nature both intellectual and sensible powers, this fact must mean, not that the soul has more powers than the intellect, but that the human intellect is not fully an intellect *without the sensible powers*. St. Thomas is thus asking us to consider that the *intellect and the senses taken together* constitute in their togetherness the adequate intellectual power of the human soul as an intellectual substance. Seen in this way, the intellect and the senses in man do not constitute more than an intellect that would be adequate to its work as an intellect; rather, in their togetherness, they constitute a complete intellect, capable of accomplishing through their co-operation a complete intellectual work.

If this conclusion is correct, we are on the way to understanding the unity of man and his nature. Let us therefore stress the point we are making, since it is both important and

---

[21] See *Q. D. De Anima,* aa. 8 and 15.

astonishing. The human soul is wholly an intellectual substance, and this in virtue of its immateriality. But it has powers that are less than the intellect — the senses, which need corporeal organs for their operation. Of course, if we were Cartesians, we could say that thinking is the essence of the soul; in that case, we would be suppressing the present problem since we would be eliminating sense powers from the soul. This is precisely what St. Thomas does not do. For him, the human soul, which is an intellectual substance, has intellectual *and* sensible powers. The soul is undoubtedly an intellectual being; but it is one in a very peculiar way. It is intellectual through the work of the intellect which depends on sense powers that must themselves use bodily organs. Intellect, senses, and bodily organs together constitute in man a complete intellect. This is, without any doubt, a most unusual intellect; but it is an intellect.

The only way in which to account for this fact is to consider the power in man we call the intellect. We are saying that, to do its work adequately, man's intellect must be joined to senses and their organs. Why is not the human intellect *by itself* adequate as an intellect? Because by itself it cannot do the work of an intellect. Why not? Because it falls short of verifying within itself all the conditions necessary to its work. For an intellect to know, it must possess adequately within itself that which it knows. Knowledge is by assimilation: the knowing intellect has, within itself, a likeness of what it knows; it knows through that likeness because, through it, it *is* the thing known. The human intellect does not and cannot adequately contain within itself the likeness of what it knows.

By itself the human intellect knows universally, but not concretely; it knows *man,* not *John* or *Thomas.* Yet it is the individual that exists, the individual with all its concrete conditions. In the presence of the individual, which is what is to be known, the human intellect abstracts in order to know: it considers, not the concrete in its concreteness, but the concreteness without its concrete conditions. Now it is true that in man abstraction makes intellectual knowledge possible; but it is also true that, from the point of view of the thing to be known, abstraction yields a knowledge which, in order to be intellectual, is abstract, but which, by as much as it is abstract, is incomplete. To know not only *man* but also *John Smith;* indeed, to know *man as John Smith* and *John Smith himself as a man,* the human intellect must work with the senses, so that the co-operative whole of intellect and the senses knows the individual John Smith adequately.

And St. Thomas further thinks that he has experiential evidence of the diminished nature of the human intellect and of its completion as an intellectual power through the senses. Our intellect gives many signs of depending on the senses: its concepts come only by abstraction, and it depends on images to use these concepts. Its judgments are built up by combining concepts, and its reasoning proceeds slowly from judgment to judgment through concepts. The intellectual life of the human intellect is naturally adapted to growing and developing, through the senses, in the world of material things. The human intellect *qua* intellect is an incarnate intellect, and it is incarnate in order to be adequately an intellect.[22]

Such, briefly and in outline, is the last line of defense that St. Thomas would adopt. The answer to the unity of man's nature lies in the soul, in the soul it lies in the intellect, and in the intellect it lies in the fact that, by itself, the human intellect is not the complete intellectual power of the intellectual substance that the soul is. Hence arises the notion of an intellect incarnated in the senses in order to be adequately an intellect; hence also the notion of soul and body as forming together an intellectual substance, wholly intellectual, but of a diminished intellectuality.

VII

Have we answered Averroës? We have, if we are willing to accept an astonishing interpretation of an astonishing fact. It would have been easier to say with Averroës that a form of

---

[22] On the rational and diminished intellectuality of the human soul, including the principles governing the location of the human intellect at the bottom of the hierarchy of intellects, St. Thomas was in full possession of his doctrine from the time of the *Commentary* on the *Sentences.* See *In II Sent.*, d. 3, q. 1, a. 6; q. 3, a. 1–3, ed. P. Mandonnet (Paris: P. Lethielleux, 1929), pp. 101–106, 112–122. The constructive use of Averroës in these texts should be noted.

matter cannot have an intellect as one of its powers. In that case, man should not even exist. But he does exist, in all his astonishing mystery. Hence, after all, St. Thomas' view of man does in fact answer Averroës. There is a proportion between the immaterial substance that the soul is and the body to which it gives existence. The soul is suited to being an intellectual substance through the body. In and through the body, it is an intellectual substance; which is why we may say of the whole man that he is in a real sense an intellect.

What is extraordinary about this conclusion is not the notion itself that man, in his very compositeness, is an intellect. Extraordinary as this Thomistic notion of man is in itself and in the history of Aristotelianism, what is even more extraordinary is its nearness to St. Augustine. St. Augustine knew nothing about Averroës and his problem; he never asked himself how a form of matter could have an intellect as one of its powers. But St. Augustine knew man, and especially he knew himself. Having defined man as a soul using a body, St. Augustine knew rather well how difficult it was to live up to his own definition. For if man is a soul, he is a soul that must slowly and laboriously build himself, with God's help, into the intellectual and spiritual being that he should be. Knowledge comes slowly, error and uncertainty are common, and growth in understanding is no less slow and troubled. Even more, man's constancy in holding to the truth is often feeble, and often he will make many false starts before he gives his allegiance to the truth with stability and fidelity. *Quando solidabor in Te?*

Seen in the perspective of St. Augustine's doctrine, the Thomistic notion of man is not so astonishing as it might seem. Man is an intellect, an incarnate intellect, and this by nature. He is an intellect needing a long existence — the "longer way"[23] — in the world of matter in order to complete his intellectual nature. St. Augustine knew man in his history, and he knew the intimate secret of that history. For not only is man born into this world. In this world he must, through his history, achieve his humanity, which is to make a mind of his turbulent self. Or rather, he must pray that God will gather

[23] See *S. T.*, I, 62, 5, ad 1.

his turbulent self into a mind turned toward eternity. To become such a mind, a mind living within its growing memory of God, was the prayer that St. Augustine began at Ostia. To explain man in his nature as such a mind, and to do so with Aristotelian philosophical tools and by observing Aristotelian philosophical principles in an Aristotelian age, was the revolutionary achievement of St. Thomas Aquinas in the thirteenth century.

Pontifical Institute of Mediaeval Studies
Toronto, Ont.

Part Four   ETHICA

LAW AND MORALITY

BY GERALD B. PHELAN

The once unquestionable fact that laws, no matter what authority they emanate from, impose a moral obligation to observe them upon all persons subject to that authority, is no longer, it seems, an unquestionable fact. To the minds of many of our fellow citizens, even among those who hold exalted positions on the bench, at the bar, and in administrative offices of government, it is nonsense to talk of any relation between that "instrument of social control," which we call Law, and the personal obligation of conscience, even if we presume that there exists such an obligation. Because this question is an acute problem today, and one which touches important principles of Christian moral teaching, I have chosen it for the topic of this paper.

To begin with a simple illustration. In this country, the law requires that the driver of a vehicle refrain from crossing an intersection while the traffic signal light is showing red. Law-abiding citizens feel bound to observe that law and do, on the whole, observe it. If you asked them, they could probably provide you with many good reasons why they should. Most persons would agree that the strongest reasons, whether or not they would happen to be the first to occur to their minds, would have something to do with the moral obligation incumbent upon everybody to avoid willfully endangering life, inflicting bodily injury, or causing damage to property.

The rank and file of our fellow men are keenly conscious of a connection between legal enactments and moral responsibility, although they may not be able to give all the reasons why it is so, or to state the precise principles upon which that conviction rests and/or provide an accurate philosophical explanation of the relation of law to morality. They are firmly convinced, however, that such a connection exists and that there are good reasons for it although they may not know them all.

They realize, of course, that there is no necessary *physical* connection between a red traffic signal and the movement of a vehicle or between the color of a light and the moral duty of a motorist to bring his automobile to a full stop. If the law prescribed that a red light meant "Go!" and a green light meant "Stop!" the driver's duty in respect to the color of the signal would be the exact opposite of what it is at present. He would now feel obliged to stop on the green light as formerly he was obliged to stop on the red. And for precisely the same reasons. The moral obligation would remain unaltered. The legal circumstances in which it becomes binding would alone have changed.

The case is not quite the same when the law forbids every person within its jurisdiction to assault or murder any other person. The ordinary decent citizen does not need to be told that he must not wantonly injure or kill his neighbor. Even if the law contained no enactment prohibiting such action, he would still feel bound to refrain from indulging in it.

Moreover, supposing that the law of the land forbade the killing of any white Aryan adult but encouraged, or even permitted, the murder of Negroes, Jews, babies, and the physically unfit, the vast majority of citizens of this country, and of most other countries for that matter, would not feel justified in taking advantage of the law and murdering such persons. Rather they would feel that the law was at fault for not providing due and adequate protection for all the members of the community. The law may say, "You may park your car in such and such an area between 6 p.m. and 8 a.m., but not between 8 a.m. and 6 p.m." But it cannot say, "You may commit murder on Mondays, Wednesdays, and Fridays, but not on Tuesdays, Thursdays, and Saturdays."

There you have the substance of the problem of the relation of law and morality in a nutshell. An adequate philosophy of law and morals would, of course, have to seek out the basis of the common conviction that law imposes moral obligations, work out in detail the reasons why this is so, examine the extent and degrees of responsibility imposed by law, investigate with the help of history, the social sciences and jurisprudence, the various conditions and circumstances of time, place, and person in which specific obligations actually apply; in a word, make a thorough and accurate study of the whole question.

That is precisely what philosophers and theologians have been doing from the time when the Greeks, seeking stable norms in the realm of ethical and political life which would somehow parallel the regulating principles that governed the physical world, discovered the natural moral law; through the Romans, who built upon that principle a body of laws which proved to be one of the greatest civilizing influences in history, then down on through the theologians of the Middle Ages, who emancipated natural law from its slavery to Greek physics and restored it to freedom in the mind of man, made to the image and likeness of his Creator,[1] and even long after that, until the "pseudo-Christian naturalism of a Jean Jacques Rousseau," the cynical pessimism of a Nicolo Machiavelli and the moral autonomism of an Immanuel Kant sowed the seeds of divorce between law and morals. In the historical and analytical jurisprudence of the eighteenth and nineteenth centuries, moral concepts played but little part, although a distinct realm of purely personal and private morality continued to be recognized, as may be gathered from the writings of

---

[1] What St. Thomas did in freeing the Christian world of being and knowledge from the necessitarianism of Greek and Arabian thought (cf. Anton C. Pegis, *St. Thomas and the Greeks* [Milwaukee: Marquette University Press, 1943]) he likewise did for the Christian world of law and morals. Professor Roscoe Pound, the erudite champion of traditionalism in legal thought and practice, slips from his customary eminence of erudition when he attributes to St. Thomas a Neo-Kantian conception of the laws of social development. He writes: "The trouble which led the juristic left to give it over and to turn so generally to Neo-Kantian relativism was that it thought of the laws of physics and of physical astronomy and hence of the laws of social development as enactments of the Supreme Ruler of the universe; as a sort of code of Justinian imposed upon physics, and if upon physics, then quite as truly upon politics and jurisprudence as social physics. This would be exactly in the manner of St. Thomas Aquinas." Cf. Roscoe Pound, *Contemporary Juristic Theory*, Pomona College, Scripps College, Claremont College, 1940, p. 41.

thinkers like von Ihering, Austin, Bentham, *et alii*. But morality in the traditional sense of the term is not even recognized by the purely pragmatic, sociological, behavioristic, and Freudian philosophies of law, which infest the law schools of this country today, and have even reached the courts and administrative agencies of the law. For evidence in support of this statement refer to the symposium, *My Philosophy of Law*, published some years ago in Boston.

If, for instance, you were to ask Professor Underhill Moore or Professor Charles C. Callahan,[2] of the Yale University Law School, to tell you what, in their opinion, would be the real reason (for they claim to be *realists*) why the driver of a vehicle stops at a red traffic signal, they would in all probability tell you that it has nothing to do with what you call morality, but is, to all intents and purposes, the same reason why a dog, which has been submitted to the appropriate training in the laboratory of Bechterev and Pavlov, secretes saliva when he sees a certain color or hears a certain sound. Your driver has been "conditioned" by fear of punishment or hope of reward to give the appropriate "reinforced" response to a particular stimulus situation in which the red light is the "sign," and the punishment and reward the "reinforcing agents." What you call his moral conviction of responsibility is only a response to a stimulus, either a purely reflex response of an emotional type or a learned, i.e., reinforced response conditioned by previous stimulus situations in which a purely reflex response has been linked with an imaginary and mythical reward and punishment situation arising from the "behavior patterns" (or *culture* [?]) of an unscientific and outmoded past.

They contend that a process of experimentation designed to determine the number of instances in which a law is violated and to measure the degree of pain or reward by which the desired response to the reinforcing signs are learned, followed by an interpretation of results on the basis of this theory, is the only way in which the relation between law and social

---

[2] Cf. *My Philosophy of Law* (A Symposium) (Boston: Boston Book Company, 1941), pp. 203–225. A statement prepared jointly by Professors Moore and Callahan.

behavior — since one does not speak of "morality" — can be ascertained.

They call this an "operational theory" and vigorously maintain that an "operational theory" of law is the only theory that has any validity whatsoever, all philosophical, theological, or other theories to the contrary notwithstanding. It may appear fantastic to the readers of this essay that such a crass materialistic theory could be seriously propounded by responsible representatives of the legal and academic professions. But I assure you that the two gentlemen whose names I have mentioned rank as eminent jurists and prominent professors in one of the country's greatest law schools, that they have been engaged for years in research along these lines in the Yale University Institute of Human Relations, and that they seriously contend that this

> theory construction and experimentation . . . have as their end the acquisition of precise knowledge of the specific effect of law on behavior. It is believed [i.e., we believe] that until such knowledge is available, any discussion of the relative desirability of alternative social ends which may be achieved by law is largely day-dreaming.

To state the matter bluntly, these gentlemen hold that there is no such thing as morality apart from behavior responses: men are just brute beasts, possessing a more complicated response mechanism than other animals: an investigation of their responses to various stimuli situations by methods of scientific experimentation is the only way to discover how they normally behave: the statistical treatment of the results of experiments so conducted permit us to discern general social behavior patterns and to predict with reasonable accuracy how like stimuli will be responded to in the future. These approximate generalizations are the only norms for the guidance of lawgivers, judges, administrators, advocates, and clients in all that pertains to their respective dealings with the law.[3] And law itself has no other end or function than to declare, on the basis of these experimental findings, that citizens on the whole

---

[3] It has been facetiously — but perhaps not untruly — said that lawyers nowadays are trained how to bet on which way the cat will jump ("the cat" being "the judge").

respond thus and so to given stimulus situations and to "rein-
force" those modes of response until they are imposed on all
the members of the social group.

I should not have burdened my readers with this excursion
into one of the contemporary "realist" theories of law, were it
not important to note how prevalent it is becoming among the
younger generation of lawyers trained in the law schools of
today and who, tomorrow will be the legislators, the jurists,
and the judges in this country. For, I repeat, this is not a
theory evolved by some obscure and half-witted crank but by
eminent representatives of the legal profession and prominent
contemporary teachers of law in this country.

I may add that this is but one of several equally pernicious
theories taught in the law schools of today and poisoning the
minds of young lawyers and jurists. I might have chosen to
illustrate my contention by reference to the robust pragmatism
of Professor Emeritus John Dewey, for whom "law is through
and through a social phenomenon; social in origin, in purpose
or end and in application"[4] or to the somewhat weaker version
of the same theory propounded by Professor Walter Wheeler
Crook of Northwestern University School of Law, who submits
that the pragmatic method ought to be tried out in this field
since (as he thinks), "all other methods have failed dis-
astrously in bringing about the desired agreement."[5] My
choice might have fallen on the pessimistic skepticism of Professor Emeritus Albert Kocoureck, also of the Northwestern
University Law School, for whom "our illusions are for us the
sole reality" (if that makes any sense) and who proclaims
that "Natural law and an ultimate standard of justice . . . are
examples of illusion on 'illusion,' "[6] or on the professed "icono-
clasm'"[7] of Professor Joseph Walter Bingham of Stanford
University, who asks us to banish from the tenets of the legal
profession the absurd dogma that nations are governed by
laws, for, real government is government *by men,* all influenced
as they are in the choice of the objectives of government by

---

[4] *Op. cit.*, p. 76.
[5] *Ibid.*, p. 64.
[6] *Ibid.*, p. 175.
[7] *Ibid.*, p. 6.

personal, social, and political prejudices.[8] Each or any of these theories of law would serve equally well to illustrate the trend of modern jurisprudence toward doctrines of a naturalistic stripe, all ultimately culminating in a Hobbesian appeal to force as the ultimate principle of law.

Contemporary thought in the field of the philosophy of law is radically opposed to the traditional Christian conceptions of law and morals in which the culture and civilization of the Western world is rooted.[9] Unless we wish to see that civilization come crashing down about our ears to be swallowed up in chaos and confusion, the spiritual traditions which are its foundations must be maintained, restored, and strengthened. Those foundations are the teachings of Christ, cemented together by the speculative wisdom of Greek philosophy as transfigured in the minds of Christian sages, and by the practical wisdom of the Roman jurists and lawgivers as transformed through the influence of the Church of Christ and of Her Canon Law, into the body of legal traditions, at once rigid in principle and yet flexible enough in application to sustain the social fabric of Western culture for nearly 2000 years.[10]

---

[8] *Ibid.*, p. 16.

[9] In the articles published by Ben W. Palmer in the *American Bar Association Journal* ("Hobbes, Holmes and Hitler," *A.B.A.J.*, 21, 11 [Nov., 1945] p. 569; "Defense against Leviathan," *A.B.A.J.*, 32, 6 [June, 1946] p. 328; "Reply to Mr. Charles W. Briggs," *A.B.A.J.*, 32, 10 [Oct. 1946] p. 635), the author raises serious objections against contemporary American juridico-philosophical thought, particularly as it is exemplified in the outlook of the late Justice Oliver Wendell Holmes, Jr. Mr. Eugene L. Garey, of New York, delivered a vigorous and eloquent address indicting the authors of the confusion and atheism prevalent in the teaching of jurisprudnce and legal theory in the great law schools of this country at the meeting of the American Women Lawyers Association held in Atlantic City, October 26, 1946 (privately printed). Professor Roscoe Pound has likewise raised his voice again in protest against these trends in legal philosophy in his *Contemporary Juristic Theory* (cited above, note 1). Despite the vast learning, urbane eloquence, and acute critical acumen of the Dean Emeritus of Law at Harvard University, one is never quite sure where he stands. His partially avowed uncertainty regarding the validity of any philosophy of law and his proposal that the best available "measure of values" is to be found in a type of "legal-engineering" (cf. his contribution to the symposium, *My Philosophy of Law* [cited above, note 2] especially p. 259 ff.) and (*Contemporary Juristic Theory*, p. 259) which looks dangerously like a pragmatic theory adapted to the defense of established order) make one uneasy and uncomfortable when reading his otherwise masterful studies.

[10] In the midst of the prevailing atheistic and materialistic mood which

Those Christian, spiritual traditions rest upon three great historical events which are of paramount importance for the understanding of any and every human problem and without a knowledge of which any and every effort to find an adequate solution of those problems is foredoomed to failure. The historical events to which I refer are too often regarded simply as articles of faith or theological postulates, when they are not summarily dismissed as superstitious myths or legendary folklore. I refer to the facts of the Creation, Fall, and Redemption of man. These historical events are likewise articles of faith[11] but that does not prevent them from having happened,[12] and

has visited professors and practitioners of the law, it is heartening to know that there is still wisdom in high places. Witness: the words of General Douglas MacArthur in his speech accepting the surrender of Japan. "The problem basically is theological and involves a spiritual recrudescence and improvement of human character that will synchronize with our almost matchless advance in science, art, literature and all the material and cultural development of the past two thousand years. It must be of the spirit if we are to save the flesh." Cf. *Vital Speeches of the Day,* New York, Vol. XI, 23 (September 15, 1945), p. 707.

[11] An historical event, i.e., something happening in time and affecting human life, can be an article of faith without ceasing to be an historical event. The methods of modern scientific history may not be adapted to deal with such facts, and have no means of testing their claim to historicity, but that does not rule them out of history. It only indicates the inherent inadequacy of those methods to deal with *all* the material that forms part of the study of the past. Scientific history *does* employ very accurate methods of investigation and not infrequently establishes beyond question the existence of certain sequences of events which defy explanation except on the basis of those historical events which are likewise articles of faith. History, like philosophy, needs the assistance of divine revelation and the aid of theology for the full accomplishment of its appointed task.

[12] "Seeing God everywhere and all things upheld by Him is not a matter of sanctity, but of plain sanity, because God *is* everywhere and all things *are* upheld by Him. What we do about it may be sanctity; but merely *seeing* it is sanity. To overlook God's presence is not simply to be irreligious; it is a kind of insanity, like overlooking anything else that is actually there.

"It is part of the atmosphere in which we live and which, therefore, we too must breathe — to take for granted that these considerations are edifying and possibly even relevant if one happens to be of a religious temperament; but not otherwise. It may be a first step towards a fumigation of the atmosphere if we see the fallacy of this too easy view. If you were riding in a car, saw it heading straight for a tree, and called out to the driver to swerve or he would hit it; and if he answered, 'It is no good talking to me about trees; I'm a motorist, not a botanist,' you would feel that he was carrying respect for the rights of the specialist too far. A tree is not only a fact of botany; it is a fact. God is not only a fact of religion: He is a fact. Not to

since it is a fact that they have happened, every human thing
— birth, death, marriage, love, labor, law, and life — is molded
by their influence.[13]

In the world of today, there are multitudes of men, many
of them great scholars and great thinkers, who deny that these
things ever happened. Others never advert to their importance,
and consequently neglect to take them into account when dealing with fundamental problems like the one we are dealing
with today — The Relation Between Law and Morality. This
they frequently do in the name of freedom — freedom of
thought. But what actually *is* does not depend upon what we
may choose to think. *E converso* (as the logician would say)
what we think, if we want to think straight, depends upon
what actually is.

The widespread rejection of, or indifference to, these facts of
history and articles of faith stems from the repudiation in the
fifteenth and sixteenth centuries of the God-centered culture
of medieval Christendom and the substitution of man-centered
culture in its place, with the result that all life, all thought, all
culture has been progressively secularized.[14]

---

see Him is to be wrong about everything, which includes being wrong about
oneself" (F. J. Sheed, *Theology and Sanity* [New York: Sheed and Ward,
1946], p. 6 f.).

[13] I recall the striking statement which an eminent scholar once made to me
in a conversation about the effect of the Incarnation of the Word of God
upon the life of man. "Everything is changed," he said, "Even the washing of
one's hands is not the same since God became Man."

[14] "We are looking on at the liquidation of the modern world, of this
world which Machiavelli's pessimism has made to take unjust force for the
essence of politics, which Luther's secession has thrown off balance by cutting
Germany off from the European community, where the absolutism of the
Ancient Regime has little by little changed the Christian order into an order
of compulsion which was increasingly separated from the Christian sources of
life, which the rationalism of Descartes and the Encyclopedists has thrown
into an illusory optimism, which the pseudo-Christian naturalism of Jean
Jacques Rousseau had led to confuse the sacred desires of man's heart with
the expectation of a kingdom of God on earth secured by the State or by
revolution, which Hegel's pantheism taught to defy its own historical movement, and of which the advent of the bourgeois class, the capitalistic profit
system, the imperialistic conflicts and the unbridled absolutism of national
states have hastened the decline. This world was descended from Christendom
and owed its deepest life's forces to Christian tradition. It was to be all the
more severely judged for it. Its error, in a word, was in believing that man
works out his salvation only by his own power and that human history is

But the errors and heresies which have led many modern thinkers to reject God, the Creator and Redeemer of men, do not alter the true condition of man as a creature of God, fallen from grace, and redeemed by Christ. Nor do the erroneous conceptions of those who would not go so far as explicitly to deny God, but take no account of Him when dealing with social problems, change the fact that man's life is governed, in the last analysis, by Divine Providence and makes no sense, has no meaning, or (in the expressive slang of the day) "does not add up," when God is excluded from consideration.

Moreover, the fact that the intellectual temper of the age in which we live is unfavorably disposed, when not openly hostile, to the introduction of theological principles into the discussion of questions touching man's social relations with his fellow man and with the agencies of government provides no justification for any attempt to adjust one's attitude toward those questions in order to achieve an illusory harmony and a dubious common ground of understanding.

It is undoubtedly true that many high-minded, earnest, honest, sincere, and learned men and many others, though not so learned are no less admirable for their character and qualities, do not believe that what we know to be true is actually so, because they have not been given the light which God has given us (though, God knows, they appear to me to be much more worthy to receive it than I have ever been). Charity, which, may I remark, is no smug and supercilious condescension, but is the humble love of God for His own sake and of His creatures for the love of Him, charity dictates ways and means of maintaining friendly relations with such persons without betraying truth. There is no limit to the charity, tolerance, and benevolence we must inwardly foster and outwardly show toward all our fellow men. But a robust charity may well prescribe what a weak-kneed kindness would condemn. There is no charity in ideas. Truth is unyielding and utterly intolerant of error. To compromise with truth is to betray it. And, as Gilson once wrote, it is an act of charity to tell the truth to someone who does not know it and, even if he

---

made without God" (Jacques Maritain, *Pour la Justice*, Editions de la Maison Francaise [New York, 1945], p. 137).

reject it, a frank disagreement is much healthier than a false and deceptive compromise.[15]

The teaching of St. Thomas Aquinas on the nature of law and its relation to morality is cast in a mold which modern jurisprudence and philosophy of law have set aside in favor of one or other type of naturalistic approach to the problems involved. However, those who still stand for the traditional thought and culture of the Western world and the Christian principles upon which they rest, not only contend, but also know, that no other pattern of thought can take full account of, and do full justice to, the facts of history and at the same time conform to the strict exigencies of an authentic philosophy of law and morals and give stability to the science of jurisprudence. In the light of these considerations, I make no apology for presenting these remarks on the teaching of St. Thomas Aquinas on the question of law and morals without regard for any of the criticisms which have been raised against it by those who do not accept the fundamental Christian truths upon which it is based.

The order in which St. Thomas Aquinas develops his theological teaching reflects the order of things in the universe as a whole and within that order, the problems of morality and law occupy their appropriate place. The aim of sacred science, says St. Thomas, is to furnish knowledge of God, not only as He is in Himself, but also as He is the Origin and End of all things, especially His rational creatures. Consequently, theology must deal, first, with God, second, with the movement of rational creatures to God, and third, with Christ, who as Man, is the Way to God.[16] It is precisely that "movement of rational creatures to God" which constitutes the moral order.

All things issue from God by that primordial dynamic im-

---

[15] Cf. Et. Gilson, *Réalisme Thomiste et Critique de la Connaissance* (Paris: Vrin, 1939), p. 238 f.

[16] "Quia igitur principalis intentio huius sacrae doctrinae est Dei cognitionem tradere, et non solum secundum quod in se est, sed etiam secundum quod est principium rerum et finis earum, et specialiter rationalis creaturae, . . . ad huius doctrinae expositionem intendentes, primo tractabimus de Deo; secundo, de motu rationalis creaturae in Deum; tertio, de Christo, qui secundum quod homo, via est nobis tendendi in Deum" (*S. T.*, I, 2, 1 Prologue).

pulse by which they receive their being and which we call "creation." It is important, however, to prevent the imagination from foisting upon our minds a false and misleading conception of creation. God did not cut His creatures off from Himself, so to speak, and cast them out to leave them thenceforth to shift for themselves. On the contrary, the initial impulse imparted to things by creation is prolonged uninterruptedly in God's conservation of all His creatures in being, in His concourse with all that He has made, and in His ever governing providence.[17] The act by which God gives being to things outside Himself is identical with the act whereby He brings them back to Himself. Creation is, as it were, a grand cycle. That initial impulse or movement, if one can call it such, sets all God's creatures on the way to their appointed destination and carries them forward to the end assigned for them by the Creator, which end is God Himself. The study of this movement in creatures endowed with reason and free will, constitutes the study of morality. The moral order, therefore, embraces all that concerns the movement of rational creatures toward their ultimate end. According to the thought of St. Thomas, morality is the character or quality which human acts possess from belonging to this order.[18] As Gilson has well expressed it, "The study of morality may be reduced to the

---

[17] "Dicendum quod Deus est in omnibus rebus, non quidem sicut pars essentiae, vel sicut accidens, sed sicut agens adest ei in quod agit. Oportet enim omne agens coniungi ei in quod immediate agit, et sua virtute illud contingere; unde in VII Phys. probatur quod motum et movens oportet esse simul. Cum autem Deus sit ipsum esse per suam essentiam; oportet quod esse creatum sit proprius effectus eius; sicut ignire est proprius effectus ipsius ignis. Hunc autem effectum causat Deus in rebus, non solum quando primo esse incipiunt, sed quandiu in esse conservantur; sicut lumen causatur in aere a sole quandiu aer illuminatus manet. Quandiu igitur res habet esse, tandiu oportet quod Deus adsit ei, secundum modum quo esse habet. Esse autem est illud quod est magis intimum cuilibet, et quod profundius omnibus inest, cum sit formale respectu omium quae in re sunt . . . Unde oportet quod Deus sit in omnibus rebus, et intime" (*S. T.,* I, 8, 1. c).

[18] I say "according to the thought of St. Thomas" because, although he describes all that belongs to the realm of morals as *moralia* ("ita nihil *moralium* erit praetermissum," *S. T.,* II–II, Prol.), I am not aware that St. Thomas ever used the word "morality" (*moralitas*). But he does use the word *bonitas* to describe the characteristic quality of the *bonum. Moralitas,* therefore, ought to mean the characteristic quality of the *morale,* i.e., the free act of men and all that appertains thereto.

following metaphysical question: what happens to the efficacy and direction of the movement imparted by God to His creatures when it reaches human beings?" or "How may and must a reasonable creature utilize the movement towards God which he has received from Him?"[19]

That initial movement or impulse is given to *all* God's creatures. Indeed, it is their very being (*esse*). The question of morality, however, does not arise until we reach the level of creatures endowed with reason and enjoying freedom of will. All other creatures are blindly borne along their respective paths inexorably to fulfill their appointed purpose. Only rational beings can know and judge that movement, choose freely to submit to it and to allow themselves to be voluntarily carried along by it. Only they can interfere, by the exercise of their free choice, to rob that impulse of its efficacy and divert it from its initial direction. In other words, only creatures endowed with reason can discern right and wrong and choose to act well or ill. Only rational creatures can have morality. But, because they never cease to be rational creatures, their every act, once they have attained the age of reason (i.e., when they can freely *use* their freedom) is stamped with a moral character, either good or bad, according as it bears them forward in the direction of the original movement imparted to them in creation or voluntarily deflects them from its normal course. This is the reason why every branch of study, research, or investigation dealing with the personal life and conduct in society is fundamentally a part of moral science. It is impossible to strip social, economic, legal, and political facts of their moral (and ultimately metaphysical and theological) character without not only distorting the facts themselves, but also spoiling the sciences which deal with them.

To the mind of St. Thomas, therefore, the realm of morals comprises the whole vast area of human activity in which man, moved to act by God's creative act, takes the initiative, and, in virtue of his power of free choice, enjoys the mastery over his own acts.[20] Brute beasts, he teaches, because they lack

---

[19] Cf. Et. Gilson, *St. Thomas d'Aquin* (in the collection Les Moralistes Cretiens), 5 ed. (Paris: Gabalda, 1930).

[20] "Postquam praedictum est de exemplari, scilicet de Deo, et de his, quae processerunt ex divina potestate secundum ejus voluntatem, restat ut con-

reason and freedom of choice, are acted upon rather than acting;[21] they react to the stimulus of things perceived but cannot be initiators of their own activities nor exercise control over them. Men, on the contrary, do not simply react but, under the impulse of the initial act of being communicated to them in creation, may freely exercise or withhold certain specific activities and determine their direction and specification.[22]

Here is how St. Thomas himself says what I have been laboring to express.

We have shown . . . that there is one First Being, possessing the full perfection of all being, Whom we call God, and Who, of the abundance of His perfection, bestows being on all that exists, so that He is proved to be not only the first of beings, but also the beginning of all. Moreover He bestows being on others, not through natural necessity, but according to the decree of His will. . . . Hence it follows that He is the Lord of the things made by Him, just as we are masters over those things that are subject to our will. Now it is a perfect dominion that He exercises over things made by Him, for in making them He needs neither the help of an extrinsic agent, nor matter as the foundation of His work. For He is the universal efficient cause of all being.

Now everything that is produced through the will of an agent is directed to an end by that agent, because the good and the end are the proper object of the will; and therefore whatever proceeds from a will must needs be directed to an end. But each thing attains its end by its own action, which action needs to be directed by Him Who endowed things with the principles whereby they act. Consequently God, Who in Himself is perfect in every way, and by His power endows all things with being, must needs be the Ruler of all, Himself ruled by none; nor is anything to be excepted from His ruling, as neither is there anything that does not owe its being to Him. Therefore, as He is perfect in being and causing, so He is perfect in ruling.

The effect of this ruling is seen to differ in different things, according to the difference of natures. For some things are so produced by God that, being intelligent, they bear a resemblance to Him and reflect His image. Hence, not only are they directed, but they direct themselves to their appointed end and by their own

---

sideremus de ejus imagine, idest de homine: secundum quod et ipse est suorum operum principium, quasi liberum arbitrium habens, et suorum operum potestatem" (*S. T.*, I, II, Prol.).

21 "Omnia quae ratione carent aguntur tantum et non agunt seipsa" (*C. G.*, III, 110). Cf. *De Verit.* XXIV, 11, e; *De Malo,* VI, q. unic.

22 Cf. *Sum. Cont. Gent.* III, 1.

actions. And if in thus directing themselves they be subject to the divine ruling, they are admitted by that divine ruling to the attainment of their last end; but they are excluded therefrom if they direct themselves otherwise. Others there are, lacking intelligence, which do not direct themselves to their end, but are directed by another.[23]

Having laid this firm foundation for his doctrine, St. Thomas proceeds in an orderly fashion to study both in general and in detail, the problems of morality, or as he would say, "the movement of the rational creature to God." Since, in the moral sphere, men are moving onward (under the influence of the act of creation), by virtue of their own free choice, St. Thomas naturally asks: "Whither are they bound? What is the end towards which rational creatures tend?" His answer is, "the fullest happiness which man can attain — beatitude."[24] Next he inquires what means can man use to reach that end? And he answers: "Only their own free acts[25] and if they direct those free acts to their due end, their conduct is morally good, but if they abuse their freedom to pervert those acts and turn them away from that end, they do wrong, they sin."[26] But, since all the free acts which men perform, whether good or bad, are concrete and individual acts, they are conditioned by man's concrete nature, that, namely, of an individual animal endowed with reason. Consequently, besides the acts which emanate from the specific nature of man as man, human beings have passions, as all other animals have, and these, too, must be studied in their relation to the movement of man toward his end inasmuch as, when properly regulated, they may aid his progress and, when unruly, impede it.[27]

Now while all human acts spring from some inward source within man's soul, they may likewise be initiated, motivated, or controlled by external influences. Hence, St. Thomas asks what are the inward sources, and outward influences, which thus affect all human conduct? What are the intrinsic and

---

[23] C. G., III, 1. This is the English translation published in *The Basic Writings of St. Thomas*, ed. Anton C. Pegis (New York: Random House, 1945), Vol. II, p. 3 f.
[24] Cf. *S. T.*, I, II, 1; I, II, 5.
[25] Cf. *ibid.*, I, II, 6; I, II, 22.
[26] Cf. *ibid.*, I, II, 18; I, II, 22.
[27] Cf. *ibid.*, I, II, 49; I, II, 89.

extrinsic principles of human acts?[28] His answer is that human
acts issue from the reason and will of man[29] and from the
virtues and gifts or the vicious habits with which those faculties may be clothed.[30] These are the intrinsic sources of human
moral conduct. The extrinsic principles of morality are the
devil who tries to lead men to evil by inducing them to sin[31]
and God who draws men to good by instructing them through
law[32] and aiding them by grace.[33]

This is the first time in this hurried outline of St. Thomas'
moral doctrine, that we have encountered his teaching on law
and I beg you to note the exalted place St. Thomas assigns[34]
to law in the government of the moral lives of men. For him,
the voice of law is the voice of God instructing men in their
use of liberty and guiding their freedom to fulfillment.

St. Thomas is here making a statement about law in general.[35] When he describes law as one of the two agencies by
which God stirs men on to the pursuit of the good, his statement applies to all law, not only to the divinely revealed Law
of the Old and New Testaments. God does not instruct us only
in the thunders of Mount Sinai, and in the sweet accents of
His only-begotten Son made Man, on the hills and plains of
Galilee, but also through the Eternal Law, the Natural Law,
the Positive Law of the Church, and the Positive Law of the
State.

For St. Thomas, as for St. Paul, all who speak with author-

---

28 Cf. *ibid.*, I, II, 48, Prologue, and I, II, 90, Prologue.

29 Cf. *ibid.*, I, 77–89.

30 Cf. *ibid.*, I, II, 49; I, II, 89.

31 Cf. *ibid.*, I, 114.

32 Cf. *ibid.*, I, II, 90–109.

33 Cf. *ibid.*, I, II, 109–114.

34 "Assigns" is, perhaps, not the best word to use in this connection. St.
Thomas simply discovers that that is the place law occupies in the order of
God's universe and says so.

35 "Principium autem exterius movens ad bonum est Deus qui . . . nos
instruit per legem . . . " (*S. T.*, I, II, 90, Prologue).

Lest there arise some ambiguity in regard to the universality of this statement, it would have been preferable to omit the word "His" (which does not
appear in the original Latin) from the English translation of this passage in
The Basic Writings of St. Thomas (cf. *supra*, note 23) which runs as follows:
"But the extrinsic principle moving to good is God, Who . . . instructs us by
means of *His* law . . . " (italics mine).

ity speak with the voice of God. Every legislator instructs[36] the people for whom he legislates, as a representative of God; every judge who has authority to decide the issues before him, does so by the authority of God; and every enforcement officer who carries out the duties of his office acts in the name of God.

If once the functions of legislation and the administration of law were surrounded by an atmosphere of great reverence, awe, and majesty — which they have lost, alas! today — it was because that Christian vision had not yet faded from the minds of men; the vision of the Creator of the world (immanent in His universe though still transcending it) guiding and directing His creatures by the instrumentality of human agents, through the myriad intricacies and contingencies of day-to-day existence to the fullness of life and happiness. Those human agents, fallen men, weak and fallible, at best, vicious and perverted, at worst, are still God's instruments. The laws they make and the purposes they pursue may often be inadequate, unfitting, or unjust, but, in the long run, what is right and just and good will finally prevail. As Paul Claudel has aptly said, "God writes straight with crooked lines."

In our myopic view, we squint at all the crooked lines and fail to see the glorious scroll in all its beauty and magnificence. But God not only instructs us by law. He also aids us by grace, and by His grace we may discern His guiding hand in all the works of men and thus we may preserve intact the vision that has given, and still gives meaning and significance to Christian culture.

As a whole, men, it seems, were not able to keep their eyes

---

[36] The term which St. Thomas uses — "Deus . . . instruit . . . per legem" offers at once, a striking evidence of the intellectualist pattern of St. Thomas' thought on law and morals, as well as a clue to his teaching on the educational function of law in society. In his doctrine, law is far from being a harsh or inhuman force robbing men of their God-given freedom, but a gentle and reasonable solicitation, at once enlightening the mind, and moving the will to the knowledge and practice of what is right and good, or expedient and helpful toward the preservation of order in society. The sanctions of the law do not form part of its instructive character. They are invoked only to prevent the lawless from hindering the lawful in the pursuit of the end envisaged by the law. Cf. *S. T.*, I, II, 95, 5, and in Rom. 13:1.

fixed on that great vision, and, at the same time, perceive that the philosophy of law, the science of jurisprudence, the practical adaptation of legal precepts to the varying circumstances of persons, times, and places, as well as the progress and development of the juridical process, judicial procedure, and legal practice, might all develop, flourish, and increase, and steadily grow toward the relative autonomy, which belongs by right to every subordinate order, and which they all should enjoy, within the all-embracing order of God's universe.

Yet, there was that in St. Thomas' doctrine on law, which offered every opportunity for such development without, in the least, destroying, but, on the contrary, enhancing his sublime vision of the whole order of the movement of the rational creature to God.

In his succinct and comprehensive definition of law, St. Thomas Aquinas has gathered together and put in order all the significant aspects and elements of the nature of law, embodied in the writings of the Roman jurists, the philosophy of Aristotle, the Fathers of the Church, and the theologians of the Middle Ages,[37] thereby opening the way for the fullest development of the philosophy of law. According to this definition, law (though not "a social phenomenon") is essentially a social and political matter. Law, says St. Thomas, is a rule or measure of human acts, inducing men to perform or to refrain from performing certain actions; it is an ordinance or dictate of the practical reason issued for the purpose of promoting the common good, and promulgated by the duly established authority in society.[38]

All the elements are there. Law is of reason; yet, it is not mere logic. Speculative reason may argue from the truth of a

---

[37] Dom Odin Lottin has written an important study on the sources and meaning of St. Thomas' definition of law, which appeared under the title of "La Définition classique de la loi" in *La Revue Neo-Scholastique,* Louvain, 26, 2nd series, Numbers 6 and 7 (May and October, 1925), pp. 129–145, 243–273.

[38] Cf. *S. T.,* I–II, 90, *passim* but especially *art. 4,* where St. Thomas sums up his previous discussion on the nature of law in these words: "Ex quatuor praedictis potest colligi definitio legis: quae nihil est aliud, quam quaedam rationis ordinatio ad bonum commune, ab eo, qui curam communitatis habet, promulgata."

universal proposition to a necessary conclusion. But not so the practical reason from which law emanates. For, the practical reason deals, in the last analysis, with concrete individual acts, posited in time and subject to many and various circumstances and conditions. However true a general proposition in moral matters may be, no rigid deduction can determine how and when it should be applied to the concrete conditions it is destined to regulate. Only the wisdom which men acquire by the experience of life (but which God, of course, has by His very nature) linked with a knowledge of the order of creation, can approximate the due ordering of the individual free acts of men by law. Prudence, not science, presides over lawmaking, the adjudication of causes, and the administration of law. Prudence is of the intellect, indeed, but it is not science. The conclusions to which it leads are "reasonable" conclusions rather than the "reasoned" conclusion reached by scientific and metaphysical methods.

Law is for the common good, the welfare of the whole body politic. Its aim and purpose is the social well-being of the community. It must, therefore, take due cognizance of all the factors and influences which give direction, shape, and form to the social life of a community. Geography, history, the social sciences, and all the resources of ethnology and anthropology contribute to the knowledge, which is required to determine the reasonableness of particular laws. For, customs, habits, traditions of thought and culture vary from place to place, and from time to time, and laws must be adapted to these differences and changes, else it will not enable men to pursue their course toward God, the Supreme Common Good, along the most reasonable paths. Law emanates from authority; yet, it is no irresponsible and arbitrary dictate of a despotic ruler. Whether a community be ruled by many or by one or by all, it belongs to the duly constituted authority, whatever it may be, to instruct (and, by instructing to prescribe) the people in the appropriate means to the achievement of the common good. Nevertheless, that authority is never absolute. For human rulers are God's agents, or, better, His instruments, and themselves subject to the whole order of God's universe and, in particular, to the order of "the movement of the rational creature to God" in which movement they are privileged to play a truly effective, though subordinate, role.

Law must be made known to all those for whom it prescribes. For, unless one knows what is to be done, one cannot be held accountable for not doing it. By the natural gift of reason, men know, in general, that good is to be pursued and evil avoided. But, in the concrete circumstances of life, especially where two courses of conduct are, in the abstract, equally good, only the promulgation of the law can enlighten the private person what the duly constituted authority has decided to be, under the circumstances, the appropriate way of acting. Obviously, the individuals who are bound by the law must make reasonable efforts to learn what they have been instructed to do, and, conversely, lawmakers must adopt reasonable means to make their decisions known to all.

The legitimate aspirations of each and all the conflicting schools of jurisprudence, and the philosophy of law can find full scope for their development within the Christian teaching on law and morals, which St. Thomas has so ably expounded. Those partial insights, which the advocates of historical, analytical, metaphysical, sociological, or psychological methods have disfigured by erecting them into mutually exclusive systems, can and should be integrated into the larger vision of the whole. But, there are dark and hidden influences at work, which no philosophy can cope with yet, which must be overcome before the hope of reconciling tendencies so disparate can reasonably be entertained. Original sin has inflicted a dreadful wound upon the souls of men, and Satan is still abroad in the world. But we know that Christ has overcome the Prince of this World, and the Ruler of Darkness. There are three historical facts, which are likewise articles of Faith, and we know that they are still true: God made man! Man fell from God! Christ has redeemed him! No pessimism can shake the confidence which is born of this knowledge and this faith. Our world is indeed a sorry world, but it is still God's world, the world which Christ redeemed and which the Holy Spirit can restore. Today, we may be witnessing the strife of many minds, the war of men upon the truth, the betrayal of all that the culture of the Christian world has stood for and all that can give human grounds for hope, for confidence, for peace. But what of tomorrow — "Send forth Thy spirit and they shall be created, and Thou shalt renew the face of the earth."

St. Michael's College
Toronto, Ont.

Thomistic Thoughts on Government and Rulers

BY   IGNATIUS   SMITH,   O.P.

There is little need for giving reasons for dealing with government and rulers in these days of political unrest. There is more need of stating the restrictions that must be placed on such a presentation. For restrictions must be delineated lest the paper become top-heavy with trite political philosophy and untimely political diagnoses. Perhaps the need of presenting pertinent points of Scholastic social and political philosophy is very evident to some, but a huge sector of our American population is very unaware of the deterioration that has set in even in American government and of the special qualities and principles which government must adopt to save itself for the people as well as from the weaknesses of the people. The seeds of dissolution, of course, are our national crimes against all government and especially against democratic government. Our salvation lies in the recovery first of all by government and political leaders of the virtues necessarily associated with successful and enduring ruling. It is worth while, in this hour, to pass in review some of the national weaknesses that threaten our permanency.

Two facts must be stressed as preambles. Our government, federal, state, and local, has not created its own political weaknesses; it has acquired them through the infiltration of wrong thinking and disastrous living in the nation at large. However, these cankers are nonetheless devastating because they have been caught by pandemic contagion rather than by incubation. The second preliminary but important fact is that we are, as nations go, still a very young people and that in the eyes of world historians our democracy is just as much on trial as is the Communism of the Soviet. National infection so far advanced in the youth of a nation demands the careful attention of philosophical diagnosticians and perhaps of political surgeons.

From a merely political point of view there is no national crime in the United States quite so subversive of national integrity and perpetuity as the nonreligion of so many teeming millions of our American people. They are not deserving yet of the terms godless, agnostic, or antireligious. That will come later. But too many dozens of millions of them have lost all knowledge of the real nature of man, of the nature of human destiny, and of the sovereignty of the Omnipotent. They are worse than indifferent; they are religiously ignorant. They and their children have lost the religious sanctions which check both governments and citizens, and they have wiped out of their lives the one court of appeal outside of government itself to which nations and their peoples should have recourse. They have created, by their own and their parents' neglect of God, faith, and religion, the danger of the same State absolutism and State worship which has become so irrational and inhumane a tyranny in totalitarian states. They have left nothing above the State and have surrendered the religious devotion which the Fathers of our democratic nation deemed an essential requisite for the success of the democratic experiment. Our government is not antireligious and it does not hesitate to call on God and religion in emergencies. Our executives and legislators are not all agnostics and materialists but men who often forget the importance of the natural law and of the Decalogue.

The basic presumption of democracy is self-government and close to this is the presumption that the people themselves are a force restraining democratic government from becoming absolutistic. Many see this sovereignty of the people disappearing paradoxically in their surrender of their self-reliance. It may be true that in national emergency like defense and war democratic processes are too slow when competing with totalitarian lightning wars and that democratic privileges must be suspended for the duration. It is also true that while democratic names and formalities remain, much of the reality of self-government has disappeared. The government has become even above God as a reality to many and it has superseded the individual as a source of control and direction. In earlier days, when self-reliant in the conviction of their own dignity, confident of the help of Divine Providence in their religious convictions and worship, living in the presence of divine law and enlightened conscience, and filled with a responsibility to help themselves and their neighbors, they really possessed democratic virtues. Now, with the collapse of their religion, their self-government and mutual help have disappeared on a staggering scale. Problems, social, economic, and otherwise, which they handled themselves conscientiously, are now thrown at the doorstep of government. Paradoxically, with many, side by side with their total surrender to government legislation and government care, has developed a fear that democratic government cannot carry the load and that to do the job another form of government may be necessary. It is not questioned that enlargement of government, more political government, was necessary when self-government waned. It is not questioned that economic and social development demands a flexible political form. It is questioned by many, however, as to how much of the sovereignty of a democratic people remains. Whatever be the answer to this question, it is evident that godlessness and irresponsibility have made us a less desirable nation.

Another source of dissolution in our form of government is the materialistic standard so evident in our unreligious education. No government can go further or higher than its youth. The best that can be said of our public-school and much of our private-school education is that it is naturalistic. By compulsion our public-school system is nonreligious; by choice most of its educational philosophy has become materialistic. The neglect of the spiritual and the supernatural usually leads to the denial of them. Such a philosophy gives an incomplete and base idea of human personality and its ethics is descriptive rather than normative. The self-realization of this pedagogy becomes the self-annihilation of political life. Such a philosophy and psychology belittle the individual, depreciate citizenship, affect legislation, determine political leadership, and weaken government.

Few nations of history have been able to survive their indecencies. When this form of immorality contaminates and enervates the home a nation is doomed. Under the name of liberalism, our homes have been devitalized as national assets by indecent divorce and lustfully planned parenthood. Under the banner of realism, literature, the stage and the screen would march to utter lasciviousness unless decent forces prevailed. Under the name of freedom, body cult and lust rule the debased lives of youth that has been taught that there is no objective standard of moral right and wrong. Common consent, which is often universally depraved opinion, presents lust and illicit sex relations as progressive. Juvenile delinquency grows and the nation grows weaker and more flabby.

It is bewildering that the millions who have discarded the laws of God and the norms of complete human nature as the guides of conduct and have anchored their destiny on the laws of the State should manifest such disregard of civil law and such irreverence for its authority. This is not strengthening democratic government; it is preparation for anarchy. The very multiplication of silly laws has engendered disdain for all law. Our penal institutions are overcrowded despite our high percentage of literacy, and the crime age is very low. The self-will that comes from undisciplining education, no indoctrination, and self-realization frets under any restraint and makes the evasion of law a mark of cleverness. Age and experience count for little among the young who take over the government of their homes, insist on student government in their schools, and paradoxically make democratic civil government impossible by their lack of self-government and by irreverence for authority. This anarchistic lawlessness is not confined to the young. The example of their elders has been vicious. Perhaps the weakening of government pursuant upon such lawlessness and irreverence for authority is due to the failure of government to discover suitable substitutes for the divine sanctions which it has discarded. The omen of future disaster is clear.

The United States of America has made tremendous prog-

ress in economic adjustment and social reorganization. But a
nation merely economically organized and socially planned
around economic motives cannot last. The Russian government has as much chance of enduring as the Greek city-states
have possibility of reappearing. One reason is that they are
erected not on the real human nature of the individual but on
a fantastic man. Too many of our evaluations are on a dollar
basis: our greatness, individual and national, is interpreted
too often in terms of wealth. We have lost, with the placing of
God as a spectator at the arena of American life, the idea of
the real functions of wealth, the perspective of voluntary
self-denial, and the advantages of sturdy toil for daily bread.
Poverty has become criminal and even our civilization is measured in terms of creature comforts and of mass production.
All this threatens government and nationhood because it di-
verts government from its real and most enduring duties to its
citizenry.

The glorification of greed and the power of wealth eat deep
into the vitals of government because they cultivate the
assassin of all governments and the nemesis of all rulers, injustice. Greed and power tend to establish the supremacy of
extremes and to nurture the principle that might is right. In
politics, to the victor belong the spoils; in industry, one generation believes that capital can do no wrong and the next
generation tends to believe that only organized labor can be
right. Justice, commutative, legal, social, and distributive, is
exiled. This means that God-given natural rights are violated,
very often by the judiciary as well as by the legislature. This
means the alienation of a substantial section of worth-while
citizens from government, the loss of confidence, and the creation of class antagonism that tears the very vitals out of a
nation. This source of possible destruction is too general in our
country. Taking sides quickly, our people often take sides
against justice. The American way, the middle way, the virtuous way, is abandoned and disaster lies ahead. It is a greater
menace to the endurance of our nation than the hazard of
extermination by foreign aggression.

This all too brief diagnosis of national or governmental
pathological conditions has been made from the viewpoint of

scholastic, social, and political philosophy. By a process of elimination and substitution, one can learn that governments and their rulers, to create a nation to which a citizenry can be rationally loyal, must place great premium on religion, self-control, spiritual and supernatural relations, purity, obedience, self-denial, and justice. One might interpose that these are qualities of citizens rather than those of government and governors. So they are, but the emphasis here is on the fact that governments and rulers have the obligation to promote these qualities and the fact that they cannot endure lastingly unless they do promote them.

There are other phases of government and other qualities of rulers that can be linked more formally to the Angelic Doctor, who saw the first beginnings of modern self-government, who had such a comprehensive understanding of Aristotle's *Politics* and who wrote extensively on the political aspects of social life. A few of his principles in their relevancy may help set the background for a sound patriotism.

Man is not only naturally a social animal; he is also naturally a political animal.[1] By the postulates of his nature man builds cities, creates states, establishes government with authority to legislate, to judge, to administer, and to enforce. Government is natural to man and it is necessary wherever there is a multitude.[2] Hence, government was introduced among men by human convention and law.[3] Government which is organized for the commonweal neither prejudices nor injures human liberty.[4] This fact about government and its relation to liberty is interesting and important. Not all government promotes liberty or even saves it. Excessive government and a deluge of unreasonable laws leave very little to human political freedom. In a tyrannical government, regimentation and coercion attempt to reach down even into the inner acts of the citizen and to control thought. Only good government preserves human liberty.

All government or principality is derived from God[5] since He

---

[1] *S. T.*, I, q. 96, art. 4.
[2] Opus 20, L. 1, c. 1.
[3] *S. T.*, II–II, q. 10, a. 10.
[4] *In II Sent.*, d. 44, q. 2, art. 2, ad 1.
[5] *In II Sent.*, d. 44, a. 1, art. 2.

alone from His very nature has dominion over men. Such dominion is not intrinsic or innate in any man even a king; it is derived. This is not, as will be seen later, a pledge that God is totally on the side of even a vicious ruler and against the people. The divine right of kings and rulers in this sense is absurd and only tyrants attempt, in emergencies, to draft their neglected God in the support of such an interpretation. How this power is derived from God is a matter of debate. The following theories are defensible. The people receive the power directly from God and confer it on the hereditary or elected ruler. The ruler receives the designation and the authority from God. The people designate the leader of the government either explicitly by election or implicitly by accepting an hereditary ruler, and the power to govern is conferred on him directly by the Lord of the universe. While some serious problems of justice have been associated with this discussion, it is largely theoretical and speculative. The power to govern comes from God either immediately or mediately; it is not an inborn natural right of a few.

The general and inescapable function of government is to give happiness or the instruments of happiness to the people.[6] This is the purpose of every political group or form, and this happiness must be commensurate with the human dignity of citizens and consonant with human destiny. This principle makes it difficult to hold that political government is responsible only for the material welfare of citizens as individuals and that their spiritual welfare falls under a higher jurisdiction. The political form cannot be absolved from the responsibility of removing obstacles to the spiritual development of its people even if its secularism and Caesarism make it legally impossible for the State to constructively promote religious agencies through which spiritual development is advanced. Neither can spiritual agencies be refused the right or absolved from the responsibility of effecting a material reform in which higher spiritual progress and happiness are more likely to be secure. The political community, like the State, differs from the family in that it is relatively self-sufficient and

---

[6] Opus 20, L. 4, c. 18.

therefore relatively perfect.[7] It is constituted to emphasize and realize the communal factors of human nature and to develop human capacities and happiness on the most comprehensive scale possible.[8]

The function of government is to promote the welfare and happiness of its people. This is supposed to be more than a vote pulling platitude of candidates for political office. It is a basic principle of rational living. The function of government is to make good citizens by *leading* them to the practice of virtues and to the performance of good works.[9] Government must keep in mind the commonweal, the general welfare and satisfaction of all the needs of all the people. As necessary steps to the fulfillment of its mission, it must establish an order of justice and virtue or it is an unnecessary imposition on human freedom.[10] Our own nation is increasingly unsuccessful in this task because it leans, for virtuous character development, on private religious and spiritual forces that have lost much of their power and grip. It takes care of its task in the armed forces through the multiplication of chaplains and of facilities for religious welfare. It is inconsistently inefficient or inefficiently inconsistent when it refuses aid to religious education and even embarrasses it with persecution in the form of lethal taxation. This devotion to the commonweal through the construction of justice and virtuous living creates the peace, the unity of peace, for which nations and states function and without which they cannot last.[11] The promotion of virtuous living is not a work of supererogation for any nation. Neither is religion alien to ordinary democratic government. The Fathers of the American nation were astute politicians in their hope that democracy would be successful because of the moral virtues which faith and worship would inculcate. Our present chief executive has on many occasions requested a religious revival and conscientious moral virtue. Scientific investigation and scholarly research have discovered

---

[7] *S. T.,* I–II, q. 96, art. 2.
[8] Opus 20, L. 4, c. 2.
[9] *S. T.,* I–II, q. 92, art. 1.
[10] *S. T.,* I–II, q. 100, art. 8.
[11] Opus 20, L. 1, c. 2.

no substitute for faith and worship as stimulants of moral deportment. There are no substitutes. Virtuous living against a religious background is not merely an emergency defense measure, like a super policeman; it is a condition vital to peace at all times and essential to the fulfillment of governmental duty.

Political government is composed of many elements which become matters of serious consideration in a democracy and in democratic effort to create and sustain patriotism. Perhaps the most important element in government is power or authority. This is the principle of both action and unity. It is the essential condition for the protection of the people and the commonweal against the rugged individualism, the selfishness, of minorities or individuals.[12] Such unity, through the power of government, postulates one head to whom power is entrusted, one flag that symbolizes it, one body of laws for all, and one well-defined and common purpose.[13]

Political power must create political order and social order through its devotion to a common purpose.[14] Only by this can it justify its existence. The totalitarian philosophy that all human rights are the gift of States which followed men in existence in point of time and can be abolished by the State is reprehensible. The practice of totalitarian government in offering the State, which is usually the dictator, as the ultimate goal of human existence is political suicide. It is possible that while all power may be from God, neither the method of acquiring or using it may have divine approval.[15] The abuse of political power is an evil that is difficult to match.[16] A wicked ruler, personally corrupt, but who gives good government by using his power rationally is preferable to a saintly ruler whose government is bad because his power is wrongly used.[17] The abuse of governmental power warrants the deposition or recall of the executive.[18] The corruption of an entire nation can follow as

---

12 *Ibid.*
13 In Eph. 4, lec. 2.
14 *De Potent.*, q. 7, art. 10, ad. 4.
15 In Rom. 13, lec. 1.
16 *S. T.*, I–II, q. 2, art. 4, ad 2.
17 *Ibid.*
18 *Ibid.*

the result of the abuse of power by a ruler since the body politic depends on the head.[19]

The correct use of authority implies several conditions without which failure may confront government. While virtuous living is essential so is material welfare, and authority, with its power, must be solicitous for public health and its own health and strength. Food, water, and healthful atmosphere and housing must be the objects of concern for political powers.[20] Political authorities must also manifest constancy of purpose and must be prepared to protect the people against enemies within or outside the nation by developing familiarity with the art of war.[21] Only by such solicitude does authority work correctly in the fulfillment of its duty to provide with intelligent foresight.[22] These duties of authority as presented by Thomistic social philosophy will indicate the direction to be taken by the answer to the query often advanced about the lag in social reform and social work among many peoples whose civilization is supposed to be Catholic. In many cases this lag is nonexistent. In many cases it does exist but because of insufficient instruments, financial and otherwise, the slack cannot be taken in. In some cases the lag is due to the venality and other criminality of political government and its apostasy from its basic duties. In some cases this evil persists because of blindness and neglect.[23]

Political government needs not only centralization in one or more chiefs of government but also counselors.[24] Soldiers are also necessary and they should enjoy special privileges.[25] The distribution of honors, occasionally, and not in perpetuity, is also valuable for the solidarity of government and the peace of the citizens. No complete analysis of law and its sanctions can be attempted here. But from the standpoints of legal sanctions and governmental rewards a word might be injected. America, as a sanction for law, might take world leadership in

19 *Ibid.*
20 *Ibid.*
21 In Isa. 3.
22 *In IV Sent.*, d. 49, q. 1, art. 2, a. 5.
23 In Ps. 50.
24 Opus 20, L. IV, c. 14.
25 *Ibid.*, c. 25.

emphasizing rewards along with punishments. We have not been entirely successful in producing law-abiding citizens through the sanction of fear of punishment. We have neglected almost entirely rewards as a sanction for high civic righteousness. Smaller groups like Scouts and schools use this procedure with great success. It is advisable that city, state, and national governments have recourse to it also.

Peoples have a choice in the types of government to which they may entrust the promotion of their terrestrial felicity. Aristotle and Aquinas list three general kinds of government, that ruled by one, that directed by a few, and that directed by many or all. Each of these types may be either efficient or vicious. If government by one is efficient it is called monarchy, if vicious it is called tyranny. If government by a few is good it is called aristocracy, if bad it is oligarchy. If government by the many or the multitude is good it is "politea," if evil it is called democracy.[26] A warning must be given that what is contemporary democracy is not necessarily what Aristotle and Aquinas classified as bad mob rule. The meaning of the terms has changed. Government of, by, and for the people is closer to the old polity than to the vicious type of popular government called democracy by the Stagirite and Aquinas.

Tyranny is a form of government which is not consonant with human nature whether it be the tyranny of one or of many. Tyranny, thought Aquinas, arises more often in the government by many than in a government by one.[27] For this reason popular government was suspect. Aquinas showed preference sometimes for monarchy or regal government because that was the government of heaven where Ruler and subjects were perfect.[28] The final resolution of the practical problem in his theory as well as in life was in favor of a mixed form of government in which all have a part.[29] He chose to live his life in such a form of elective representative regime in the Order of Preachers. Such a government has the centralization of monarchy in one chief executive, the balance of aristocracy

---

[26] *S. T.*, I–II, q. 95, a. 4.
[27] Opus 20, L. 4, c. 8.
[28] *S. T.*, I, q. 103, art. 3; II–II, a. 105, art. 1, ad 2.
[29] *Ibid.*

in the wisdom of an advisory council, and the stimulus of democracy in the elective and initiatory processes of the people.[30] It would be represented factually though not nominally today in the republican political form of the United States and in the constitutional monarchy of England. The form of government must be in harmony with the condition of the people. The world at large cannot be given a democratic or representative government because some peoples are not ready either temperamentally or intellectually for such a regime. Perhaps it might be advisable for democracies at times to change their regime. Many think that in lightning wars democracy must suspend many of its privileges and adopt dictatorial procedure in order to keep abreast of the speed of the totalitarian governments. That is debatable, but it is certain that a people's form of government must be related to its intelligence, its environment, its age, and to world conditions. Any government that people want, that brings them happiness, and respects their human rights and liberties is good government and best for them. Despotic tyranny is only for slaves.[31] A perfect government is one in which citizens are in agreement with the ruler and co-operative with one another,[32] but it is always necessary that restrictions be placed on imperial power to keep it from devolving into the arrogance of tyrannical dictatorship,[33] and from becoming remiss in the duty of dispensing the common good in a peaceful and orderly manner by law, judgment, and defense.[34]

The dissolution of political power and the disintegration of government are conditions against which a people must be on guard constantly, since erosive forces begin to operate suddenly and rapidly. Vicious and immoral rulers are a menace to good government, and civic virtue in leaders is a first line of internal defense[35] since otherwise the protection of the commonweal is impossible.

Perpetuation in office is not good. The universe is constantly

---

[30] *S. T.,* I–II, a. 105, art. 1.
[31] Opus 20, L. 2, c. 8.
[32] Opus 20, L. 4, c. 23.
[33] *Ibid.*
[34] *Ibid.*
[35] *S. T.,* I–II, q. 92, art. 1, ad 3.

changing; so are men and their environment. Nature is constantly replacing the old with the new; so ought men to do. In the State a very important responsibility of government, and of the people in a democratic government, is to carefully select replacements in the various offices of government.[36] New, alert, and progressive blood is needed. Government also protects itself against collapse by discovering penalties that will really deter men from breaking laws by depriving them of privileges they really prize.[37] Fining a rich drunken driver is not likely to reform him; making him walk for a year might correct him. Government, to guarantee its success and endurance, must be prepared for war. What doth it profit a nation to avoid all internal dangers if it is unable to defend itself against external perils.[38]

Erosive factors of government must be eliminated from every political form. A nation must be on guard against the ambition of dishonest and inefficient men who reach for public office. This does not mean that citizens are not to aspire to public service. They are obliged to contribute of their talents to the commonweal. But reprehensible ambition, as opposed to magnanimity, is not a desire to serve the public but an unrestrained craving for honors[39] that so blinds men as to make them unfit for office.[40] Infidelity to government by the use of their office for their own profit and not for the happiness of the people is an attack on all government.[41] Fraternization of government officials with crooks is the indication of the disintegration of the power of authority.[42] Graft and neglect of the indigent are further indication that government is weak.[43] Punishment ought to be meted out to these men by revealing their inquity and inefficiency, and the Almighty has frequently punished such defection in other generations by depriving them of authority and power and by blinding their minds.[44]

---

[36] Opus 20, L. II, c. 15.
[37] Ibid.
[38] Ibid.
[39] S. T., II–II, q. 131, art. 2.
[40] In Mt. 2.
[41] In Isa. 1.
[42] Ibid.
[43] Ibid.
[44] In Isa. 3.

Defects due to ignorance, age, or viciousness are assassins of good administration.[45] The defects of stupidity and injustice in administration are as fatal to good government as is disobedience in the people.[46] To strengthen government and advance its successful care of the people the authorities must be lovable and creditable. Hateful characteristics and insincerity are dangerous.[47] Rulers should serve God by living rightly and serve the people by legislating wisely.[48] They must create conditions that make for health, long life, intelligence, and civic righteousness.[49]

In these dire days, along with totalitarian philosophy of government has come the tyrannical dictator. How he differs from the tyrants of earlier centuries is irrelevant. The horrible fact is that some nations seem to thrive temporarily under tyrants and under the extermination of their human liberties. Material welfare and territorial expansion are an anesthesia that dulls the pains of totalitarian absorption. Another horrible fact is that tyranny is contagious. Even sane political leaders grow envious of wider powers enjoyed by other political executives. National emergency fans tyrannical flames and privileges are surrendered temporarily. No small task of democratic government is to see that it is not caught up in the tyrannical tornado. No small task of democratic people is to be alert that their free and independent institutions of republican government are not wiped out. Tyranny and its advocates must be kept from these shores and the tyrants of those nations who do not want them must be removed.

A tyrant who comes to power by usurpation can be run out of office by the people while they have the power. If they accept him then this right ceases.[50] The condemnation of tyranny and tyrannical dictatorship can scarcely become excessive because it is the worst possible form of government.[51] Yet a government easily degenerates into a repulsive tyranny on

---

[45] *Ibid.*
[46] *De Malo,* q. 7, art. 7, ad 9.
[47] In Ps. 44.
[48] In Ps. 2.
[49] Opus 20, L. 2, c. 1.
[50] *In II Sent.,* d. 44, q. 2, art. 2.
[51] Opus 20, L. II, c. 3.

account of the great power of the ruler and because of his cruelty and avarice. The remedy against this tendency in a ruler is his own perfection of virtue.[52] Evidently tyrannical dictators, with pride, greed, and cruelty, showed the same tendencies seven hundred years ago that they show today. Aquinas believes them to be despicably unjust because they desolate cities, steal sacred things, and loot great institutions — like libraries and art galleries. How often the question is asked today why God permits such destructive tyrants to prosper even for a time. A partial answer is that God permits them to rule for their own damnation and for the punishment of evils.[53] If that be the consequence of godless thinking and living, our own republic ought to be alarmed because self-government is doomed.

People have in right, if not the actual opportunity, many remedies against tyranny. Historically penalties have been visited on tyrants[54] for their hatred of law, for their cruel reprisals, and for their spoliation.[55] Historically also, and ethically, peoples have taken steps against tyranny and re-established rational government.[56] They have the right and the duty to revolt. This uprising would not be sedition if reasonable, but rebels must be sure that greater evils will not follow in the wake of their uprising.[57] Tyrannicide is permissible only when ordered by public authority even though the tyrant is unjust.[58]

These are merely pertinent high spots in the principles of Thomistic social and political philosophy dealing with the forces that strengthen and those that weaken government. It stands out clearly that the keel in the ship of state is the ruler. Upon his character, to no small degree, hangs the fate of a nation and the security of his regime. A people, therefore, is justified and should be compelled to take inventory of their potential rulers before either accepting them or electing them.

---

52 *S. T.*, I–II, q. 105, art. 1, ad 2.
53 *In II Sent.*, d. 44, q. 1, art. 2, ad 2; ad 3; and ad 5.
54 Opus 20, L. 1., cc. 11, 12, 13.
55 In Isa. 9.
56 Opus 20, L. II, c. 6; c. 11.
57 *S. T.*, II–II, q. 42, art. 2, ad 3.
58 *In II Sent.*, d. 44, a. 2, art. 2, ad 5.

They must be worthy of their positions. Some qualities ought to be outstanding in them and others ought to be conspicuous by their absence.

Men possessed of an exaggerated sense of their own importance and addicted to the vice of bluffing (*jactantia*) are to be kept out of office, because they extol themselves above their real worth and above what prudent and general opinion deems them to be.[59] For this same reason liars and arrogantly proud men ought to be kept out of political life.[60] Bluffers in public life are a menace because they have no respect for the glory of God, they resent the fame and happiness of their fellow citizens, and they reek with vainglory and pride.[61] It may be dangerous to place a poor man in public office because of the possibility that he will be corrupted and sell out his subjects,[62] but it is also dangerous to entrust the distribution of the commonweal to the rich because opulence and wealth cause the pride and the vanity which lead to dangerous bluffing and insincerity in political life.[63]

Rulers may collect in taxes what is necessary for the commonweal and also they may impose fines where they are just.[64] National wealth is at the command of the executive for purposes of government. This wealth he ought to have, and both he and his administration are entitled to economic and financial protection. But he may not collect taxes merely for his personal aggrandizement or that of his friends. This would be tyrannical.[65] Unjust confiscatory taxation or seizure is rapine even in a ruler and he is obliged to make restitution.[66] Taxation collected but not used for the advantage of the people, taxation that is illegal or more than the ability of the people to pay is criminal.[67]

Prudence as a quality of mind and as a moral habit is

[59] *S. T.,* II–II, q. 110, art. 2.
[60] *S. T.,* II–II, q. 132, art. 5, ad 1.
[61] *Ibid.*
[62] Opus 20, L. II, c. 2.
[63] *S. T.,* II–II, q. 112, art. 1, ad 2; ad 3.
[64] Opus 20, L. 3, c. 1.
[65] Quodl. 12, art. 25.
[66] *S. T.,* II–II, q. 66, art. 8.
[67] In Isa. 1.

vitally necessary in a ruler. There are five kinds of prudence: monastic, economic or domestic, political, military, and gubernatorial.[68] The last three of these are intimately involved with the functions of good government.

Physical health and stability of character have already been mentioned as part of the necessary equipment of a good ruler.[69] Sagacity or wisdom in ruling is even more essential in gubernatorial equipment,[70] and happy can be that ruler who enjoys this sagacity not as an endowment from the devil but as the result of human learning and divine revelation.[71] Reverence for his position, the reverence that promotes obedience, is stimulated if the ruler is conscious of the dignity of his office, if he is skilled in moral virtues, and if he be of dignified demeanor.[72] He should decline office if he feels he is unable to carry out its duties.[73] This is especially true if he feels unable to correct the erring and to punish defection mercifully and with clemency.[74]

In the hierarchy of virtues which a successful ruler must possess, mercy and clemency which protect him from being cruel or ruled by maudlin pity hold a high place[75] and are different from the *mansuetudo* which should rule the conduct of citizens with one another.[76] Clemency moderates punishment because of the sweet and amiable disposition of the ruler.[77] It need not be stressed that in all of this catalogue of virtue, prudence and justice must prevail since they are most becoming in a ruler.[78]

A good ruler must be absolutely a good and virtuous man whose virtue differs in kind and degree from that of a good citizen.[79] With virtue, with humility he will win all; with pride

---

[68] *S. T.*, I–II, q. 57, art. 6, ad 4.
[69] In Isa. 3.
[70] *Ibid.*
[71] *Ibid.*
[72] *Ibid.*
[73] *Ibid.*
[74] *Ibid.*
[75] *S. T.*, II–II, q. 157, art. 2.
[76] *S. T.*, II–II, q. 157, art. 1.
[77] *S. T.*, II–II, q. 157, art. 2, ad 2.
[78] *S. T.*, II–II, q. 50, art. 1, ad 1.
[79] *S. T.*, I–II, q. 92, art. 1, ad 3; II–II, q. 47, art. 11, ad 1.

he will lose his office and ruin his government.[80] Let him rule citizens with mercy but let him treat enemies of the nation with severe justice.[81] Let him be truthful, humble, and kindly in correction.[82] The reward of such a ruler is more than the honor and glory of this world; it is the blessed and eternal happiness of the next life[83] and he will obtain greater reward there than any of his subjects.[84]

Government and rulers are important to the fulfillment of man's mission on earth and to the development and expression of both the social and the sociable nature of man. The suffering peoples under the domination of Communism are plagued and are under the heels of tyrants. Their personalities are cramped and earthly felicity is difficult of attainment. Here in the United States some special protection of Divine Providence has kept us mindful of our freedoms and hating the tyranny from which we have escaped. Our government is essentially sound and we have been blessed with a succession of rulers who, in the main, have met the qualifications just outlined from the content of Thomistic political philosophy. The example of the best of them may serve as a model for the rest of them. Of such a government and of such rulers a nation may be proud. On the foundations of such a government and the example of such rulers our future can be erected safely. To such a government continued and to such rulers multiplied can we link that love of country called patriotism. The faults of our system and the failures of our officials serve merely to stress the truth of what has been said.

The Catholic University of America
Washington, D. C.

[80] Opus 20, L. 3, c. 14.
[81] In Ps. 32; in Ps. 2.
[82] *Ibid.*
[83] In Eth. 5, lect. 11.
[84] Opus 20, L. 3, c. 10.